AF479273

The Challenges of Ethno-Nationalism

The Challenges of Ethno-Nationalism

Case Studies in Identity Politics

Edited by

Adrian Guelke
Professor of Comparative Politics, Queen's University, Belfast

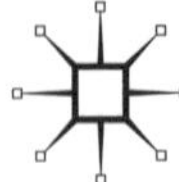

First published 2010 by
PALGRAVE MACMILLAN

Palgrave Macmillan in the UK is an imprint of Macmillan Publishers Limited, registered in England, company number 785998, of Houndmills, Basingstoke, Hampshire RG21 6XS.

Palgrave Macmillan in the US is a division of St Martin's Press LLC, 175 Fifth Avenue, New York, NY 10010.

Palgrave Macmillan is the global academic imprint of the above companies and has companies and representatives throughout the world.

Palgrave® and Macmillan® are registered trademarks in the United States, the United Kingdom, Europe and other countries

ISBN 978–0–230–22410–0   hardback

This book is printed on paper suitable for recycling and made from fully managed and sustained forest sources. Logging, pulping and manufacturing processes are expected to conform to the environmental regulations of the country of origin.

A catalogue record for this book is available from the British Library.

A catalog record for this book is available from the Library of Congress.

10   9   8   7   6   5   4   3   2   1
19   18   17   16   15   14   13   12   11   10

Printed and bound in Great Britain by
CPI Antony Rowe, Chippenham and Eastbourne

Contents

List of Figures

List of Tables and Graph

Tables

Graph

Notes on Contributors

Rob Aitken is a social anthropologist and a senior lecturer in the Department of Politics at the University of York. His research interests focus on forms of belonging, including locality and ethnicity, and how these interrelate with nationalism, state institutions and changing systems of ethnic and cultural distinction. His current research focuses on the relations between ethnicity and conflict and the comparative study of processes of ethnicization during and after conflicts. He is currently writing a book *Ethnicity and Conflict: Ethnicization, Cultural Identities and Post-War Reconstruction.*

Emel Akçalı is Honorary Research Fellow at the Department of Political Science and International Studies, University of Birmingham. She holds a PhD in Political Geography from Paris IV-Sorbonne, and an MA and a BA in International Relations, respectively from Galatasaray University and the American University of Paris. Among her recent publications are *Chypre: un enjeu géopolitique actuel*, (l'Harmattan, Paris, 2009) and '"Nature Knows No Boundaries"– A Critical Reading of UNDP Environmental Peacemaking in Cyprus', *The Annals of the Association of American Geographers, special issue on Geographies of Peace and Conflict* (with M. Antonsich, 2009).

John Coakley is a professor in the School of Politics and International Relations at University College Dublin. He has published extensively on Irish politics, comparative politics and nationalism, and is contributing editor or co-editor of *Politics in the Republic of Ireland* (5th edition, Routledge, 2009), *Crossing the Border: New Relationships between Northern Ireland and the Republic of Ireland* (Irish Academic Press, 2007), *Renovation or Revolution? New Territorial Politics in Ireland and the United Kingdom* (UCD Press, 2005), *From Political Violence to Negotiated Settlement: The Winding Path to Peace in Twentieth-Century Ireland* (UCD Press, 2004) and *The Territorial Management of Ethnic Conflict* (2nd edition, Frank Cass, 2003).

Ksenia Gorbenko is a doctoral candidate in sociology at the University of Pennsylvania. Her current research examines visual representation of non-violent social movements in the media from a historical perspective. She has studied in Russia, Hungary, Ukraine and the US.

Adrian Guelke is Professor of Comparative Politics in the School of Politics, International Studies and Philosophy at Queen's University, Belfast. He is the director of the School's Centre for the Study of Ethnic Conflict. Recent publications include *The New Age of Terrorism* (IB Tauris, 2009), *Terrorism and Global Disorder* (IB Tauris, 2006) and *Rethinking the Rise and Fall of Apartheid* (Palgrave Macmillan, 2005). He is the chair of the International Political Science Association's research committee on politics and ethnicity.

Cillian McGrattan is Government of Ireland Post-Doctoral Fellow in the School of Politics and International Relations, University College Dublin. His most recent publication is '"Order out of Chaos": The Politics of Transitional Justice' in *Politics* (2009), and he is currently completing a monograph titled *Northern Ireland, 1968–2008: The Politics of Entrenchment* to be published by Palgrave Macmillan (2010).

Diarmuid Maguire, PhD, is Senior Lecturer in Government and International Relations at the University of Sydney. His current research centres on the development of social movements, ethnic conflict and geopolitics.

Ramón Máiz is professor of Political Science at the University of Santiago de Compostela. His main fields of research are comparative nationalism and federalism and political theory. Recent books include *Democracy, Nationalism and Multiculturalism*, co-edited with Ferrán Requejo (Routledge 2004); *Ethnicité et Politique*, co-edited with Jean Tournon (L'Harmattan 2005); *Nación y Literatura en América Latina* (Prometheo, Buenos Aires 2007); *Nación y Revolución: la teoría política de Emmanuel Sieyès* (Tecnos, Madrid 2007); and *La Frontera Interior* (Ediciones Tres Fronteras, Murcia, 2008). He is vice-chair of the IPSA research committee on politics and ethnicity, editor of the *Revista Española de Ciencia Política* and on the board of *Nationalism and Ethnic Politics*.

Olga Malinova, PhD, is the leading fellow of the Institute of Scientific Information for Social Sciences, Russian Academy of Sciences. She is the author of several books and articles about nationalism and national identity, political discourse and political ideologies, including *Liberal Nationalism (the Middle of the Nineteenth – the Beginning of the Twentieth Century)* (Moscow: RIK Rusanova, 2000) (in Russian) and *Russia and 'the West' in the Twentieth Century: Transformation of Discourse about Collective Identity* (Moscow: ROSSPEN, 2009) (in Russian).

Klaus-Jürgen Nagel is Professor of Political Science at Pompeu Fabra University, Barcelona. He teaches political theory and comparative politics. Nagel studied social sciences and history in Münster and Bielefeld (Germany). He obtained his PhD from the University of Bielefeld in 1989 for a thesis on the Catalan working class and the national question. Before he moved to Pompeu Fabra University, Nagel worked in the history department of Universität Bielefeld and in the department of social sciences of Johann Wolfgang Goethe-Universität Frankfurt am Main. His current research interests include nationalism, federalism and European Integration. He has also published on Catalan history.

Niall Ó Dochartaigh is college lecturer in the School of Political Science and Sociology at the National University of Ireland Galway. He is the author of *From Civil Rights to Armalites: Derry and the Birth of the Irish Troubles* (Cork UP 1997; 2nd edition, Palgrave Macmillan 2005) and two books on Internet research as well as articles and book chapters on the politics of conflict in Northern Ireland, and the use of new technologies in conflict situations.

Sangit Kumar Ragi is Associate Professor in Political Science at Maharaja Agrasen College, University of Delhi, India. He has been teaching Indian politics and comparative politics to both undergraduates and post-graduates in the University of Delhi and other Indian universities for the last 15 years. He has published widely in books and journals and is currently working on a book on the BJP's concept of cultural nationalism. He is on the editorial boards of the journals, *Eternal India* and *Indian Journal of Social Enquiry* (published in New Delhi).

Jennifer Todd is Professor in the School of Politics and International Relations, University College Dublin and Director of the Institute for British Irish Studies. She is co-author of *Dynamics of Conflict in Northern Ireland* (Cambridge University Press, 1996) and has published widely on Northern Ireland politics, and on ethnicity, identity and identity change, including in *Political Studies, Archives Européennes de Sociologie, Theory and Society* and *Nations and Nationalism*. She is presently working on a new book on the Northern Ireland conflict and settlement.

Acknowledgements

This book had its origin in a colloquium of the International Political Science Association's research committee on politics and ethnicity. The colloquium was held as a curtain-raiser to a major conference at Queen's University of Belfast on the theme of 'Beyond the Nation?' I am particularly grateful to my colleague Dr Keith Breen who was the organizer of the main conference but who took care to ensure that participants in the IPSA colloquium received all the benefits of involvement in the larger event. My thanks are also due to everyone who took part in the colloquium, including those who presented papers and participated in the discussion, but who for one reason or another were unable to contribute a chapter to this book. The exchange of opinions in Belfast helped all the authors in developing their conference papers into chapters for the book. I would also like to thank Alexandra Webster at Palgrave Macmillan to whom I submitted the proposal for the book, as well as the anonymous reviewers she sent it out to for their evaluation. I got valuable feedback from these readers at different stages of the process. Her colleague Renée Takken oversaw the production of the book after the acceptance of the proposal and I am grateful for her help, not least for choosing the cover along with Alexandra Webster. The photographs in the chapter on Ukraine are reproduced courtesy of a licence obtained from the Ukrainian Independent News and Information Agency, while acknowledgement is made that the mental maps in the chapter on Cyprus first appeared in the author's monograph published by l'Harmattan. Macmillan Publishing Solutions in India did the copyediting. This task was carried out efficiently and I thank them for getting everything done ahead of schedule. I also received help with the book from Alessia Bisson who was based at Queens for a three-month internship in the Centre for the Study of Ethnic Conflict through a generous arrangement with her university in Venice. She assisted in particular with the index. My wife, Brigid, helped me in the final proofreading of the book and I am most grateful for her assistance in identifying typographical errors that I had previously missed.

Adrian Guelke, Belfast

1
The Multifaceted Nature of Ethno-Nationalism

Adrian Guelke

Hopes that the end of the Cold War world might usher in an era of peace between and within the nations of the world were quickly dashed by new sources of domestic and international tensions. Two stood out: there was a resurgence of ethnic conflict in a number of parts of the world, particularly during the 1990s, while the assault on America on 11 September 2001 underscored the threat that the new menace of mass-casualty terrorism posed to the world. Often blamed for the first of these challenges to a new world order was ethno-nationalism. The phenomenon was commonly associated with the horrors of ethnic cleansing, a term that originated in the Balkans in the early 1990s. This gave ethno-nationalism a bad name and also meant that it tended to be linked with secession and the break-up of states, as well as with political mobilisation leading to war. Ethno-nationalism also tended to be associated with minorities dissatisfied with their place in an existing polity. But, in fact, the phenomenon was much broader than simply providing recourse for rebellious minorities. This volume explores the challenges presented by ethno-nationalism in a wide range of different contexts. While the primary focus of the book is on the post–Cold War context, the analysis in a number of the chapters extends well before this. This is most particularly so in the Irish case, where conflict not merely long predated the end of the Cold War, but where this watershed in world affairs arguably contributed to its resolution.

However, it is difficult to understate the importance of the end of the Cold War as an influence on the salience of ethno-nationalism. Practically everywhere in the world, political mobilisation on the basis of class has been on the wane since the end of the Cold War. The collapse of Communism in Eastern Europe and the demise of the Soviet Union underlined that for the time being at least, the forces of capitalism had triumphed. The class struggle's lack of credibility opened the door to other agendas, centred on the environment and on issues of identity, including gender and ethnicity. So prevalent were the latter that the post–Cold War era has been dubbed 'the age of identity.'[1] This volume examines how ethnic political mobilisation played out in a variety of circumstances, though without neglecting cases where it did have violent manifestations or the means by which states and the international community sought to provide constitutional political answers to ethnic conflicts.

Before summarising the arguments put forward in individual chapters, let me briefly discuss the changes in the international political system that placed ethnic conflict at the top of the political agenda in the 1990s and the consequences that flowed from the prominence of the issue. When Mikhail Gorbachev came to power in the Soviet Union in March 1985, the Soviet system was in crisis. Among the problems Gorbachev faced were a stagnant economy, a costly intervention in Afghanistan and a serious challenge to Communist rule in Poland from the trade union movement, Solidarity. Gorbachev sought to address these problems through fundamental reform of the Soviet system, but in the process triggered far-reaching changes that brought about the collapse of Communist rule in Eastern Europe in 1989 and ultimately the dissolution of the Soviet Union itself in 1991. Gorbachev hoped to revitalise the Soviet economy through the twin approaches of *perestroika* (restructuring) and *glasnost* (openness). To create space for his reforms, he also sought from the outset to improve relations with the West. This led to his agreeing in April 1988 to a timetable for the complete withdrawal of Soviet troops from Afghanistan by February 1989.

The consequences of the abandonment of Communist orthodoxy within the Soviet Union itself were far-reaching. It led ultimately to permission being granted for the holding of multi-candidate elections in the Soviet Union in March 1989. When this liberalisation of the political system was copied in Eastern Europe it proved sufficient to bring about the rapid collapse of Communist political control. In August 1991, orthodox Communists made a last-ditch attempt to reverse the changes Gorbachev had introduced. The failure of their coup accelerated the collapse of the Communist system, with power shifting from the centre to the republics that made up the Soviet Union. Almost everywhere the ideological vacuum created by the demise of Communism was filled by nationalism. In most cases, the new political forces accepted the existing international boundaries or those bequeathed to them as a result of the break-up of the Soviet Union. But in some, conflict did arise as a consequence of internal communal divisions that were reflected in competing ethno-nationalisms.

Remarkably, the political transformation of a region stretching across a number of time zones was achieved both rapidly and with relatively little violence. Ironically, the main exception to this generalisation was Yugoslavia where, for most of the Cold War, Soviet influence had been weakest. Another region where ethnic differences gave rise to a series of conflicts was the Caucasus. While Communist rule survived in China, Vietnam and Cuba, Communism was no longer credible as a global alternative to capitalism. Further, not only was Communist ideology discredited, but there was also a waning in the influence of socialist ideas more generally. Notions such as class struggle and the promotion of equality achieved through the redistribution of wealth fell into abeyance. Other ideologies came to the fore, not least ethno-nationalism and politicised religion, conveniently if not entirely accurately labelled as religious fundamentalism. In a number of cases, the two occurred in combination. However, generally, religious affiliation tended to be transnational and gave rise to movements that were transnational in their ambitions.

There was no automatic reason why the rise of these ideologies should have resulted in violent political conflict. And, indeed, in many instances, movements espousing these ideologies were accommodated within democratic political systems. But these ideologies did contain the potential for generating violent political conflict, particularly in areas of the world subject to geo-strategic competition. A factor compounding the potential for conflict was the impact of the end of the Cold War on international norms. In the wake of the ending of the bipolar international political system, the interest of the major Western powers in upholding norms such as non-intervention and territorial integrity (particularly the anathema against secession) diminished. The readiness to accept the creation of new states was reflected in an increase in the membership of the United Nations from 159 member states in 1990 to 189 in 2000. Admittedly, there is scope for debate over the direction of causation, so it might be argued that the change in the interpretation of international norms was more a product of the impact of ethno-nationalist movements than a factor that facilitated their success. Or it might reasonably be contended that the two ran in tandem.

While the disintegration of the Soviet Union could be rationalised as the belated dismantling of the Tsarist Empire, no such rationalisation was available in the case of Yugoslavia. Yugoslavia had come into existence as the result of the collapse of the Austro-Hungarian Empire in the course of the First World War. The new entity barely survived the Second World War from which it emerged as a Communist state, but unlike most of the states of Eastern Europe, this status was not the outcome of occupation by Soviet forces. During the Cold War, Yugoslavia had remained a non-aligned state outside the Soviet bloc. Even under Communist rule, ethno-nationalism had been sufficiently powerful to ensure the devolution of considerable power to its six republics under a federal system, though the boundaries among the republics by no means neatly coincided with ethnic divisions.

The fact that the first multi-party elections in Yugoslavia took place within individual republics boosted the forces of secession since it meant that the elected governments of the republics had greater international legitimacy than the country's federal institutions, boosting the prospect that if secession were proclaimed it would secure international recognition within a relatively short period of time. This set the scene for a violent contest for power in the country among competing ethno-nationalisms compounded by geo-strategic rivalry between the West and Russia. Constraining factors included the fear that events in the Balkans would set a precedent for secessionist movements elsewhere in the world and the spillover effects of the violence, including the flow of refugees from the region. The major Western powers sought to limit the impact of the break-up of Yugoslavia by insisting that this should proceed on the basis of the pre-existing boundaries among the republics to avoid the implication that force could provide an effective and legitimate way of redrawing borders. But this rule was modified so as to permit the secession of Kosovo from Serbia, though in this case the international community remained divided as to whether to accord recognition to a new entity that largely owed its existence to military intervention by NATO forces.

Events in the Balkans in the 1990s propelled ethnic conflict to the top of the international agenda. Further, developments elsewhere in the world, most particularly the genocide in Rwanda in 1994, ensured that it was seen as a global problem and not one that simply arose out of the collapse of Communism in Eastern Europe and the Soviet Union, large as that area was. The implications of the break-up of Yugoslavia for the rest of the world were mixed. On the one hand, it gave encouragement to movements seeking secession that success was possible, both in terms of establishing a new state and, just as importantly in the long term, in gaining international recognition. For example, the Kashmiri militants involved in the Kargil incursion in 1999 that threatened to detonate a war between the nuclear weapons states of India and Pakistan pointed to the war over Kosovo in justification of their actions.[2] On the other hand, the bloody events in the Balkans were also a warning to states and regionally based nationalist movements of the very high costs if they failed to reach a political accommodation.

The assault on America on 11 September 2001 changed international priorities and the issue of terrorism displaced that of ethnic conflict as the major concern of most states. It also meant that states were able to portray insurgents as terrorists undeserving of any international support and state authorities benefitted from the reinterpretation of some violent conflicts that had previously been seen in ethnic terms as problems of terrorism. But a complicating factor was the international unpopularity of the Bush Administration's conduct of the global war against terror. Further, not all states were successful in persuading the outside world to accept their characterisation of their rebels as terrorists, particularly where the actions of the rebels did not spill over international boundaries or could not plausibly be linked to groups such as al Qaeda. And counterbalancing the picture of rebels as terrorists was a developing readiness to condemn state authorities for their violation of human rights, extending to the advocacy of intervention in the most serious cases of states that abused their own citizens. Admittedly, beneath the use of this moralistic language, geo-strategic calculation and rivalry often lurked just below the surface. It is striking that both NATO and Russia contentiously invoked the concept of genocide when justifying interventions in ethnic conflicts in the Balkans and in the Caucasus in 1999 and 2008, respectively.[3]

This book arose out of a colloquium under the auspices of the International Political Science Association's research committee on politics and ethnicity held in Belfast, Northern Ireland, in September 2007. That is to say, the chapters in this book, apart from this introductory chapter, had their origins in papers delivered on that occasion, though it should be stressed that they have all been revised and updated for this book, as will be evident from their content. The book is divided into three parts following this introductory chapter. The first comprises six individual case studies from a very wide range of divergent societies. The second part consists of three contrasting, though by no means contradictory, perspectives on the Irish conflict, while the three chapters in the third and final part take a comparative approach.

Individual case studies

In the first of the individual case studies, Ramón Máiz analyses the success of Evo Morales and the ethno-nationalist movement he headed, in the Bolivian presidential elections of December 2005. Latin America is a region of the world that tends to be neglected in studies of ethnic conflict. For example, the region is entirely absent from Stefan Wolff's global study of ethnic conflict.[4] A common, but mistaken, assumption by scholars without specialist knowledge of the region is that ethnic divisions are of little or no importance, because they see it as a region dominated by conflict between left and right and by clashes between populist movements that transcend ethnic differences and the military. While the tumultuous politics of Venezuela and the military coup against a populist president in Honduras in 2009 might appear to justify this impression, other developments point to a more complex reality. Through charting the rise of Morales's indigenous movement in Bolivia, Máiz shows the growing importance of identity politics in the region. In this context, the name of Morales's party, *Movimiento al Socialismo* (Movement Towards Socialism) is misleading in suggesting continuity with parties of a previous era. But the name does underline Morales's inclusive approach, in contrast to the exclusive approach of the party's indigenous and much less successful rival, *Movimiento Indígena Pachakuti* (Indigenous Pachakuti Movement), as is demonstrated by Máiz in his detailed analysis of the discourse of the two parties.

The second case study focuses on one of the world's longest-running and intractable ethnic conflicts. This is the dispute over Cyprus, partitioned since 1974 after Turkey invaded the island to protect the Turkish Cypriot minority. Hopes of an end to what since 1974 has very largely been a bloodless conflict grew with the prospect of the island's membership of the European Union. In particular, the European framework allayed Turkish Cypriot fears that they would be vulnerable as a minority under any settlement that ended the partition. But the opportunity for a negotiated deal was lost when a large majority of Greek Cypriots voted against the terms of a complex set of proposals that came out of international negotiations on the issue in a referendum. The referendum preceded Cyprus's admission to the European Union in May 2004, but this was not made dependent on a favourable outcome to the referendum.

There have continued to be talks between representatives of the two communities on possible terms for the reunification of the island since the Greek Cypriot rejection of 2004, but without the urgency that preceded Cyprus's entry into the European Union. Emel Akçalı uses an innovative, interdisciplinary approach to explore the different mindsets of the two communities. Her fieldwork was conducted in 2005 and 2006. She uses mental maps to bring out people's emotions, perceptions and values, thus underscoring the psychological dimension of their relationship with the territory. Greek and Turkish Cypriot respondents were asked to draw the country they would like to live in, as well as the one they hoped to live in. The results show revealing differences not just in how the two communities perceive the territory in which they live but in their aspirations for the future as well.

The third case study examines the role that the notion of empire has played in the political discourse of post–Soviet Russia. Empire tends to be counterposed to nation and imperialism to nationalism, but these concepts are by no means as contradictory as they might appear at first sight. In the first decade after the fall of the Berlin Wall, the concept of empire was generally applied to the past in Russia. However, it re-emerged in contemporary political discourse as the country's relations with the West deteriorated, especially after the war against Serbia over Kosovo in 1999. Olga Malinova distinguishes five different meanings of empire in Russian political discourse, ranging from the conception of Russia as a country that is bound to encompass many peoples and ethnic groups to Russia's right to be a major power exercising influence beyond its borders. She also distinguishes between the use of the term by a cluster of perspectives that she describes as 'imperial nationalists' and by liberals.

The link to ethno-nationalism is to be found in the notion propagated by a number of nationalist writers that it is specifically the mission of the Russian people as an ethnic group to dominate the empire, while sustaining its multi-ethnic character through their capacity to bind in other peoples. The territorial ambitions of nationalists vary and at the most extreme there are those who imagine a future in which a new empire would stretch beyond the boundaries of the Soviet Union. Some even imagine reviving the nineteenth-century idea that Russian soldiers might one day be able to wash their boots in the Indian Ocean. Of course, such speculation bears no relationship whatever to the realities of power now or in the foreseeable future or, for that matter, to any expectation in the government in Moscow that the reconstitution of the Soviet Union might become possible in any shape or form. The mirror image of Russian ultra-nationalists is to be found among alarmist Western commentators warning that Russia should not be allowed to 'Finlandise' Western Europe.[5] For liberals, the key to Russia's recovery of its international influence is to be found in its becoming a member of the club of democratic world powers. Malinova also shows how the discourse on empire in Russia during the last decade has influenced the thinking of the country's leaders through analyses of speeches by Putin and Medvedev.

The dramatic events in Russia's neighbour, Ukraine, in 2004 when non-violent mass mobilisation forced the authorities to accept the re-run of Presidential elections reversing the outcome and leading to a change of government, form the subject of Ksenia Gorbenko's case study. While both the evidence of electoral fraud in the initial outcome and its political orientation ensured that the Orange Revolution, as it was dubbed, received wide international support, Gorbenko's analysis of the photographic representation of these events in Ukrainian newspapers underlines the country's deep linguistic and regional divisions. But while these divisions continue to play a central role in Ukraine's politics, they have not hitherto given rise to widespread inter-communal violence or, what would be likely to follow such an eventuality, the threat of secession or partition. A constraining factor is that it remains very evidently in Ukraine's interest to maintain good relations with both the West and Russia, as far as that is possible.

The next case study analyses the political fortunes of Hindu nationalism, which in combining the criteria of indigenousness and religion is best described as an ethno-religious movement. Sangit Kumar Ragi demonstrates how the impact of market liberalisation and globalisation was a factor in the rise to power of Hindu nationalists in the 1990s, but he argues that in the last decade it has contributed to *Hindutva's* relative decline, paving the way for the victory of the Congress party in India's national elections in 2004 and 2009. In particular, he points to the failure of the India Shining campaign that formed the centrepiece of the Hindu nationalist government's campaign for re-election in 2004. Ragi also shows how the impact of the market has dented the appeal of left-wing opposition to the Congress party. At the same time, India faces considerable problems in its regions, most particularly the long-running insurgency in the state of Jammu and Kashmir. It is nonetheless striking that Hindu nationalists proved unable to capitalise politically on the government's handling of serious terrorist atrocities, such as the attack on Mumbai in November 2008.

The final case study examines Catalonia's political evolution since Spain's transition to democracy. Klaus-Jürgen Nagel employs a detailed examination of the electoral programmes and conference resolutions of Catalan political parties to show how the institutional architecture established after Spain became a democracy to accommodate regionally based ethno-nationalisms has taken root in the case of Catalonia. The result is that parties across the political spectrum have moderated the radical stances they adopted at the outset of the transition and, though differences remain in their attitude towards the devolution of power, they have come broadly to accept the rules of Spain's multi-level politics. This achievement should stand Catalonia and Spain in good stead to meet the very severe challenge that the global economic downturn poses both to the region and the country.

Irish perspectives

The next part of the book consists of three studies regarding the Northern Ireland problem. The first of the three by Jennifer Todd examines the role of the equality agenda in the Northern Ireland peace process. She argues persuasively that this aspect of the peace process has not received the attention it deserves. Much of the focus of those writing on the peace process has been on the political institutions created under the Good Friday Agreement. However, the peace process has clearly not depended on their operation, since the functioning of the institutions has been beset by frequent crises so that in practice Northern Ireland has been governed under direct rule from London for much of the time since 1998. Todd draws a distinction between equality as a steady state and equality as a threshold. The former, she argues, involves the enforcement of equality across the board between the two communities, whereas the latter focuses simply on the removal of the inequalities under which Catholics had laboured. In practice, the latter view has been the one adopted by the British and Irish governments, correctly in Todd's view, since she contends that this approach makes it possible for the society to move towards a plural and participatory polity.

Niall Ó Dochartaigh employs the example of Northern Ireland to demonstrate a very significant difference between state-framed nationalism and counter-state nationalism, which is that in the case of the former, the state possesses the wherewithal to embed itself on a national scale, whereas naturalising an alternative national territorial framework presents a much larger problem for counter-state nationalists. Taking this distinction as his point of departure, Ó Dochartaigh gives a detailed account of the local focus of militant Irish nationalism during Northern Ireland's troubles, the period of violent instability in the province dating from the late 1960s. He shows how dependent Republican paramilitary organisations were on pockets of local support in sustaining their campaigns of violence and he illustrates the crucial importance of local solidarities by describing the hostile reaction to the Official Irish Republican Army when it abducted and murdered a British soldier who was at home on leave in a Catholic estate in Northern Ireland's second city of Londonderry/Derry.

Cillian McGrattan argues that the approach taken by constitutional Irish nationalists in Northern Ireland, in other words nationalists who have sought to advance the cause of a united Ireland by wholly peaceful means, have been maximalists practically throughout the course of the troubles. He disputes the argument associated with the theoretical work of Donald Horowitz that ethnic outbidding by a radical competitor in the form of Sinn Féin accounts for the stance taken by the main constitutional nationalist party, the Social Democratic and Labour Party (SDLP).[6] In particular, he shows that decisions taken in the early 1970s that committed the party to a maximalist position preceded any challenge from Sinn Féin. He uses the case study to underline the theoretical point that key decisions of political actors play a crucial role in the construction of ethnic contention. McGrattan notes that some of the leading figures within the SDLP recognised the adverse impact that the party's stance had on the prospects for an accommodation with Unionists. It is worth emphasising that these were figures in the party who gave a higher priority to socialism than to nationalism and had a different conception of equality than just that between Protestants and Catholics.

Comparative analysis

The final part of the book comprises three comparative studies. The first by John Coakley assesses the capacity of federal systems to accommodate a set of territorially concentrated ethnic groups. To this end, he examines the functioning of the federal model, noting that there is relatively little disagreement in the literature on which countries have federal systems and which do not and, despite disagreement over a small number of borderline cases, the consensus is that there are currently about 24 federal systems, the majority of them being long-established federations. In most cases, the internal boundaries of federations and those of putative ethnic homelands do not coincide. Further, a number of ethnic federations, that is, federations in which the units have been designed to coincide with ethnic divisions have failed. But the pressure from ethno-nationalists for recognition of ethnic communities through autonomy or the institutionalisation of federal arrangements remains unrelenting. Consequently, there is every reason to expect further experimentation in this area. Coakley concludes that ethnic federations sometimes survive and sometimes fail but the full explanation requires a case-by-case analysis.

Diarmuid Maguire's chapter explores the dynamics of protest mobilisation and state response within what he calls ethnic-national locales. To analyse the use of space in such conflicts he examines the cases of

Northern Ireland and Israel. He argues that the battle between the state and protestors to control space tends to be especially fraught in divided societies. He contrasts the actions of Israel to delineate the living space of Palestinians through the construction of a separation wall with the efforts of the British state to bring the two communities in Northern Ireland together in a post-national framework. The former reflects a policy of containing and isolating the Palestinians in the absence of a negotiated settlement, while the latter arises out of the province's peace process.

The final comparative chapter by Rob Aitken examines the application of consociationalism in the peace processes of Northern Ireland and Bosnia-Herzegovina. The term 'consociationalism' was coined by the Dutch political scientist Arend Lijphart to describe a combination of devices – power sharing, proportional representation, segmental autonomy and mutual vetoes – deployed to create stable governments in a number of small European states. Consociational devices, and most particularly power sharing, have proved popular with external mediators seeking to create stable governments in ethnically divided societies in the wake of violent conflict. While Aitken accepts that consociationalism can contribute to peace and an end to violence in the short term, he argues that this approach runs the risk of entrenching and therefore perpetuating the ethnic polarisation that occurs in the course of violent conflict. But he identifies differences among consociational settlements, contending, in particular, that the Good Friday Agreement is more flexible than the Dayton Peace Agreement.

The authors of this book share a common commitment to the scholarly study of the relationship between politics and ethnicity that is the objective of the IPSA Research Committee. But, as will be very evident to any reader, there is a wide divergence not only in how they approach the study of the relationship but also in their political viewpoints. These differences are as sharp from within particular societies as they are across continents, so they should not be put down to the fact that scholars from many different countries are represented in this volume. What is more important, particularly in relation to individual case studies, is the expertise that scholars living in and/or from the societies being examined are able to bring to their analysis.

Some common themes of the contributions are worth highlighting. Perceptions are vitally important to an understanding of ethnonationalism, whether these take the form of the discourse political leaders or parties use, how the other side in a conflict is represented in the media or the images people have of the society in which they live. The point is perhaps most obvious in societies that are deeply divided along ethnic lines. But it also has significance in states in which the domination of a particular ethnic group is taken for granted or is masked by a commitment to civic nationalism.

Another theme that runs through the book is the importance of both geography and history, not necessarily as such, but in the interpretations of leaders, commentators and ordinary people. In this form they are intimately bound up with who people think they are. But, as a number of the chapters emphasise, people's identities are not fixed. They are subject to change, though in this context a concern is that they may become fixed if institutions are not sufficiently receptive to the possibilities of change. Reactions to globalisation, both positive and negative, also receive attention. However, the colloquium took place before the global economic crisis in the autumn of 2008, so the opposite of globalisation, deglobalisation, finds no place in any author's analysis. In any event, it still remains too early to speculate as to how long the downturn will last and if any recovery will prove durable.

Further, the political implications of the crisis have only just begun to be painted in very broad brush-strokes. Thus, it is commonly argued that the pendulum has swung back to the state,[7] giving it a central role in the regulation of the economy, and away from the market as a self-correcting mechanism operating transnationally. Also important is how the crisis will affect the international balance of power. If there is a shift away from the West and towards the new Asian powers of China and India, as some commentators contend,[8] that is likely to have profound implications for ethno-nationalism, at least where it is connected to separatist objectives. In particular, neither China nor India has any reason to view secessionist movements favourably and that may influence whether the multiplication of states that has occurred since the end of the Cold War will continue.

But even if the fragmentation of states should continue, nonetheless, much effort will still be needed to achieve political accommodation within states, since most ethnic groups do not inhabit self-contained homogeneous spaces that can readily be transformed into viable political entities. The requirement that people with different ethnic identities should be able to get along in the same locality, as they by and large do, is not going to disappear. At the same time, it is important not to view the phenomenon of ethno-nationalism negatively as if all ethno-nationalists were intent upon expulsion, transfer or ethnic cleansing and the destruction of multi-ethnic societies. As this volume underlines, ethno-nationalists themselves vary very considerably in their approach to promoting the politics of identity. Indeed, ethno-nationalism takes so many different forms that there is room for argument as to which movements or parties should be included within the term's scope. But whether it is narrowly or broadly defined, ethno-nationalists seem likely to continue to pose significant challenges to the prevailing order within states and internationally.

Notes

1. Ilan Peleg, *Democratizing the Hegemonic State: Political Transformation in the Age of Identity*, Cambridge: Cambridge University Press, 2007.
2. See, for example, B. Bearak, 'Kashmir a Crushed Jewel in a Vise of Hatred', *New York Times*, 12 August 1999.
3. Quentin Peel, 'Russia's Reversal: Where Next for Humanitarian Intervention?' *Financial Times*, 23–24 August 2008.
4. See Stefan Wolff, *Ethnic Conflict: A Global Perspective*, Oxford: Oxford University Press, 2006.
5. See, for example, Edward Lucas, 'Do Not Let Russia "Finlandise" Western Europe', *Financial Times*, 9 October 2009.
6. See particularly, Donald L. Horowitz, 'The Northern Ireland Agreement: Clear, Consociational and Risky' in John McGarry (ed.) *Northern Ireland and the Divided World*, Oxford: Oxford University Press, 2001, pp. 89–108.
7. See, for example, even before the failure of Lehman Brothers, John Plender, 'The Return of the State: How Government is Back at the Heart of Economic Life', *Financial Times*, 22 August 2008.
8. See, for example, Dominique Moïsi, 'A Global Downturn in the Power of the West', *Financial Times*, 6 October 2008.

Part I Case Studies

2
'We aren't the peasants of the seventies' – Indianism and Ethnic Mobilization in Bolivia

Ramón Máiz

In December 2005 the Aymaran Indian Evo Morales, at the head of the *Movimiento al Socialismo* party (Movement Toward Socialism or MAS), won the Bolivian presidential elections with 53.74 per cent of the valid votes. That in Latin America a native Indian should attain presidential office with a pro-Indian programme of government constitutes a striking novelty; that he should do so with the massive, nationwide support of white and mixed-blood voters as well as Indians is amazing. This chapter attempts, albeit very schematically, to identify the factors responsible for the success of the indigenous movement in Bolivia; to explain why it was Morales's MAS rather than Felipe Quispe's *Movimiento Indígena Pachakuti* (Indigenous Pachakuti Movement, MIP) that gained the ascendancy within this movement; and to do so by reference to interpretational aspects of the indigenous discourse that have generally not been remarked on but which throw new light on previous accounts.

More specifically, we will develop an analysis of MAS's success that takes into account the following four components:

1. The ethno-cultural inheritance (culture, language, history, territory, etc.), though always bearing in mind the extent to which perception of this inheritance is itself the product of previous generations of 'awareness builders'.
2. The existence of socioeconomic circumstances favouring awareness of a collective identity, of an 'us' as distinct from a 'them'. Such circumstances may include a network of common interests that actually or potentially conflict with those of some other group or groups; subjection to neoliberal economic policies that erode social ties, destroy the traditional territory of the group and generate rootlessness and

the need for an identity; and the existence of a sufficient degree of social mobility and/or supra-local communication that facilitate the perception of a common social space.

3. A propitious political opportunity structure, which may be formal – including various kinds of political decentralization (federalism, municipalization, etc.) and the existence of effective access to the political arena – or informal (electoral realignments, crises in the traditional party system, the emergence of new potential allies, etc.).

4. A political machine that is organizationally and *rhetorically* efficient, creating new opportunities to generalize identification with the ethnic group to a broad social segment on the basis of shared interests and specific objectives of self-government.

Below, I deal in turn with these four components in the case of the MAS in Bolivia, and in Section 2, I use frame analysis to focus in greater detail on the aspect to which least attention has hitherto been paid, the political discourse.

1. Indianist ethno-politics in Bolivia: Searching for a pluri-causal explanation

Of all Latin American countries, Bolivia has the largest proportion of indigenous inhabitants: 62 per cent in the 2001 census, which is generally regarded as reliable, claimed to belong to some indigenous ethnic group, a figure that can be compared, for example, with 25 per cent in Ecuador. Nearly 31 per cent identified themselves as Quechuans, and over 25 per cent as Aymarans, the remaining six per cent being distributed among Chiquitanos (2.2%), Guaranies (1.6%) and others. This has of course been an important factor in the rise of the indigenous movement and its electoral success: as Evo Morales repeatedly reminds us in his speeches, the indigenous population of Bolivia is not a marginal minority, but constitutes the majority of the country's whole population. However, it is not by itself a sufficient explanation, because this majority is not homogeneous.

Firstly, there is the division into Quechuans, Aymarans and other groups. Secondly, there are a number of socially relevant geographical variables that divide this majority into subgroups: rural Indians vs city dwellers (currently more than 50%); highland vs lowland communities; Eastern Bolivians (*cambas*) and Western Bolivians (*collas*). Thirdly, bearing in mind the poverty of the indigenous population and the labour insecurity it suffers, it should be remembered that traditional left-wing parties and labour unions, in addressing native Indians, have for long subordinated their ethno-cultural identity to the conventional classification as 'peasants' or 'workers', a practice that has played an important role in impeding Indianist mobilization in Peru and, to a lesser extent, in Chile. That the success of Indianism in Bolivia may be due to other factors in addition to the size of the indigenous population is also suggested by the fact that the first South American indigenous parties to achieve a degree of success appeared in Colombia in 1990 in spite of only 2.7 per cent of the Colombian population being indigenous.[1]

The first factor that must be examined to explain the realization of the potential of the indigenous majority of Bolivia is the ethno-cultural inheritance that has been exploited by the indigenous movement.

The ethno-cultural inheritance

The Indianism of the high Bolivian plateau possesses an extraordinarily rich and powerful source of myth in the Great Andean Rebellion led between 1780 and 1783 by the Quechuan Tupac Amaru, who besieged Cuzco, and the Aymaran Tupac Katari, who besieged La Paz for six months.[2] These were historically decisive uprisings in that they put an end to the system of undertakings upon which Spanish dominion was based and, for the first time, placed the Empire in jeopardy; the insurgents included not only Indians, but also mixed-bloods, creoles and even a few Spaniards (though fewer than in Peru). More importantly for our present purposes, they became the basis for a comprehensive mythology surrounding the figure of the 'new Inca', the restoration of Incan rule and the revenge of the native peoples subjected to Spain since the fifteenth century. In a different vein, the Great Andean Rebellion was later reinterpreted as a precursor of the Bolivian war of independence, and even as a precedent of militarist nationalism.[3] This mythico-symbolic capital survives today, and in the speeches of Felipe Quispe and Evo Morales is constantly invoked,[4] for example, by references to the indigenous peoples' '500 years of resistance'.

A second historico-mythical reference for Indianism relates to the Bolivian Federal War of 1898–9. The conflicts that resulted in the capital of Bolivia being moved from Sucre to La Paz led the Federalist Pando to seek the support of the now-legendary Aymaran leader Pablo Zárate Willka, offering in return the restitution of formerly Indian lands that had been nationalized some 30 years previously – a promise that was promptly broken once the Federalists had gained power following a battle in which the Aymarans had played a key role. The memory of these events has been zealously kept alive and exploited by Felipe Quispe, who propounds an 'imitation of Zárate's armed uprising'.

In spite of the mythogenic vigour of these two episodes, they have traditionally been relegated by the republican rhetoric of the Bolivian state,
which completely excluded Indians from participation following independence from Spain in 1825. Not until the traumatic loss of most of the
Gran Chaco in 1935 did the idea of a mixed-blood nation find a place
in Bolivian nationalism, and even the National Revolution of 1952 only
recognized the indigenous population as peasants, denying their ethno-
cultural identity. The system that the Revolution took as its model was
that of Mexico, in which the transformation of the indigenous population into a peasantry by redistribution of the land in exchange for votes
through the mediation of corporate labour unions was accompanied by
its acculturization and assimilation into a mixed-race national identity –
the 'cosmic race' of Vasconcelos – in schools, in the army and in the
media. The corporatist Bolivian state constructed during the 1950s by
the MNR (*Movimiento Nacionalista Revolucionario*) thus had two facets: on
the one hand, the establishment of state-controlled labour unions and
other top-down mechanisms mediating the standardization and control
of local community institutions through the exchange of favours; and
on the other hand, the attempt to generate a Bolivian nationality in the
sense of a collective identity shared by all Bolivians, a nationality centred
on a common language, a common view of history, a common external
enemy (Chile) and common symbols and myths such as the national
flag. There was in principle no room for indigenous collective identities.
And when Barrientos came to power in 1964, the Peasant–Military Pact –
supplemented with outright dictatorial repression – served to continue
the erasure of Indian identity.

Only with the suppression of Indian autonomy in the region of La
Paz, and the massacre of Tolata, did there arise an opportunity for novel
processes of political identification. The first indigenous movements
of this kind were the *Movimiento Nacional Tupac Katari* (1968) and
Luciano Tapia's *Movimiento Indio Tupac Katari* (MITKA, 1978), and the
more moderate, union-oriented *Centro Campesino Tupac Katari* (1971)
and *Confederación Sindical Única de Trabajadores Campesinos de Bolivia*
(CSUTCB, 1979). It was at the 1983 National Congress of the CSUTCB
that it was first publicly proposed that Bolivia should recognize itself as
a 'plurinational state'.

Socioeconomic preconditions

The second requisite for political ethnification is a propitious socioeconomic environment. To evaluate this aspect, we must look back
to the agrarian reforms and associated measures introduced between

1952 and 1964 as part of the MNR's National Revolution. These reforms redistributed large amounts of land to Indian owners, thus converting Indian communities into communities of peasants, that is, individual proprietors of small-holdings. Dialogue with this sector was organized chiefly through corporate peasant labour unions, and these organizations did indeed sometimes work reasonably well on behalf of their members in those parts of the country, such as Cochabamba, where the Indian population was already concentrated in nuclei and there was already a certain tradition of peasant unions on the model of workers' unions.[5] In the Andean highlands, however, where many communities were allowed to retain certain common property and a degree of political autonomy, the lowest levels of the union structure were in fact traditional Indian community structures – the union *was* the community; these latter structures thus survived relatively unscathed, but were ineffective within the overall union structure.

In spite of their de-Indianizing nature, for a large proportion of Indian communities, the MNR-led reforms afforded access to at least a minimal level of socioeconomic resources, including not only land but also suffrage and the right to education, a right previously actively opposed by many of the four per cent of the landowners who had hitherto possessed 82 per cent of Bolivian land.[6] However, the mechanisms and ideology through which the MNR achieved these socioeconomic improvements militated against the indigenous identity deriving from Indians' ethnocultural inheritance – as in Peru (de la Cadena, 2000), a class of 'half-blood Indians' emerged, persons of Indian appearance speaking indigenous languages and observing indigenous cultural traditions who nevertheless considered themselves, implicitly or explicitly, as of mixed race.

After the MNR years, de-Indianization was intensified by successive military régimes, but gratitude to central government for the economic advances of the 1950s was slow to wane. The post-revolution economic measures that did most to pave the way for the success of the indigenous movement were those of the New Economic Policy of 1985, which sacrificed the remnants of officialist unionism by doing away with support for the rural economy in the form of subsidies, price regulation and so on. There were also drastic cuts in health services and education, and the autonomy of those communities that enjoyed any was further eroded by measures such as the privatization of common land.[7]

The inoperancy of the peasant labour unions, and the further destruction of traditional community structures, facilitated among the indigenous population a renewed perception of itself as Indian rather than peasant. Furthermore, large numbers of indigenous miners were made unemployed when the New Economic Policy–dismantled Comibol migrated to coca-growing areas, and in doing so they rejected the ideas of unionism and class struggle from which they had hitherto benefited, turning instead, in their disillusionment, to an identification with local indigenous culture and traditions.

Political opportunity structure

The formation of a favourable political opportunity structure, as regards both political institutions and relationships with competing forces, has been decisive in Bolivian indigenous mobilization in general and the success of the MAS in particular. The most salient institutional aspects include the democratization and broadening of the political spectrum consequent on the breakdown of traditional corporatism; the institutional reforms of the 1990s, especially the constitutional reform of 1994; and the process of decentralization set in motion by the People's Participation Act of 1994. With regard to the relationships among agents, the most salient features of the political context have been the crisis of traditional parties, electoral realignments and the availability of non-indigenous potential allies. Let us take a brief look at these factors.

It should first be emphasized that it was not only the previously mentioned economic effects of neoliberalism that favoured the indigenization of Bolivian rural politics; the breakdown of the corporative patronage system whereby votes were exchanged for political support also provided an opportunity for the formation of 'horizontally' organized movements based on links that were nominally ethnic, albeit in a broad sense that I shall analyse in greater detail in Section 2. Networks created in relation to the common interests of diverse indigenous groups, and which in the case of the MAS were subsequently extended to include non-indigenous groups, progressively replaced the divisive, de-mobilizing hierarchical corporative systems of political organization that dated back to the MNR (see Fig. 2.2).

In spite of insufficient enforcement and implementation, the legal and constitutional recognition of ethnic plurality in the 1990s undoubtedly constituted a very significant step forward as regards the 'respectability' of the claims of the indigenous movement. The ratification of the ILO's Convention 169 on the self-determination of indigenous and tribal peoples in 1992 was followed in 1994 by constitutional reforms in which Bolivia is defined as a multiethnic and pluricultural State (Art. 1), the 'natural authorities' of indigenous communities are recognized for administrative purposes, limited application of indigenous common law is allowed (Art. 171), collective property rights are acknowledged and bilingual education is accepted.[8] The establishment of new electoral constituencies in 1995 also played an appreciable role,[9] since some of the one-seat constituencies introduced in the lower house alongside proportionally represented multi-seat constituencies coincided with ethnic boundaries, and thus allowed the representation of ethnic minorities. However, the principal administrative novelty favouring the growth of indigenous movements and their transformation into efficient political parties was the People's Participation Act of 1994, which created 311 new municipalities.[10] In fact, this Act included the first legal recognition of indigenous communities, therein referred to as Basic Territorial Organizations. When the MAS and other Indianist parties won power in several of these municipalities, they took full advantage of the opportunity to obtain resources for their localities and gain a reputation that served as a foundation for their subsequent assault on central government. Finally, it should be borne in mind that the 1996 Act that set up the National Institute for Agrarian Reform enabled indigenous communities to register common land as 'Original Community Land', which within these communities created a motive for organization to exercise this right, and thereby provided an important opportunity for the construction of a political discourse centred on the key concept of 'territory'.

The constitutional reforms of the 1990s were thus fundamental in the rise of indigenous political parties because of the new rights and opportunities they afforded to Indians. However, they also assisted this process in more negative ways. The new pluralism of the Bolivian state was in many ways insufficient, and in the light of what it did provide for, its shortcomings provoked more ambitious indigenous aspirations, aspirations that the movement was now confident of its power to satisfy. In the 'water war' in Cochabamba in 2000, and the 'gas war' in La Paz in 2003, the indigenous movement showed its muscle and proved its capacity to force concessions through disruptive mobilization.

Vis à vis the electorate, political Indianism thus took full advantage of the opportunities to exhibit itself that it was offered or created for itself, but it also benefited enormously from the crisis suffered between 1989 and 2002 by the MNR and by the relative newcomers, *Acción Democrática Nacionalista*, and *Movimiento de Izquierda Revolucionario*, both of which were created during the 1970s. This is evident in the fact that the MAS grew precisely in the most volatile electoral districts,[11] where it was turned to by its natural audience following the organizational and electoral collapse of the traditional left wing as the result of external influences (the post-1989 crisis of socialism[12]), the turn to the right of the MIR (manifested in the neoliberal coalition government formed by Paz Zamora and former dictator Hugo Banzer), and the crisis of Bolivian unionism brought on by neoliberal economic policies. The break between the indigenous movement and the traditional left-wing allies that as class-bound organizations were unresponsive to Indianist demands allowed the MAS, as a non-exclusive Indianist party, to attract not only disaffected left-wing voters but also to steal disaffected militants from these former allies, thus reinforcing its organizational capacity. These converts included leaders such as the Guevarist journalist Antonio Peredo, Gustavo Torrico (formerly a member of the Socialist Party), Manuel Morales (formerly of CONDEPA) and the Trotskyite miners' leader, Filemón Escobar. Additionally, this growth in some cases allowed the MAS to reach agreements with residual left-wing groups, thus further broadening its potential electorate.

It was not only strictly political parties and groups that were affected by the crisis of the traditional Bolivian parties in the 1990s. The crisis orphaned numerous organizations that, though not themselves political parties, had traditionally supported and had been supported by these parties: rural teachers' unions, small business associations, craftworkers' associations, business federations and so on. These organizations were now receptive to the possibility of reaching an understanding with indigenous parties. In particular, the MAS attracted lowland indigenous organizations, including both religious groups and the CIDOB (which by then had extended its influence outside the lowlands). In spite of the difficulties associated with such heterogeneity, and the need for those with a union background to adapt to the new ethnically oriented discourse, such alliances afforded the MAS an invaluable plurality of material, organizational and reputational resources.[13]

A final component of the political opportunity structure that favoured the rise of the MAS was the international context: the fall of the Berlin wall in 1989, the break-up of the Soviet Union, the ILO's Convention 169 (which was ratified by Bolivia in 1991 following the March for Territory and Dignity, and was partially incorporated in Article 171 of the 1994 Constitution) and the celebrations surrounding the 500th anniversary of Columbus's discovery of America, which together with the increasing presence and activity of international NGOs provided Indianists with an international showcase that they took advantage of with the '500 years of resistance' campaign. It is noteworthy that this campaign made a major contribution to coherence between the demands of Eastern and Western Bolivian Indians, as is shown by its inclusion of a defence of traditional uses of coca leaves that would subsequently become a national symbol of resistance to US policy in Latin America.[14]

Political mobilization and the repertoire of contention

The final decisive factor in the success of the MAS was the mobilization policy it inherited from its precursors, the way in which it created and exploited opportunities. This approach differentiated Bolivian Indianism from, for example, its Peruvian or Guatemalan counterparts. Here and in the next part I shall focus on two closely interrelated aspects of this policy: the organization of collective action, and political discourse.

Efficient organization is essential for any party to exploit and build on the political opportunities that circumstances provide it with. From this point of view, two features of the history of the MAS stand out: the prior existence of a rich network of organizations and movements and the willingness of the MAS to take this plurality on board and make use of its organizational experience and capacity.[15] As I insinuated previously, Indianist political mobilization required the establishment of strong horizontal organization in order to combat division and demobilization, tendencies that had not only been promoted by the virtually defunct vertically organized labour unions, but which were also favoured by the weakness of territorial structure, community isolation, local rivalries, inward-looking communities and a general lack of social communication. Thus the MAS (but not the MIP) coveted and welcomed the organizational structure and capacity of existing groups such as the lower levels of vertical unions, independent unions, religious congregations and, of course, Indianist groups that had survived from the 1970s; although these latter had failed to thrive in the pre-1993 political context, they were nevertheless fundamental in the organization of successful post-2000 mobilization.

It is also true, of course, that the split in the indigenous movement between MAS and MIP had its origins in the 1970s. Firstly, the indigenous organizations that had arisen in the highlands differed widely from their counterparts in the lowlands. More importantly, the 1970s already exhibited divergence between the radical Indianism of leaders such as Luciano Tapia and the pluralist Katarism of Genaro Flores, for example, which was explicit in the Manifesto of Tiahuanacu. Both currents were strengthened by the Tolata massacre of 1974, but it was the Katarists who, following the foundation of the CSUTCB in 1979, created a political party, and who in 1982 entered the Bolivian parliament. The 1988 unification of Eastern unions and coca growers' organizations, and their subsequent control of the CSUTCB, laid the foundations for the creation of the MAS as a broad-based indigenist party.

As noted previously, the '500 years of resistance' campaign of 1992 was a landmark in the mobilization of the indigenous population of Bolivia. It was in the Assembly of the Original Peoples held on 12 October that the creation of a specifically political organization for channelling indigenous claims – the 'political instrument' – was first discussed in public. In consonance with this initiative, there was a deepening of the rift between Indianists wishing to enter the political arena, and those who proclaimed the need to fight the system from the outside, for whom the self-determination of the original peoples required a return to the *ayllu* and the *quyasuyo*.[16] A later example of these aspirations was provided when the National Council of Ayllus and Markas of the Quyasuyo, constituted in 1997, proposed – in opposition to the CSUTCB – that the legal device of the Original Community Land be employed to reconstruct the ancient Andean territories.

In the case of the MAS, there was an inversion of the traditional order of events in the relationship between social movements and revolutionary left-wing parties in Latin America: instead of an urban party sending out expeditions to rural areas to organize peasant disturbances, the MAS, a political party, was the result of the unification of peasant and indigenous organizations and their subsequent adoption of urban allies and goals so as to extend their influence nationwide in both geographical and political senses. Even the anti-bureaucratic style of the MAS leaders proved attractive to voters who were tired of bureaucracy, corporatism and the makeshift dealing among neoliberalist parties, and to militants in the traditional left-wing parties that were now in downright decadence. This novel relationship between party and movement led to the MAS being constituted by a multiplicity of different organizations. In fact, the 'political instrument' discussed at the Assembly of the Original Peoples was from the start realized as a federation of heterogeneous social movements that would be controlled from the bottom up, and Evo Morales's leadership has thus always been subject to the will of this variegated web of independent organizations, as he continually indicates by such far-from-rhetorical phrases as 'never stop correcting me.'[17] Not only does the party *not* replace the movement; the party is in principle just one more component of the movement's organizational repertoire.[18] This operative plurality of the political instrument and the MAS, together with the discourse to be examined in Section 2, is what makes it wrong to regard the MAS as populist in the classical sense.[19]

It was in 1995, at the Santa Cruz Congress, that the CSUTCB finally decided to create a 'political instrument' to compete in municipal elections. The Assembly for the Sovereignty of the Peoples (ASP) and the IPSP (*Instrumento Político por la Soberanía de los Pueblos*) were constituted, but since the electoral authorities refused to recognize the IPSP it fought the elections under the banner of United Left (*Izquierda Unida*), an uneasy coalition of residual left-wing parties headed by the Bolivian Communist Party. Thus the inclusive, pluralist organizational strategy I have just described was complemented by a strategy of action based on three decisions: unequivocal rejection of armed conflict, acceptance of representative democracy and entry into electoral politics. The electoral fruits of these strategic policies and decisions began to be gathered in the municipal elections of 1995, in which ten mayorships were won, and in the general elections of 1997, in which IPSP/IU achieved 18 per cent of the vote and four seats in Cochabamba. One of these seats was won by Evo Morales, who was already known nationwide following his arrest and subsequent release from gaol as a leader of the 1994 coca growers' march,[20] and who now obtained 60 per cent of the vote in his constituency. In 1999, to become legal, IPSP took over the name of an existing but inactive party, so becoming the MAS.

As I hinted earlier, the organizational development of what was to become the MAS was hindered not only by competition with agents external to the Indianist movement, but also by perpetual strife with Indianists who radically rejected association with non-indigenous agents. This internal conflict within the Indianist movement, which was far more than a question of personal antagonism between Evo Morales and Felipe Quispe, dated back to the beginnings of Katarism in the early 1970s, and was acutely manifested in 2000 when Quispe, who had led MITKA in the 1980s and the Red Offensive of Tupakatarist Ayllus since 1986, founded the MIP with an anti-white programme that established as its objective the reconstruction of the Incan dominions (Quyasuyo) under mono-ethnic Aymaran rule. However, these extreme proposals, which excluded not only whites and mixed-bloods but also indigenous Quechuans and Guaranies, were met by an electoral débâcle, the MIP obtaining only six per cent of the vote in the 2002 elections (which did not stop Quispe from continuing to fragment the movement in 2004, when he gave up his seat in order to continue to 'fight for Quyasuyo' from outside the system). Meanwhile, the MAS thrived with its policy of appealing not only to Aymarans and Quechuans but also to mixed-bloods and whites, and its willingness to form broad alliances with left-wing groups and even to include mixed-blood and white politicians among its own candidates and leaders, the most striking example of this being the Vice-Presidency of García Linera. In the 2002 elections, it received 19.4 per cent of the vote (almost as much as the 20.8% of the winning party, the MNR). The MAS therefore successfully differentiated itself from the exclusive Indianism of the MIP, and established itself as a 'catch-all' left-wing party in keeping with its slogan *Somos incluyentes*:[21] by 2005 it had managed to attract not only the miners and the urban left (in crisis since 1985), but even middle-class professionals and intellectuals. To achieve this required not only organizational success, but also a political discourse that appealed to these wider audiences and avoided raising the fears raised by the attitudes of the MIP and others. Let us now take a closer look at this discourse, and how it differed from that of the MIP.

2. The divergent discursive strategies of the MAS and the MIP

The ideologies of both the MAS and the MIP include all the elements typical of nationalism: humankind is divided naturally into nations; each nation is internally homogeneous, with an identity defined by differential ethnic traits that differentiates it from other nations; a person's freedom and authentic existence depend on his or her identification with a nation; loyalty to one's nation takes priority over loyalties to class or other groups; a nation is only free to develop if it controls its own sovereign, independent state; the state should serve the interests of the nation, its language and its culture; the world as a whole will only be free and at peace when all nations are free and independent. Nevertheless the inclusive *Bolivian* nationalism of the MAS, in which Indian ethnic groups are just the nucleus of a project to re-found the Bolivian nation for the benefit of all Bolivians, is clearly distinguishable from the exclusive, strictly *Aymaran* nationalism of the MIP, which denies the reality of Bolivia as a nation and aspires to the reconstruction of the Incan Quyasuyu under the slogan 'The Two Bolivias'.

Although the framing strategies of the MAS and the MIP (see Table 2.1) have shared a number of common features (anti-neoliberalism, defence of resources, defence of indigenous languages and autonomy), in other respects they have differed radically with regard to all three kinds of frame. In what follows, I subject the discourse of the MAS and the discourse of the MIP to comparative frame analysis, taking as my raw material, a corpus comprising speeches by and interviews with Evo Morales and Felipe Quispe, together with official programmes, proposals and statements of the MAS and the MIP (see the list of references in the notes).

As can be seen in Table 2.1, in which all entries correspond to literal fragments from the sources just mentioned, there are differences between MAS and MIP right from the beginning, in the definition of the problem to be resolved. Granted, both discourses include colonialism as a general descriptor of the Bolivian Indian's plight; but whereas the MAS

Table 2.1   Comparative analysis of interpretive frameworks

MAS: *To re-found Bolivia*	MIP: *The two Bolivias*
Problem	**Problem**
Bolivia: Sold, split, subjected	*Destruction of the original Indian national heritage*
Destruction of the Bolivian State	Domination and exploitation by the q'ara
Extermination of original peoples	White culture
Exclusion of the indigenous population in the founding of Bolivia in 1825	Colonialism, capitalism
Spoliation of natural resources	Denaturalization of the indigenous nation
Colonization	Loss of ancestral culture
Discrimination, hatred, disdain	
Subjection to imperialism	
Diagnosis: Causes	**Diagnosis: Causes**
500 years of plunder and extermination	*Bolivianization of the Aymaran nation*
Neoliberalism, the New Economic Policy	The capitalist, colonialist, racist and imperialist system
Imperialism	The arrival of the Spaniards
The neocolonialist State, internal colonialism	Contamination by Western ideology
Total dependence, direction from without, foreign impositions	Spoliation of indigenous assets and heritage
A fractionated, auctioned, transnationalized country	'What they call "Bolivia"'
Privatization of basic services (water, fuel)	The fact that Bolivia is not a nation
The imposition of a Western industrialist model	The republicanization of the country
US foreign policy: zero coca, the *Plan Dignidad*	Neoliberalism
Corruption, 'partiocracy', favours	The influence of drug traffickers in Bolivian politics
Imported Western democracy	Liberal representative democracy
Centralism	
Racism, discrimination	
Unemployment, emigration	
Diagnosis: Antagonists	**Diagnosis: Antagonists**
External agents and their local allies	*The traitorous white man*
Traitorous creoles (1781, 1821)	Gringos, whites, q'ara, westerners, foreigners, 'tenants', the colonial minority, the dominant caste

(*continued*)

Table 2.1 Continued

Diagnosis: Antagonists	Diagnosis: Antagonists
Imperialism, the USA	USA, imperialism
Foreign governments	Borbons, Pizarro, Almagro, Bolívar, Sucre, Banzer, Paz Zamora
Multinational corporations	Representatives of the USA: Goñi, Mesa
Local allies: García Meza, Sánchez Lozada	Creole landowners
Unpatriotic national oligarchy	Left-wing parties, those who have veered to the right
Traditional parties	MAS, Evo Morales, 'the antagonistic group'
US armed forces in Bolivia	Social-democrats and reformists, Christian socialism
Prefects, Governors	Those aiming to patch up the system, opportunists, foul play, those forming part of the system
	García Linera ('white traitor')
	White and half-caste assessors
	Pettifogging, officialistic politicians
	'The mishmash that governs this country'

Prognosis: Alternatives	Prognosis: Alternatives
A self-respecting, sovereign Bolivia with room for all	*The new Quyasuyan land*
National sovereignty, economic sovereignty, 'food sovereignty'	Recovery of the original Aymaran national heritage
Nationalization of natural resources	An Indian vision of the Nation
Renascence of the motherland	We the Tupakatarists
Refoundation of Bolivia	To sideline the *q'ara* system
A multinational State, a pluralist democratic republic	Political constitution of the Quyasuyan State
Dialogue between cultures	Tawantinsuyo: The Aymaran nation in its totality
'Union in diversity', unity and integrity	Revolutionary struggle
Rights of the peoples	Revolutionary sacred Pachakutism
Self-determination	A specifically Indian philosophy
The territorial principle (TCOs)	Resources owned by the community
Differentiated citizenship	To get rid of the colonial trash
Autonomy with solidarity	The Indian productive system, as opposed to capitalism

(*continued*)

Table 2.1 Continued

Prognosis: Alternatives	Prognosis: Alternatives
Co-officiality of indigenous languages	Communal forms of production (*ayni, mink'a, qamana*)
Representative and participative (community) democracy	Communal socialist system
Social economy, Andean capitalism	Ancestral production techniques
	Communities, *ayllus, tawantinsuyo*
	Reconstruction of the communal *ayllu*
	An *ayllu* of *ayllus*
	Self-determination
	'Self-government in accordance with our customs'
	Participative community democracy, as against representative liberal democracy
	Democratic communalism

Prognosis: Protagonists	Prognosis: Protagonists
Together we shall change history	*We the communalists*
Precursors: T. Amaru, T. Katari, B. Sisa, Zárate Willka, Bolívar, Guevara	Tupac Katari, Tupac Amaru, Zárate Willka
A. Tumpa, A. Ibáñez, M. Quiroga, L. Espinal	Aymaran Indians
The indigenous Bolivian people, majority sectors	The Indian nation, the Aymaran Nation
The indigenous and peasant movement	The indigenous movement
Indians, peasants, workers, outcasts	Indigenous pioneers
Professionals, intellectuals, the middle class	American Indianism
The national business class	The *Movimiento Indígena Pachakuti*: Authentic Indian politics
Álvaro García de Linera	A political agent with its own way of thinking
All Bolivians	Mallku
Bolivian women: Our women are dynamite	Actor político con pensamiento propio'
A government with *ponchos* and neck-ties	The Mallku of America
Andean and Amazonian culture	

(*continued*)

32

Table 2.1 Continued

Mobilizaton Repertoire	Mobilization Repertoire
Changing Bolivia with votes, not bullets	*The struggle between nations, the two Bolivias*
Pachakuti, Jach'a Uru = Democratic national revolution	Original indigenous revolution
To make the Empire give way	Antagonism between the two republics: The Indian and the *q'ara*
The power of conscience	Indian non-racism vs white racism
Democratic cultural revolution	Imitation of the armed uprising of Zárate Willka
The vote: A conquest of the people in 1952	To eradicate foreign ideology from the Indian's head
Social movements in town and country	A communal army
Unity, inclusivism	Communal modes of struggle and organization
The People's Political Instrument (MAS)	Laying siege to La Paz
Roadblocks	Mobilization, not negotiation; disobedience
The March for Sovereignty, the Ghost March, the March for Dignity	No respect for legalities
The '500 Years of Resistance' campaign	No dialogue
Thoroughgoing, pacific transformation	Armed struggle, radical positions
Defence of national resources: Oil and gas, water, land and territory	Willingness to spill blood
The sacred leaf	'Two arms, two ways' strategy: armed struggle ('the arm beneath the *poncho*')
'Coca is not cocaine'	Electoral competition
Coca = national sovereignty and dignity	Refusal to resort to allies or means foreign to Indians
Patriotic symbols: The national flag and the wiphala	Refusal to seek unity for the sake of unity
America: *Abya Ayala*	Opposition to Western representative democracy
Quyasuyo, Tawantinsuyo	Refusal to join in 'the election game'
	Refusal to participate in coalition governments
	Patience in awaiting future rebellions
	'*Pacha Mama, Coca Mama*' = The indigenous nation
	Sharp distinction between 'them' and 'us'
	Contraposition between the wiphala and the present national flag, a symbol of oppression

(continued)

Table 2.1   Continued

Mobilizaton Repertoire	Mobilization Repertoire
	Contraposition between Aymaran identity and the Bolivian national identity card
	Contraposition between the Presidency of the 'Republic of Quyasuyo' and the Presidency of Bolivia
	Tawantinsuyo = Aymaran nation

takes a decidedly *Bolivian* view of the effects of colonialism (it is *Bolivia* that has been sold, split and subjected, and the *Bolivian* national state that has been destroyed by neocolonialism), the MIP has formulated the problem in much narrower terms as the denaturalization of the indigenous nation and the destruction of the original Indian national heritage (where by 'Indian' it means in particular 'Aymaran'), the blame for which is specifically placed on the culture of white peoples (*q'ara*).

In consonance with its description of the problem, the MAS identifies its causes as basically originating *outside* Bolivia, though implemented by Bolivian nationals (Table 2.1, Diagnosis: Causes); and, as we shall see, the solution it offers is the re-founding of Bolivia *around* the Indian nucleus. For the MIP, however, Bolivia is not, and never can be, a nation; it is merely a colonial state that oppresses the true nation to which its territory, or a large part of it, corresponds. For the MIP, the Republic of Bolivia *as such* is a cause of the woes of the Aymaran people, being merely the form adopted by colonialist oppression during the past two centuries, and therefore an intrinsically artificial structure. By contrast, the Aymaran nation is an objective reality defined by its distinguishing marks: by its history, which goes back beyond the 500 years of resistance to Western invaders, to times immemorial; by its natural territory, the Quyasuyo, which does not coincide with the artificial frontiers of the internationally recognized Andean States; by its language, Aymara, which has survived in spite of the imposition of Spanish; by its culture, including in particular its traditional system of production, which does not depend on 'capital or institutionalized exploitation', but on bartering, reciprocity and redistribution[22]; by its ancestral forms of self-government and communal institutions (participative communal democracy; the network constituting the 'ayllu of ayllus'); and by its Andean religion, which preaches brotherhood, peace and harmony with Nature (the *Pachamama* or *Cocamama*) in contrast with violent imperialist Catholicism. When judged by these criteria for nationhood, Bolivia is fundamentally a contemptible artefact: in particular, it has no territory, since it merely occupies a territory that in reality belongs to the true nation, the frontiers of which it has distorted artificially to its own disadvantage (unlike modern Bolivia, the Tawantinsuyo reached to the Pacific Ocean); and it has no language of its own, since the imposition of Spanish has not managed to eradicate the native languages.

A closer look at what the MAS identifies as the causes of Bolivia's current problems shows them to have four kinds of origin: economic policies (in particular, the neoliberalism of the New Economic Policy pursued by Paz Estenssoro and Sánchez de Lozada, with its privatization of public services and resources); international politics (imperialism, colonialism, submission to external policies); internal politics (corruption, 'partiocracy', the system of patronage and exchange of favours, centralism) and cultural phenomena (the absence of a specifically Bolivian culture since the exclusion of the indigenous peoples from consideration in the original foundation of the Bolivian Republic). In spite of similarities, the MIP's diagnosis differs markedly: it is anti-capitalist, rather than merely anti-neoliberal; anti-Western; anti-Bolivian, as regards the existence of a Bolivian nation; and radically opposed to liberal representative democracy, which it identifies with 'officialism'.

These differing diagnoses of the causes of the problem bring with them different conclusions about who is to blame. For the MAS, it is basically external agents (the USA, multinational corporations), aided and abetted by traitorous local allies (the Bolivian oligarchy, the traditional parties). For the MIP, in spite of its avowedly not wishing to replace the racism of whites with indigenous racism, it is not only gringos, the USA, multinational corporations and foreign whites in general, but also all white and mixed-blood Bolivians (and even, implicitly, non-Aymaran Indians); and among the local tools or henchmen of the foreign or colonialist oppressors it includes both traditional left-wing parties (which are all accused of having veered to the right) and, in particular, the MAS, which is regarded as the agent that does most harm to the cause of the MIP[23] because of its reformism (seen by the MIP as integration in 'the system'), its social democratic nature (seen as subservience to capitalism) and its 'opportunism'. In this list of enemies of the MIP's project, a special place is reserved for Álvaro García Linera, once a comrade of Quispe's in the Tupac Katari Guerilla Army and now Evo Morales's vice-president: regarded by Morales as a paradigm of how support for the indigenous movement can be found among non-Indian intellectuals and the urban middle class, for Quispe he is prototypical of the traitorous white man.

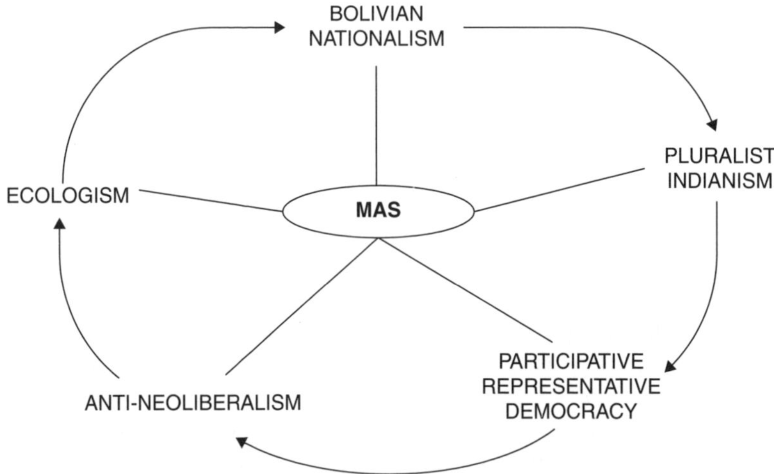

Figure 2.1   The dimensions of the discourse of the MAS

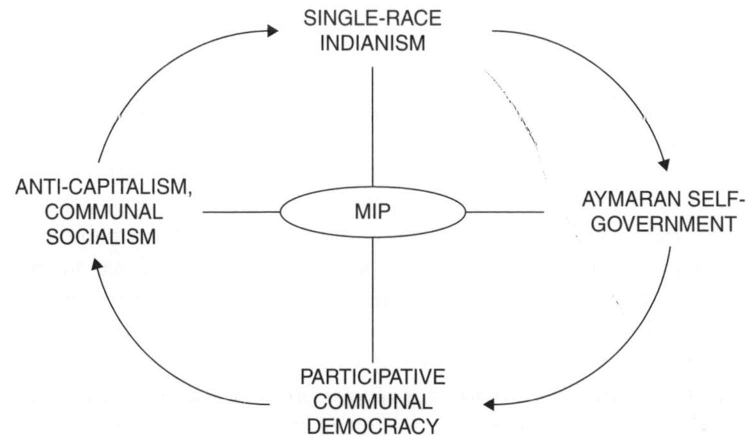

Figure 2.2   The dimensions of the discourse of the MIP

Nothing exemplifies the MIP's enclosure in a ghetto of its own making more than its invective against 'half-blood assessors' and 'the mishmash that governs this country'.

As is natural, given these different views of the problem and its causes, the prognostic frames of the MAS and the MIP also differ widely (Figs 2.1 and 2.2). The MAS proposes an alternative future consisting in the recovery of national sovereignty, hitherto surrendered to the agents of imperialism and neoliberal globalization, that is, multinational corporations and their local allies (traditional parties and the Bolivian oligarchy). It aims for Bolivia to be re-founded as a self-respecting sovereign nation by a Constitutive Assembly that will enact what it calls 'the second independence of our nation'. This recovery of national sovereignty from external agents will necessarily be accompanied by radical internal reforms of both the state and the nation that can be grouped under four headings: the concept of nation, the form of democracy, social justice and political ecologism.

Firstly, Bolivia must recognize itself as a culturally and linguistically plural nation. This does not mean a multiculturalism consisting of a collection of separate, inward-looking communities (Aymarans, Quechuans, Guaranies, mixed-bloods, etc.), but a common project that is shared by them all without attempting to obliterate their differences; a project that implicitly treats Bolivia as a nation of nations. Thus invocation of the right of the peoples to 'self-determination', 'territoriality', 'differentiated citizenship' and 'linguistic co-officiality' is accompanied by a vision of 'unity in diversity', 'unity and integrity' and 'autonomy with solidarity'. The aim is not just to set up a 'multinational state', 'a plural democratic republic', but to construct a new Bolivian nation based on 'dialogue between cultures', 'interculturality' and the inter-territorial redistribution of wealth.

Secondly, the organization of this nation of nations requires both the autonomy and self-government of the indigenous communities in their own territories, and a synthesis among three styles of democracy: representative democracy; a participative democracy realized through referenda, plebiscites, people's initiatives and the power to revoke the powers of the government; and the traditional democracy of the indigenous communities, with their communal forms of choice and decision taking. And this brings with it a relaxation of the monolithic universality of state law to allow recognition of indigenous law to the extent that it may be compatible with the equitable dispensation of justice. Democratic innovation – 'a unique laboratory for mixing distinct governing logics' in words of Donna Lee Van Cott – rather than the mere return to communal, traditional forms of self-government becomes a key feature of the MAS programme radically powered by diverse facilitating factors like a flexible and bottom-driven legal context for decentralization, a very innovative 'organic' articulation between the political party and the grass-roots civil society movements, and a charismatic and stable mayoral leadership.[24]

Thirdly, national sovereignty and pluralist democracy are means by which to execute the nationalization of resources and achieve the redistribution of wealth in accordance with a goal of solidarity, social justice and an economy at the service of Bolivians. The socialist spirit of the MAS is to be realized through sweeping reforms creating a kind of welfare state that the MIP dismisses as social democracy: a 'communal social economy' with opportunities for private enterprise, for a national, anti-neoliberal capitalism that García Linera has called 'Andean capitalism'. The constitutional proposal submitted by the MAS to the Constitutive Assembly is titled 'Re-founding Bolivia to live well'.

Finally, a non-trivial component of this discourse is its political ecologism, the goal of living in harmony with the environment, of regaining 'fraternal mutual respect between the inhabitants of Bolivia and mother Nature'. This goal does not merely refer to the nationalization of natural resources as an economic move, but ties in with the very concept of the Bolivian nation as propounded by the MAS. A relationship with Nature distinct from that perpetrated by Western civilization is to be a hallmark of Bolivian nationality, which is to recognize the biodiversity and environment of Bolivia as 'part of the original nation and hence of the *Pachamama* and the *Pacha*'. Community and Nature are viewed as a single entity that is to uphold a re-founded Bolivia as an Indian-centred but plural nation pursuing an alternative model of sustainable development, a non-essentialist model that functions, moreover, through deliberative participative democracy: 'the state shall consult the indigenous peoples regarding the uses of land and geological resources located in their territories'. By contrast with this programme, the alternative put forward by the MIP is, in consonance with its diagnosis, oblivious of all that is not Aymaran. Its proposal to 'recover the original Aymaran national heritage', to construct the 'new Quyasuyan land', stems from a view of the indigenous nation of much narrower scope than that of the MAS, specifically denying as it does the reality of the Bolivian nation. The MIP programme accordingly concentrates on eradicating 'the white system' through policies corresponding to four goals or mindsets: a single-race Indianism aiming to 'cleanse the Indian's mind of Western ideology', replacing it with a specifically Indian philosophy, and to 'get rid of colonial trash' so as to reconstruct the Incan realm separate from the rest of Bolivia; an anti-capitalist defence of 'the Indian productive system', a communal socialist system that will recover and modernize 'ancestral production techniques'; Aymaran self-determination and self-government 'in accordance with our customs', that is, rejection of and secession from Bolivia, however 're-founded'; and the replacement of liberal representative democracy with a participative, communal, deliberative kind of democracy, 'democratic communalism'.

These different proposals of the MAS and the MIP naturally postulate their realization by different protagonists. For the MIP, it is essentially only 'authentic Indian pioneers' – by which it means Aymarans – who can lead the Aymaran people in the proposed direction. By contrast, the MAS is explicitly inclusive in exhorting Bolivians to work 'all together' to change the course of history: though rooted in the indigenous left wing, its appeals to 'the great majority' are directed not only at the lower classes (Indians, peasants, workers, marginal minorities) but also at middle-class professionals and intellectuals, and even at 'national businessmen' who are not dependent on foreign capital. Its strategic objective is to form a broad alliance, a MAS-led nationwide social bloc in which indigenous claims will not be overridden or subordinated but instead constitute central objectives.

Guided by its conception of itself as a revolutionary party that will achieve 'total change', the MIP in its motivational frame preaches radical antagonism between 'white and Indian republics', confrontation between these 'two Bolivias'. In its pursuit of racial authenticity, it urges rejection of 'Western democracy' and rejection of the Bolivian nation. Bolivia, a Western artefact, is set in opposition to the wholly Andean, Aymaran Tawantinsuyo; the Bolivian flag, to the wiphala; and the presidency of Bolivia (legitimated only by the laws of the state) to the Mallku's ethno-nationally legitimated presidency of 'the Republic of Quyasuyo'. Western democracy and its elections are at best a means to an end: the openly proclaimed 'two-armed' strategy of the MIP is to coordinate electoral contest (when convenient) with armed conflict by a 'communal army', an 'imitation of the armed uprising of Zárate Willka'. Foiled in both directions, it prefers to await 'future rebellions' and exclude itself from the parliamentary system so as to be able to deride the 'mishmash' that governs Bolivia and to disdain dialogue, 'unity for the sake of unity' and association with allies foreign to Indians.

The inclusive project of the MAS requires a very different motivational frame. In order to attract and mobilize both Indian and non-Indian groups in its favour, it must sanction both the Bolivian flag and the wiphala. Though extremely active in the organization of a variety of unarmed manifestations of intent, notably marches and roadblocks, it prioritizes electoral contest, aiming 'to change Bolivia with votes, not bullets' (coherently with this attitude, universal suffrage, instituted by the 1952 Revolution, is itself interpreted as a past conquest of the lower classes). Its strategy is accordingly to construct a political party that is pluralistic yet permanently wed to the indigenous movement, which is regarded as the nucleus that can agglutinate other forces on the path towards a culturally oriented 'democratic national revolution', a radical process requiring not merely that the existing Constitution be subjected to more or less drastic reforms, but that it should be completely rewritten by a Constitutive Assembly.

In conclusion, the framing strategies of the MAS and the MIP constitute an integral part of their radically distinct alternatives as regards not only their objectives and programmes but also their political, institutional and organizational strategies, identifying the protagonists of their projects and the frontiers between friend and foe that define the collectivity that will give birth to a new nation. The radical Aymaran ethnic nationalism of the MIP has given rise to a strategy based on antagonism, on the postulation of internal, racially defined frontiers and on a severely limited group of legitimated protagonists – a strategy that has led to electoral defeat and deepening isolation. The pluralist and inclusive Bolivian nationalism of the MAS has facilitated its formation and intellectual, moral and organizational leadership of a new bloc that congregates socially diverse groups in a new national project for Bolivia. Consequently, the MAS is faced with the indisputably thorny challenge of reconciling a set of very diverse interests and preferences – notably the opposing interests of the East and West regions of the country – without relinquishing its initial raison d'être: satisfaction of the demands of the original indigenous peoples.

Notes

The author is grateful to Xavier Albó, Donna Lee Van Cott and Sarela Paz, for their contributions to and criticisms of this text.

1. D. L. Van Cott and R. Rice, 'The Emergence and Performance of Indigenous Peoples's Parties in South America', *Comparative Political Studies*, Vol. 39, No. 6, 2006, pp. 709–32.
2. F. Mallon, 'Indian Communities, Political Cultures, and the State in Latin America: 1780–1990', *Journal of Latin American Studies Supplement*, 1998, pp. 35–53.
3. M. D. Demélas, *L'invention politique: Bolivia, Équateur, Pérou au XIX siècle*, ERC, Paris, 1992.
4. X. Albó, 'Hacia una Bolivia Plurinacional e intercultural', CIDOB Congress, Barcelona, 2006.
5. X. Albó, A. Ticona and G. Rojas, *Votos y Wiphalas*, La Paz: CIPCA, 1995.
6. J. Dunkerley, *Rebellion in the Veins: Political Struggle in Bolivia 1952–1982*, London: Verso, 1984.
7. D. Yashar, *Contesting Citizenship in Latin America The Rise of Indigenous Movements and The Postliberal Challenge*, Cambridge: Cambridge University Press, 2005, p. 181.

8. R. Irigoyen, *Sometimiento Constitucional y Penal de los Indígenas en los Países Andinos*, PhD Thesis, University of Barcelona, 2005.

9. D. L. Van Cott, *From Movements to Parties: The Evolution of Ethnic Politics*, Cambridge: Cambridge University Press, 2005.

10. D. L. Van Cott, *From Movements to Parties: The Evolution of Ethnic Politics*, Cambridge: Cambridge University Press, 2005 and X. Albó, 'Hacia una Bolivia Plurinacional e intercultural', CIDOB Congress, Barcelona, 2006.

11. R. Madrid, 'The determinants of the electoral performance of ethnic parties in Latin America: The case of the MAS in Bolivia', APSA Meeting, Washington, 2005, and R. Madrid, 'Indigenous Parties and Democracy in Latin America', *Latin American Politics and Society*, Vol. 47, No. 4, 2005, pp. 161–79.

12. R. Máiz, 'El Indigenismo Político en América Latina', *Revista de Estudios Políticos*, No. 123, 2004, pp. 129–74.

13. R. Madrid, 'The Determinants of the Electoral Performance of Ethnic Parties in Latin America: The Case of the MAS in Bolivia', APSA Meeting, Washington, 2005; R. Madrid, 'Indigenous Parties and Democracy in Latin America', *Latin American Politics and Society*, Vol. 47, No. 4, 2005, pp. 161–79.

14. P. Stefanoni and H. Do Alto, *Evo Morales: De la coca al Palacio*, La Paz: Malatesta, 2006.

15. R. Máiz, 'Ethnisation de la politique et indigénisme en Amérique Latine' in R. Máiz and J. Tournon, *Ethnicisme et Politique*, Paris: L'Harmattan, 2005, pp. 213–77.

16. P. Stefanoni and H. Do Alto, *Evo Morales: De la coca al Palacio*, La Paz: Malatesta, 2006, p. 57.

17. Evo Morales, *La Revolución democrática y Cultural*, La Paz: Malatesta, 2006, p. 13.

18. D. L. Van Cott and R. Rice, 'The Emergence and Performance of Indigenous Peoples's Parties in South America', *Comparative Political Studies*, Vol. 39, No. 6, 2006, pp. 709–32.

19. P. Stefanoni and H. Do Alto, *Evo Morales: De la coca al Palacio*, La Paz: Malatesta, 2006 and R. Madrid, 'The Rise of Ethno-Populism in Latin America: The Bolivian Case', APSA Meeting, Philadelphia, 2006.

20. F. Patzi, *Insurgencia y Sumisión: Movimiento indígeno-campesino*, La Paz: Comuna, 1998.

21. Evo Morales, *La Revolución democrática y Cultural*, La Paz: Malatesta, 2006, p. 171.

22. F. Quispe, 'Organización y proyecto político de la rebelión indígena Aymara-Quechua', Interview with P. Costas, M. Chaves and A. García, 2001.

23. Ibid.

24. D. L. Van Cott, *Radical Democracy in the Andes*, Cambridge: Cambridge University Press, 2008, p. 175.

3
Reading the Cyprus Conflict through Mental Maps – An Interdisciplinary Approach to Ethno-Nationalism

Emel Akçalı

Introduction

There is a strong connection between a nation's existence and that of its individual members, in the sense that if the nation faces the threat of extinction, so do its citizens.[1] Likewise, for any nationalist project to be successful, it should first pass through the everyday life of the individual, and then diffuse its effects on a more collective and societal scale through institutional and non-institutional actors.[2] Analysing individuals' everyday lives and social relations may thus give hints about what kind of emotions and resources they invest for the future of their nation.

For Walker Connor, the essence of a nation is indeed a psychological matter rather than a fact.[3] 'It is not *what is* but what people perceive as is which influences attitudes and behaviour.'[4] According to this perspective, a nation does not rise upon individual/collective lived experiences only, but also on emotions, perceptions and representations, producing different types of markers, and promoting a certain idea of its very existence. Consequently, it occupies a strong and important space in the universe, both objectively and imaginatively.

In his work, *La région, espace vécu*[5] the French geographer Armand Frémont tries to analyse this space by taking into account the subjectivity of human beings living in it, via a multi-disciplinary method based on psychology and sociology. He calls it *l'espace vécu* (the lived space), the space directly lived by individuals through its associated images and symbols. By opening a ground for spatial analysis, *l'espace vécu* offers a deeper understanding of how individuals perceive and live the territory, as well, which is the 'appropriation of space.'[6] 'It's certainly a more vague, more individualist, more phenomenological and literary notion of geography, but more reflexive, more complete, more subjective, more colourful, and pictorial as well.'[7]

I find an intimate link between Frémont's concept of *espace vécu* – the lived space and Connor's[8] emphasis on the psychological dimension of the nation and nationalist behaviour. I further argue that this link may help to construct an inter-disciplinary methodological framework between political science and geography to study the nation, ethnicity, nationalism and ethno-nationalism.[9] Frémont's concept resonates well with Connor's analytical subjectivism which espouses the idea that a nation does not rise in the mind of intellectuals alone, but exists in the feelings and daily experiences of ordinary people, and is realized when there is a widespread belief in belonging to a nation.[10] Also, Frémont's emphasis on the space that the nation occupies brings the neglected references to territory, territoriality and the process of homeland making, as evoked by Penrose[11] and Kaiser[12] to nationalism and ethno-nationalism studies. The concept of territory may perhaps not suggest strong emotional bonds as much as place because of the scale of the concept and the lack of direct experience of individuals with territory.[13] However, when a territory is tied to human bonds, such as ethnicity and nationality, the emotional bonds can in fact be much more powerful.[14]

Drawing upon the inter-disciplinary framework introduced above, this chapter will examine the ethno-nationalist conflict on the island of Cyprus through the prism of individuals' perceptions and emotions. To this end, one hundred Cypriots' mental maps of their country will be analysed. The respondents' representations of their country will hopefully bring an insight into their perceptions, hopes, aspirations, desires and frustrations and their relationship with the political elite,[15] besides stimulating a novel way of analysis in ethno-nationalism studies.

Mental maps as qualitative methods

Mental maps refer to the psychological (internalized) representation of what we know about places, as revealed by simple paper and pencil tests.[16] By their very nature, they are qualitative representations: they are drawings, pictures or sketches and are 'hard to express in measurable units.'[17]

The world as we believe it to be is a synthesis of different types of information such as visual, auditory, olfactory and kinaesthetic, and people mix this information in varying proportions when asked to produce mental maps.[18] People's sensory capacities, age, experience, attitudes, perceptions, preferences, values and biases also play an important role in mental mapping.[19] People differentiate the good and the bad, attractive and unattractive, desirable and undesirable in their minds, at all spatial scales. This explains why physical distances on mental maps are thus often 'distorted, being under or overestimated according to the subjective importance of the destination point.'[20]

In their famous work on *Mental Maps*, Peter Gould and Rodney White[21] elaborated further on the mental map methodology to find out what conditions human spatial perceptions and what kind of consequences these have on attitudes towards migration. They explored a number of indications which can determine individuals' attraction, repulsion or accessibility to a place, such as landscape, climate, language, culture, infrastructure or zones said to be dangerous, or marked by a certain political attitude.[22] Finally, they devised a technique which, through a questionnaire, makes it possible to represent spatial preferences of a localized population. The respondents were asked a simple question: 'Where would you want to live?' They were then offered a series of places to order by subjective preference and the correlation of responses made it possible to classify people's spatial preferences. Another mental map method mentioned in this work was to ask the respondents to sketch a map of their favourite places in town.

According to Downs and Stea, the ability to represent spatial information as either words or images poses serious problems for research into the process of mental mapping.[23] When a person is asked to sketch a map, for example, the graphic medium or expression may constrain the external form of the representation people have in their minds. People vary widely in their graphic abilities, and age is a major factor affecting basic manual skills. The drawings or the sketches do not thus necessarily reflect the mental internal representation of a given space. This is true for the verbal medium as well.

> In some contexts, a picture may be worth a thousand words. Conversely, we can better express our evaluative feelings about a place in words. And should a person be forced to make a mental translation from one medium to another, the resulting external representation will probably reflect his translating skills and not necessarily how he knows Chicago or how he cognitively represents what he knows.[24]

Downs and Stea suggest that the problem of translation can be clarified if we think of the spatial knowledge as a vocabulary and the mental representation as a grammar since any representation (internal or external) is the result of an application of a mental signature (or grammar) to spatial knowledge (or vocabulary).[25]

I suggest that mental maps are inspiring qualitative assessments of the lived space/territory and the psychological dimension of nationalism/ethno-nationalism mentioned in the introduction of this chapter. A lived space or territory can directly or indirectly lead a person to be a part of a nationalist ideology or a group by its emotional power on the person and by the person's beliefs, hopes, desires, preconceptions, values and everyday experiences. Such a lived space/territory associated with a nationalist ideology can then be directly linked to the geopolitical codes of statesmen in their foreign policymaking. In this context, mental maps can easily be transformed from the individual to a collective level. This can also happen vice versa.

In his study on the boundaries as a topic in geographic education in Israel, Bar-Gar[26] argues that ideology and the state, as powers controlling society and space, channel resources in order to survive, not only through material means, like the army and economy, but also through mental processes, as in the case of territorial socialization. Schools and the educational system serve as an important source of influence over human values and beliefs, aiding in the production of consensus and standardization in the world views of the individual towards the present, the past and the future.[27] Geographical education is no exception. The creation of territorial belonging is important for the shaping of the character and world view of the individual and it is through this practice that a person finds his/her place in the world.[28] However, it is important to note that mental maps do not always reflect national ideologies diffused by the state. They can be reflections of lived experiences, individual aspirations and various other identifications. Deformations, exaggerations and blanks in the maps can also reveal a certain spatial representation of a particular place of which the origins and causes are open to investigation.[29]

In the next section, I will further elaborate on the mental map methodology by integrating it into a case study.

The ethno-nationalist conflict in Cyprus: A case study

Historically, the Cyprus conflict stemmed from competing ethno-nationalisms between Greek and Turkish Cypriot communities, in the decolonization period from the British Empire in the 1950s. Owing to Turkey's and Greece's involvement since its early stages, it has also become a regional conflict. Recently, due to the adhesion of the Republic of Cyprus (RoC) to the European Union (EU) in 2004, it is now also a European affair. Since the military intervention of Turkey in 1974 in support of Turkish Cypriots (TC), following a period of violence (1963–74) and an attempted Greek Cypriot (GC) coup d'état backed by the Greek military junta, the island of Cyprus is partitioned territorially between a de facto Turkish Republic of Northern Cyprus (TRNC), not recognized internationally, the RoC, internationally recognized, two sovereign British bases and a UN buffer zone, known as the Green Line.

While the legitimacy of the British sovereign bases and the buffer zone are recognized by both Turkish and Greek Cypriot governments, none of the sides recognizes the legitimacy of the other. The RoC government considers the territories controlled by TRNC under occupation and claims full sovereignty all over the island. However, it has not exercised any authority in the northern part of the island since 1974. This is also because Turkey still holds a substantial military presence in TRNC.

The ethno-nationalist conflict between Greek and Turkish Cypriots and the territorial partition of the island (see Figure 3.1) as a consequence led to the internal displacement of thousands of people: TCs in 1958 and between 1960 and 1963; and GCs in 1974. The GC displacement in 1974 was en masse and since then, these refugees have expected to return back to their homes. By contrast, TCs welcomed the separation

Figure 3.1 Partition of Cyprus

and the establishment of their territorial administration. Consequently, they have never really insisted on a 'right of return' to their places of origin. TC administration has also presented the territorial partition in 1974 as permanent, while GC administration has stressed its temporary nature, keeping alive the 'right of return' discourse.

The EU got involved in the conflict in the 1990s, as the RoC applied for membership. The expectations of peacemakers were that the EU negotiations and UN peace talks would go hand in hand. Finally, a UN peace plan based on a bi-zonal and bi-communal federal solution was brokered between the two sides and put to a referendum, on 24 April 2004, on both sides of the island. To the disillusion of much of the international community, the UN peace plan was rejected by 75 per cent of GCs, while being accepted by 65 per cent of the TCs. Since the implementation of the Plan was dependent on the approval of the two sides, it obviously failed and the island has remained divided. The GCs were generally dissatisfied with the territorial arrangements, property rights issues, limitations on the right of return of refugees and the fact that a part of Turkish citizens who settled on the island from Turkey after the 1974 partition could continue staying in Cyprus after the acceptance of the peace plan. In 2008, the two parties have started the negotiations again in order to find a viable solution to the partition of the island, and the talks continue to this date.

Mental Map collection in Cyprus[30]

During March–August 2005 and December 2005–January 2006, I asked 100 respondents, recruited through snow-balling or self-selected sampling techniques (50 in the cities of North Nicosia, Kyrenia, Famagousta, Morphou and in the villages of Akdogan and Yalya in TRNC, and 50 in the cities of South Nicosia, Paphos, Limassol and Larnaca in RoC), to sketch two maps: the first one of the country in which they live and the second one of the country in which they would like to live. The question was asked as such in order to stimulate the individuals to think in terms of lived territories, rather than only in terms of lived neighbourhoods, cities, towns or regions so that I could gather information about Cypriots' mental territorial representations. The sample on both sides of the island had a balanced mix of age, gender, education, income and rural/urban character of the place of residency. Among the respondents in RoC, there were one American, one French and three Greek citizens who resided in RoC, and four Cypriot Armenians, four Cypriot Maronites and one Cypriot Pontian. Among the respondents in TRNC, there were two Turkish citizens from Turkey. Thanks to my ethnic origin (half Turkish and half Turkish Cypriot), I did not have a linguistic obstacle in TRNC. Owing to the transportation facilities in this entity, I could also extend the collection of mental maps to rural areas. However, as public transportation is almost non-existent in RoC, the survey in this part of the island was conducted only in major cities to guarantee also a high percentage of English-speaking people, as I do not speak Greek. Questions were thus asked in English in RoC although in a few cases a questionnaire in Greek language was also shown to the respondents. GCs did not know about my ethnic origin during the time they were asked to sketch the maps – even though it is possible that some of them could have guessed it.

Results obtained on each side of the island vary, although the idea of territory as diffused by statesmen, school or media has emerged as the most important mental representation of 'the country' for most of the respondents on both sides of the divide. These territorial representations, however, are quite diverse, not only inter-ethnically, but also intra-ethnically, and most of the time they do not reflect the ethnic belonging of the respondents. This diversity reveals that identities in Cyprus are plural and multidimensional and Cypriots attribute diverse meanings and symbols to their country. The mental maps collected in Cyprus also show that individual emotions, perceptions and representations stem, at times, more from personal hopes, goals and desires rather than from ethnic or cultural belonging. This can help us to learn an important dimension about ethno-nationalist conflicts: personal aspirations and worries do not necessarily correlate with national or ethnic objectives.

It is important to draw attention to the fact that the mental maps collected in TRNC are more diverse. They do not en masse represent the official discourse – a bi-zonal Cyprus or an independent TRNC. This may stem from the fact that there was a regime change in TRNC, from a hardliner nationalist position to a moderate one in 2003, due to an identity transformation process within the TC society which is now more willing to compromise than in the past. The new administration in TRNC is also a supporter of a solution based on a bi-zonal and bi-communal option. However, it does not base its argument on Turkish nationalism and independentist discourses, and favours a federalist administrative framework under an EU umbrella, instead. Also, it has a territorially united Cyprus map as its political emblem as opposed to more nationalist symbols like the moon and the star symbolizing Turkishness.

In RoC, although the GC leaders had officially agreed on a bi-zonal and a bi-communal solution in 1977, their idea of a united Cyprus has always been administratively less federal and more unitary than an option acceptable for TCs. GC political discourses, national education and the media have also constantly put more emphasis on a territorially or administratively united Cyprus than a federal one. Plus, the accession of RoC to the EU strengthened the official arguments and positions of RoC governments.[31] The Orthodox Church in RoC is also very influential in keeping the Greek Cypriot identity firm and less compromising. There is not such an influential spiritual institution in TRNC which can also play the card of a political actor. However, it is true that some mental maps show a hardliner tendency among the Turkish Cypriots as well. Since the failure of the Annan Plan, the TC community is disillusioned by GCs, and EU institutions which, according to them, have not kept their promises to the TC community in return for a Yes vote for the UN Peace Plan. According to Tocci,[32] the identity transformation in TRNC before the failure of the Annan Plan was achieved through pressure and punishment rather than through EU institutional contact and socialization. This partially explains why a significant part of the TC community is less trustful towards third actors like the EU and their GC neighbours since the failure of the UN Peace Plan. As the mental maps below were collected during the post-Annan period, some of them show that a segment of TCs are keen on maintaining their militarily protected bounded space rather than living together within the same territory with GCs.

In the next two sections I will present and discuss examples of mental maps collected, respectively, in the RoC and in the TRNC.

Republic of Cyprus

In RoC, 30 respondents out of 50 preferred to draw a virgin map of Cyprus (see Figure 3.2). While 26 out of 30 left no indication or writing on the maps that they sketched, three respondents added the symbols of the RoC, representing either the GC administration discourse that there is only one legitimate government in Cyprus or wishing to prevent any misinterpretation or misunderstanding of their maps. A respondent in the city of Limassol, who was a refugee from the city of Famagusta, which is now within TRNC, indicated her city of origin and the St-Andreas point of the island on her map. These were areas mostly populated by GCs before the partition of the island in 1974 and the fact that this respondent emphasized them on her map is an important signifier of the strong 'right of return' feeling among Greek Cypriot refugees.

Figure 3.2   Virgin map of Cyprus (30 out of 50 respondents in RoC)

Figure 3.3   A divided Cyprus (11 out of 50 in RoC)

Eleven respondents out of fifty in RoC drew a geographically divided, occupied or a half Cyprus as a response to the first question (see Figure 3.3). This is, in fact, the lived experience of a major part of GCs for almost 35 years. As seen in one of the drawings, one respondent wrote 'occupied' in the North of the dividing line, to make sure that the division on his map is not interpreted as something ordinary. It is interesting to observe that almost all the respondents sketched the dividing line

in Cyprus in the form of barbed wires signifying a very hard complicated border guarded by military means. These are important signifiers
of individuals' frustration about the partition of the island. Another
respondent, besides indicating the dividing line in his map, sketched
also the tourist resorts, palm trees, hotels and beach umbrellas in the
locations of major tourist destination cities, Larnaca, Limassol and
Paphos, as a reminder that Cyprus is not only famous for its intractable
conflict, but also for its natural beauties.

Two GC people drew Cyprus within its regional space, one representing Cyprus in a hostile regional environment and the other representing it as isolated from all other continents, but making explicit that
he hopes that one day it could connect to the world. The maps are
significant to give us an idea of the geopolitical perception of Cyprus
among Cypriots.

Two young Greek Cypriot girls drew a socio-economically and ideologically divided Cyprus, rather than a territorially divided one as a
response to the first question (see Figure 3.4). The one who drew Cyprus
in the form of a star was a shopkeeper and a college student of psychology. She represented RoC through a divide between *political parties and
their followers, racists, ethnicists, the Church, people with power, people who
are the most dependent on the government and its politicians* on the one
hand and *people whom I would like to be with* on the other hand. The
other girl, who was also a half-American high school student, drew

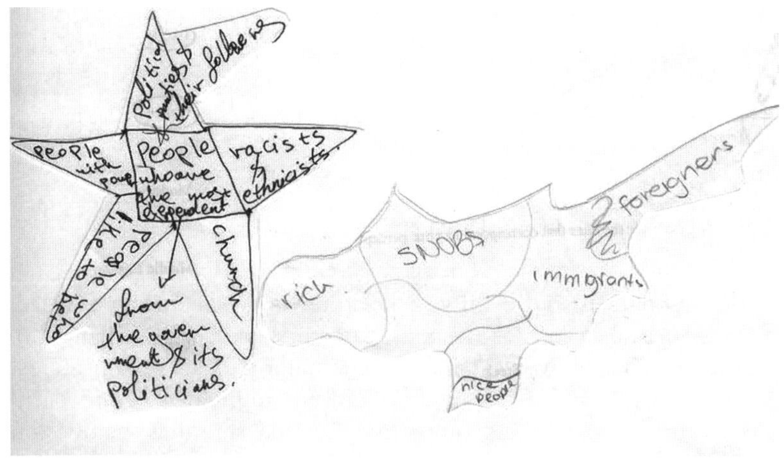

Figure 3.4   Cyprus socially and ideologically divided (2 out of 50 in RoC)

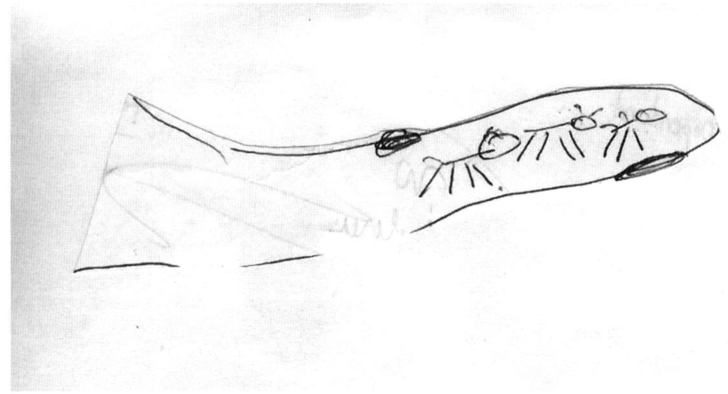

Figure 3.5   The only 'true' Cypriots (1 out of 50 in RoC)

Cyprus divided between *the rich, the snobs, the foreigners and the immigrants* on one part and *nice people* on the other part. She located this latter people in an area at the very south end of the map, which corresponds to the Akrotiri sovereign British base location in Cyprus.

A GC scholar drew donkeys from the Karpasia peninsula, making an allusion to the supposed statement of both Archbishop Makarios, the first president of RoC, and Rauf Denktas, the first president of TRNC, that the only Cypriots on the island are the wild donkeys living in the Karpasian peninsula of the island (see Figure 3.5). These two politicians were the major actors during the escalation of the ethno-nationalist conflict on the island.

A Cypriot Armenian shop owner drew clouds and birds as a mental representation of her country to show her optimist perception for both present and future Cyprus. A Cypriot Greek university student drew a beach and the sun and another 20-year-old young lady wrote only *Supara Rally*, a car race in Cyprus, giving important hints about their lived Cypriot space.

A young Greek Cypriot female graphic designer drew Cyprus like a staircase descending from the stronger to the weaker; and a male Greek Cypriot architect drew his quarter in Lefkosia (Nicosia), showing his office, *Maria's bar also*, his house and two other bars that he frequents (see Figure 3.6).

The maps shown in Figures 3.4, 3.5 and 3.6 are significant in the sense that they do not represent the lived space/territory in its classical sense, but inform us about different ways in which people live the

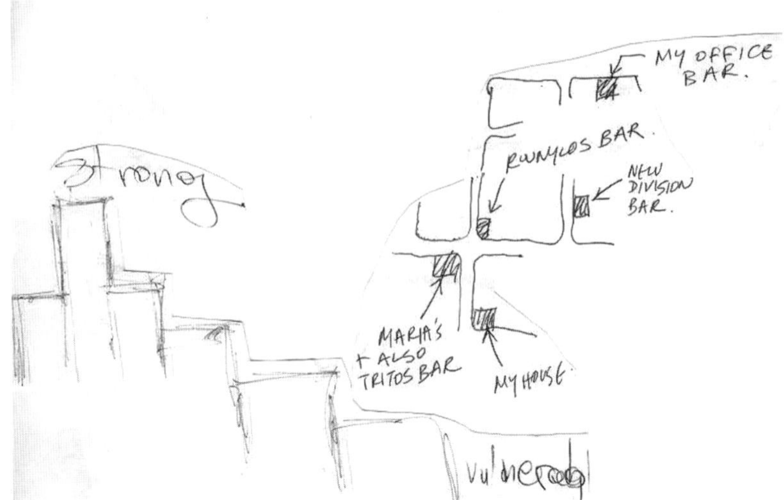

Figure 3.6   Cyprus through daily and social life (2 out of 50 in RoC)

territory and diverse meanings that they attach to their country. They are important indicators of social and individual identities rather than of ethnic or national identities. The fact that these mental maps come generally from young Greek Cypriots is important to recall in that the present and the future 'country' might have different meanings for the more cosmopolitan young generations who hold different ideas of a nation and territory than the ones held by their elders.

As a response to the second question, 40 respondents out of 50 drew a territorially unified Cyprus, representing 'the country' that they would like to live in. A unified Cyprus is certainly the idea of 'the country' diffused by GC statesmen, school or media, but it also is the physical shape and consequently the most well-known representation of the island. Finally, while five respondents did not draw any sketches, the remaining five preferred to draw a divided Cyprus, representing their support for a federal solution which was actually the solution put forward by the UN Peace Plan.

Mental Maps collected in TRNC

Thirty respondents out of fifty drew a divided Cyprus in TRNC – Cyprus divided between a TRNC and a RoC; between Turkey, Greece and Great Britain; between Turkish Cypriots and Greek Cypriots; between Turks and Greeks or between Christians and Muslims as a response to the first

Figure 3.7   Divided Cyprus (30 out of 50 in TRNC)

question, indicating as it is the case in RoC, that the territorial division of the island is the most evident lived experience of Cypriots, which also has an impact on economic and social lives of Cypriots at all levels (see Figure 3.7).

A male university student drew Cyprus divided into a Northern and a Southern part, and represented the North by night clubs and casinos, and the South, by a Tourism Office and the local siege of the EU, showing his ironical mental representation of the island and giving a hint that night clubs, casinos, the tourists and the EU officials are the real owners of the island, not the Cypriots.

Seventeen respondents drew a virgin map of Cyprus in response to both questions, representing a mental map of Cyprus without borders and any political markers. One of the respondents drew Cyprus as a boat, in response to both questions, either representing its independence or the political claim that Cyprus will never be independent from regional or global powers because it is a 'would never sink military boat'. A political activist drew his country in response to both questions, under exterior influences, especially of the US and Europe, as a response to both questions, indicating his geopolitical perception of present and future Cyprus.

A Turkish Cypriot woman drew a bottle of *zivania* (Cypriot liquor) and Cypriot *kebab* in response to both questions (see Figure 3.8), emphasizing

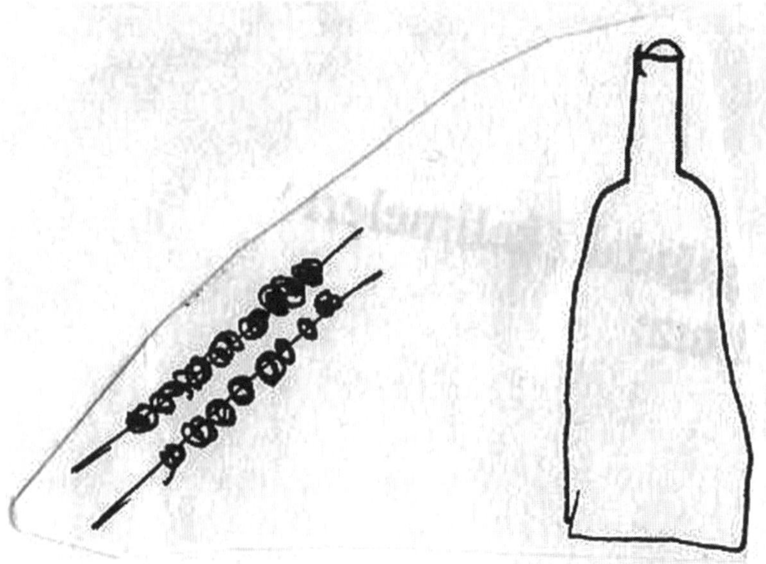

Figure 3.8   Cyprus cultural (1 out of 50 in TRNC as response to both questions)

that these are really the only things that come to her mind when she thinks about Cyprus, and giving an example about the mundane or banal symbol of a national territory.

Interestingly, among the 30 TC respondents who drew a divided Cyprus for the first question, 13 drew a reunified Cyprus as a response to the second question (see Figure 3.9). This clearly shows their aspiration to overcome the condition of division. One of these respondents drew the island reunified by railways; showing a preference for an environment-friendly Cyprus, as opposed to the actual situation where private cars are the only means of transportation on the island and almost each Cypriot who has reached the age of 18 possesses a car. These drawings reveal the development that TC mental representations have tilted a great deal from the hardliner separatist discourses. This transformation revealed by mental maps is significant since it helps to apprehend that one way to read mental maps is to analyse them as social constructions which go through a social filter prior to their entry into the individual's perceptual filter. Consequently, when the ways social groups use certain symbols, signs and discourses change, mental maps of individuals may also transform.

Among the 30 respondents who drew a divided Cyprus for the first question, 17 drew a bi-zonal Cyprus for the second question (see Figure 3.10),

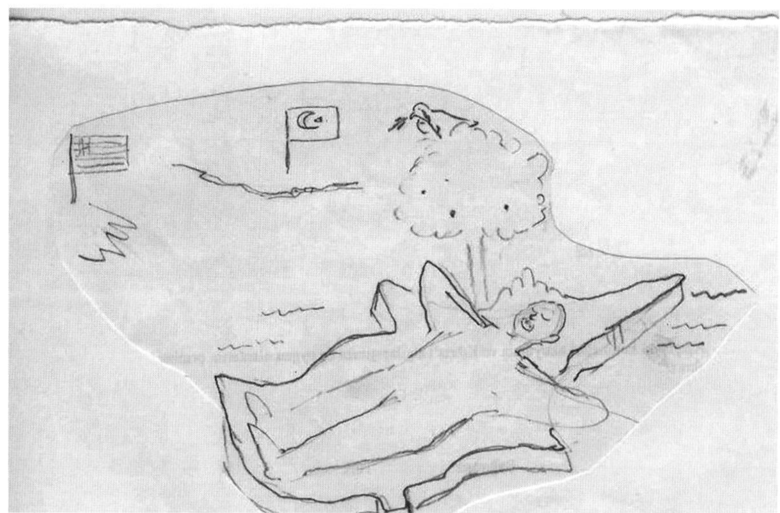

Figure 3.9 Reunified Cyprus (13 out of 50 in TRNC as a response to the second question)

indicating that the 'country that they would like to live in' is in conformity with the idea of a TC territory as diffused by TC statesmen, school or media.

This dimension of spatial/territorial attraction or repulsion is quite evident in the third mental map above, which was sketched by a TC artist. She drew only the northern part of the island, representing the country where she would like to live in. By leaving out the entire RoC from her perception of her present and future country, she clearly conveys the idea of repulsion or fear of this entity. Drawing upon such a sketch, the next step would be to learn what causes her repulsion or fear.

Conclusion

As the qualitative study in this chapter shows, the lived space and territories of Cypriots revealed through their mental maps are real (e.g. division), symbolic (e.g. kebab) and imagined (e.g. clouds). In line with the inter-disciplinary approach identified and proposed in the introduction, they do not reflect the ideologies diffused by the political elite only, but reveal people's diverse lived experiences, emotions and values. The use of mental maps as a qualitative data gathering helps grasp this plurality of views while preventing at the same time passionate debates

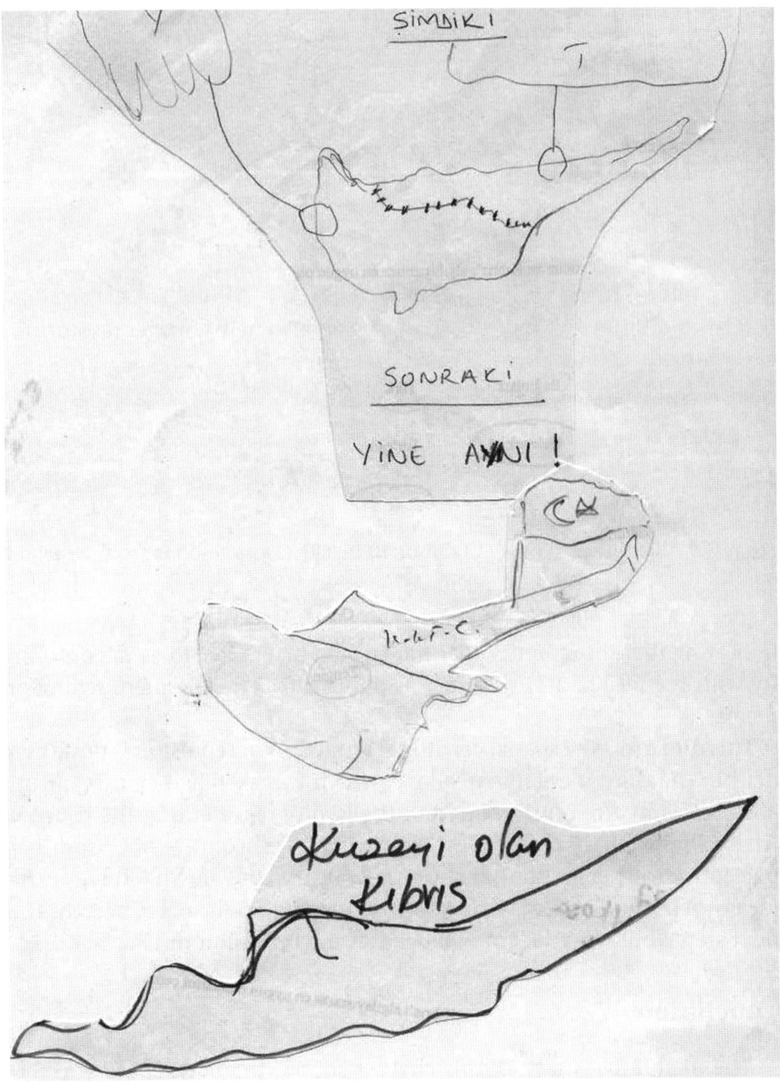

Figure 3.10 Cyprus with its northern part (17 out of 50 as a response to the second question in TRNC)

Note: The first inscription on the first map below translates as *Now* and the second *Later, the same*. The inscription on the second map indicates: *KKTC*, which means TRCN in Turkish language. Inscription on the third map translates as: *A Cyprus which has its North only*.

with the respondents. By privileging maps instead of narratives, the clarity of information about the respondents' perceptions and emotions might have been lost in the process. However, mental maps prove powerful in the sense that they provide both internal (psychological) and external representation (graphic and visual) of the lived territories thus a larger space for analysis.

The inter-disciplinary approach adopted in this chapter also proves helpful as it helps to refine studies on ethno-nationalism. It concentrates on the psychological relationship of human beings with their territory, and on what kind of meanings and signs people attribute to the country that they live in. In this way, it can also help conflict resolution. According to Miall, Ramsbotham and Woodhouse, the way that the root causes of a conflict are conceptualized usually determines the conduct of its resolution.[33] If the conflict is viewed from a competitive struggle perspective, the parties are assumed to be in a permanent confrontation. If the role of the perceptions, emotions and beliefs is highlighted, then this may open a ground for communication. If we combine these two perspectives and presume that a conflict occurs when parties find themselves 'divided by perceived incompatible interests or goals and competition for control of power and scarce resources,'[34] then we may have a clearer picture about how to develop accurate strategies for conflict resolution.

The interdisciplinary methodology proposed in this chapter facilitates obtaining such a clearer picture, as it helps to analyse not only the impact of ideologies diffused by the statesmen on shaping individuals' perceptions, but also the psychological link between individuals and their lived territory.

Notes

1. Umut Özkırımlı, *Theories of Nationalism – A Critical Introduction*, London: Palgrave Macmillan, 2000, p. 224.
2. Amaël Cattaruzza, *Le Monténégro entre Union et Indépendance – Essaie sur une géographie du nationalisme*, Unpublished PhD thesis, Université de Paris IV, Sorbonne: 2005.
3. Walker Connor, *Ethno-Nationalism: The Quest for Understanding*, Princeton: Princeton University Press, 1994, p. 42.
4. Ibid., p. 197.
5. Armand Frémont, *La Région, Espace Vécu*, Champs, Paris, Flammarion, 1999.
6. Roger Brunet, Robert Ferras and Hervé Théry, *Les mots de la géographie, Dictionnaire Critique*, Paris, Reclus, 1992; Guy Di Méo, *L'Homme, la société, l'espace*, Paris, Anthropos, 1991; Guy Di Méo, et Buléon Pascal, *L'espace social-Lecture géographique des sociétés*, Paris, Armand Colin/VUEF, 2005.

7. Frémont 1999, p. 40.

8. Connor 1994.

9. Ethno-nationalism denotes loyalty to a nation deprived of its own state and the loyalty to an ethnic group embodied in a specific state, particularly where the latter is conceived as a 'nation-state'. Daniele Conversi (ed.), *Ethno-Nationalism in the Contemporary World – Walker Connor and the Study of Nationalism*, London: Routledge, 2004.

10. Walker Connor, 'When is a Nation?' *Ethnic and Racial Studies*, Vol. 13, No. 1, 1990, pp. 92–103.

11. Jan Penrose, 'Nations, States and Homelands: Territory and Territoriality in Nationalist Thought', *Nations and Nationalism*, Vol. 8, No. 3, 2002, pp. 277–97.

12. Robert J. Kaiser, 'Homeland Making and the Territorialization of National Identity' in D. Conversi (ed.) *Ethno-Nationalism in the Contemporary World – Walker Connor and the Study of Nationalism*, London: Routledge, 2004, pp. 229–47.

13. I borrowed this idea from Nicholas Entrikin (Nicholas J. Entrikin, 'Contemporary Humanism in Geography', *Annals of the Association of American Geographers*, Vol. 66, No. 4, 1976, pp. 625–6) although in his own argument, he used the concept of 'region', instead of 'territory'.

14. Entrikin, 1976, p. 627.

15. I borrowed this idea from Amael Cataruzza (Amaël Cattaruzza, 'Les représentations de l'espace politique et culturel chez les jeunes de Bosnie-Herzegovine, in Y. Richard and A. L Sanguin (eds), *l'Europe de l'Est, Quinze Ans après la chute du mur – Des pays baltes à l'ex-Yougoslavie*, l'Harmattan, Paris, 2004, pp. 309–24).

16. David Ley, 'Mental Maps', in R. C. Johnston, D. Gregory, G. Pratt, M. Watts (eds), *The Dictionary of Human Geography*, Oxford: Blackwell Publishers, 2000, pp. 498–9.

17. See http://www.mentalmaps.info/.

18. Roger M. Downs and David Stea, *Maps in Minds – Reflections on Cognitive Mapping*, New York: Harper&Row Publishers, 1977, p. 23.

19. Ibid.

20. See http://www.mentalmaps.info/.

21. Peter Gould and Rodney White, *Mental Maps*, London: Penguin Books, 1994.

22. Cattaruzza 2005, p. 70.

23. Downs and Stea 1977, p. 85.

24. Ibid.

25. Ibid.

26. Yoram Bar-Gal, 'Boundaries as a Topic in Geographic Education', *Political Geography*, Vol. 12, No. 5, 1993, p. 433.

27. Ibid., p. 422.

28. Richard Muir and Ronan Paddison, *Politics, Geography and Behaviour*, London: Methuen, 1981, p. 39.

29. Cattaruzza 2005, p. 71.

30. The mental maps analysed in this section originally appeared in Emel Akçalı, *Chypre, un enjeu geopolitique actuel*, Paris, l'Harmattan, 2009, pp. 285–99.

31. Emel Akçalı, 'The European Union's Competency in Conflict Resolution: The Cases of Bosnia, Macedonia (FYROM) and Cyprus examined' in T. Diez and N. Tocci (eds) *Cyprus: A Conflict at the Crossroads*, Manchester: Manchester University Press, 2009, pp. 187–9.
32. Nathalie Tocci, *The EU and Conflict Resolution – Promoting Peace in the Backyard*, London and New York: Routledge/UACES Contemporary European Series, 2007.
33. Hugh Miall Oliver Ramsbotham, Tom Woodhouse, *Contemporary Conflict Resolution*, Oxford: Polity Press, 2000, p. 12.
34. Ibid.

4
Defining and Redefining Russianness: The Concept of 'Empire' in Public Discourses in Post-Soviet Russia

Olga Malinova

A reassessment of the legacy of empire is an important part of the problem of redefinition of collective identity that arose in Russia after the collapse of the USSR. Leaving aside a disputable question about how long ago Russia ceased to be an empire,[1] it is important to stress that to build the ties of national solidarity on 'the ruins of empire' is not to design them in an empty place: 'the ruins' are an uneasy substructure that significantly determines the configuration of future building.[2] So, different models of the Russian national identity offered by political entrepreneurs should in this or that way take into consideration the imperial legacy. This chapter analyses the interpretations of the concept of 'empire' in public discourses of the last decade with the purpose to reveal some problems of conceptualization of Russian identity in the post-Soviet context.

Remarkably, the symbol of 'empire' has had considerable popularity in the 2000s, which sharply contrasts with the situation at the beginning of 1990s when the concept of 'empire' was considered critically and applied mostly to the past. The rare cases of its projection to the future looked scandalous.[3] Such evident ardour for an idea of 'empire' in the 2000s is explicable. At the end of the 1980s and the beginning of the 1990s, on the wave of euphoria caused by dismantling of the Soviet system and optimistic aspirations towards the West, the critical approach to the imperial experience of the USSR was shared by a large part of the intellectual elite. Later disillusionment with post-Communist transformations, traumatic consequences of the collapse of the Soviet Union and uneasy relationships with the West paved the way for reconsideration of the imperial past. So, the symbol of 'empire' has acquired positive connotations and has become a valuable resource for politicians with different orientations.

This chapter tries to answer two basic questions: how do Russian politicians and public intellectuals with different political orientations deal with the concept of 'empire'? And how is the symbol of 'empire' used for the construction of different models of collective identity that underlie the new Russian state? The answers to these questions will be based on analysis of a significant body of statements and publications of Russian politicians as well as of texts of intellectuals written for the broad audience of non-specialists. In this analysis we will distinguish *imperial* projects that introduce some plans of revival of the empire and *post-imperial* ones that propose some decisions of present-day problems taking into account the imperial experience of the past (considered positively or negatively). Our analysis will be concentrated mostly on the former, but to give a full picture of positions presented in the Russian public space we will have to address the latter as well.

The semantic map of the concept of 'Empire' in Russian public discourses

It would be useful to start this research with clarification of different meanings in which the term 'empire' is used in Russian public discourses. We do not mean to evaluate different interpretations of 'empire' as a tool of social research – it is obvious that in public discourses this term is used not always according to the notions of contemporary political theory. We will trace how this term is represented in political discourse. The revealed variations of meaning have both cognitive and doctrinal origins: on the one hand, the Russian politicians and intellectuals derived their notions of 'empire' from different sources (history, Soviet ideology, mass media, academic literature, etc.); on the other hand, as we will try to show, there are some more or less stable combinations of basic meanings in each segment of Russian political discourse.

Drawing on the texts that were the objects of our analysis we have distinguished five basic interpretations of the term. Each of them might be paired with some 'opposite' ideal–typical concept. This procedure helps to establish the complicated system of meanings into which the concept of 'empire' is built in Russian political discourse (see Figure 4.1).

1. *The heterogeneous state*: Empire is seen as a type of polity that includes *many* communities ('peoples', 'ethnic groups', 'nations', 'nationalities', 'political entities', etc.). The ideal-typical opposite of this interpretation of 'empire' is 'the *nation*-state' (with the accent on the

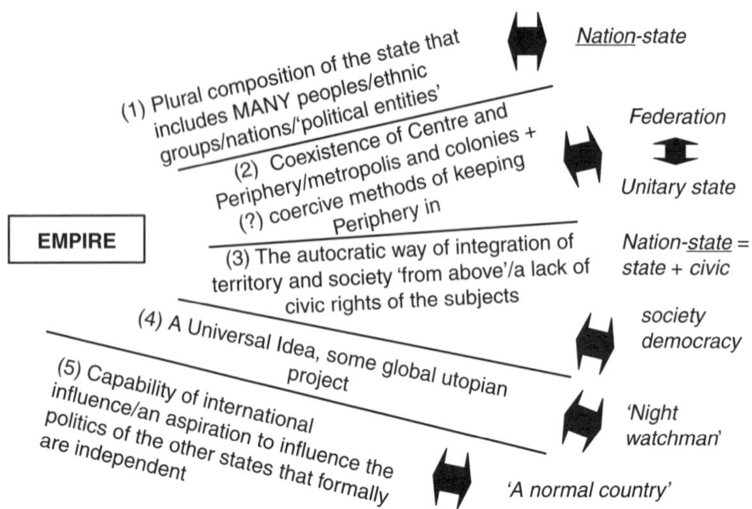

Figure 4.1   The concept of 'empire' in Russian political discourse: Basic meanings and oppositions

first part). In the Russian political discourse 'empire' is sometimes contrasted to the state 'of one nation'.

2. *Coexistence of Centre and Periphery (metropolis and colonies)*, the relationships of which are *asymmetrical and hierarchical*. Sometimes those who share this interpretation additionally stress an unequal exchange of resources to the benefit of the Centre and coercive methods of keeping the Periphery in. In this sense 'empire' is contrasted, on the one hand, to *federation* that presupposes an equal relationship between the federal centre and members of federation, and, on the other hand, to *the unitary state* where centre and periphery are not so opposed to each other.

3. *The autocratic way of integrating territory and society 'from above'*. This interpretation accentuates the 'vertical' character of political relationships in empire in the contrast to combination of the 'vertical' and 'horizontal' ones that is typical for nation *state* (the latter is seen as a tandem of democratic state and civil society). Within the framework of such interpretations, the deprivation of the subjects of empire of any civic rights is sometimes contrasted to the status of citizens of the nation state. So, 'empire' presupposes autocratic coercion not only of subjected territories but also of individuals.

4. *Presence of some Universal Idea*: some global utopian project for the sake of which an empire integrates in its body and in the sphere of its influence, different peoples and territories. 'Empire' thus is interpreted not only as a type of organization of political power, but also as a vehicle of some messianic project. In this sense it might be contrasted to the ideal type of the *night watchman state* the functions of which are limited to service of its citizens' interests.

5. *Capability of international influence*: an aspiration to influence the politics of the other states that formally are independent. In this sense 'empire' is 'a great power' that fully realizes its potential. This interpretation is not very strict (probably in this sense it would be better to speak about 'imperial rule' or 'hegemony'). It is a metaphor rather than definition, but the word 'empire' was used in this sense not only in post-Soviet Russia – see Ronald Reagan's definition of the USSR as 'an evil empire'. To determine the ideal type that might be contrasted to this meaning we will also appeal to the metaphor referring to the expression, 'a normal country', once used as a title for an article by A. Shleifer and D. Treisman.[4]

These are the basic meanings of the term 'empire' that are represented in Russian political discourse. Having at our disposal this semantic 'map' we can pass on to analyses of 'imperial' and 'post-imperial' projects presented in the Russian public space.

The issue of empire in the discourse of 'Imperial' and 'Post-Imperial' Russian nationalism

We will start with the projects for the revival of empire proposed by *imperial nationalists*. We will use this term to label the cluster of ideological projects that regard a revival of Russian empire as their primary aim. Most of these projects have a bias towards Russian nationalism, that is, they strive for valorization of Russian identity and aspire to create favourable political and economic conditions for the well-being of the community that is defined as 'the Russians' (which means – ethnic Russians, *russkie*). It should also be noted that contemporary Russian nationalism proposes not only imperial, but also *post-imperial* projects. The latter presume that the empire does not exist any longer and that it cannot or need not be revived. We will describe the positions of 'post-imperial nationalists' as well to give a fuller picture of the ideas to be found in this segment of public discourse.

In the texts of 'imperial' and 'post-imperial' nationalists we find some combinations of three basic meanings of the term 'empire'.

Firstly, 'empire' is interpreted as meaning *a plural state*, that is, as a state in which there are many nations. Following this criterion, Russia definitely should remain an empire otherwise it will have to lose a great part of its territory. According to the leader of the movement 'The Eurasian Union', Alexander Dugin, 'Russia from the very beginning was something like an empire. It combined different tribes and peoples that never turned into a homogeneous civic population.... This is a principle according to which all empires are organized – common strategic space, integration from above and diversity from below.'[5] The same criterion is used by a deputy of the State Duma, Victor Alksnis, but he comes to a conclusion that Russia cannot be treated as an empire insofar as according to data of the last census, 80 per cent of its population are ethnic Russians.[6]

While confirming that Russia is a 'multinational country', most of 'the imperial nationalists' stress the dominating role of the ethnic Russians. This thesis is often followed by reasoning about the ethnic tolerance of the Russians and their 'unique ability to understand the other peoples' that determined a specific, 'non-imperial' character of the Russian empire.[7] Many texts of this group point to 'the hard lot of the Russian people' and propose some programmes for its demographical and spiritual 'revival'. Remarkably, one of the main obstacles to this is seen in *inorodcy*, that is non-Russian ethnic groups that have certain preferences (including special national-administrative status), migrants and so on. The other obstacle is the 'anti-Russian' ruling political elite.[8] However, not all projects are so much concentrated on ethno-nationalism. Alexander Dugin, for example, constantly stresses that he is arguing not for a Russian but for a Eurasian multiethnic empire. But his project also gives to the ethnic Russians a specific role insofar as 'the Eurasian project' is regarded as their historic mission.[9]

Secondly, almost all projects of 'imperial' and 'post-imperial' nationalists connect the notion of 'empire' with the promotion of some *universal idea* that provides a basis for its development. According to the definition of the author of the book, *The Third Empire: Russia as it Should Be*, businessman and politician, Michael Yuriev, 'empire is a state that has some purposes that go further than simple maintenance of its own existence and growth of the material well-being of its subjects'. It strives 'to organize the added territories according to its own notion about proper way of life and state order.'[10] By the same token the absence of 'the sacred idea' is seen by the 'post-imperial nationalists' as one of the arguments for the impossibility of empire. According to Valery Solovej, 'the matter is that Russia had exhausted moral-psychological and ideological resources for empire-building. Today it has no ideology that could legitimize this aim.'[11]

Thirdly, directly or indirectly many 'imperial nationalists' represent 'empire' as an *autocratic way of integrating territory and society 'from above'*. They welcome the idea of 'the strong power.'[12] Many projects from this cluster argue for withdrawal of the federal principle. As Michael Smolin, the editor of the book series, *The Ways of the Russian Imperial Consciousness*, puts it, 'federalism in no way prevents separatism, it rather gives this movement an additional power fostering the new splits and future problems.'[13] This idea is also articulated by Zhirinovsky and his party in parliament. The official position of the Liberal Democratic Party of Russia (LDPR) supports transition from the present combination of national-administrative and territory-administrative principles of state arrangement to the latter one (*gubernii*).[14]

All the projects of this cluster have a more or less explicitly anti-Western orientation. They need some *dangerous Other* insofar as opposition to it is a strong argument for the integration of multi-ethnic Russia around 'the Russian nation' (*russkaia natciia*). Their other arguments – common history and culture – point to the past, while the *dangerous Other* contention is a spur to rally now to ensure a reliable future. According to A. Dugin, 'both for Russia and for many of contiguous states there is only one way to keep our sovereignty, our freedom and independence in the global world, we should become an empire again'. The logic of this conclusion is very simple: 'As soon as Russia stops to be empire it becomes an easy spoil for other empires that are built at our expense and based on our resources.'[15] Even more explicitly, this idea is expressed by M. Yuriev: he supposes that now 'humankind comes to the end of the period of peace' and in 50–100 years there will be no more than 50–100 states on the political map. In this logic there may be only one alternative: to become an empire or to die. In Yuriev's forecast Russia must become 'the fifth world power' the territory of which will cover the whole of Europe (though the destiny of Turkey is disputable).[16]

The anti-Western orientation of the projects of 'imperial nationalists' manifests itself not only in geopolitical opposition between Russia and 'the West' (or – most often – the USA), but also in the aspiration to establish the 'civilisational' self-sufficiency of Russia, its right to follow its own way, its immunity from criticism based on 'alien' standards. Remarkably, according to the interpretation of M. Smolin, 'imperial consciousness' is 'a positive sign of psychological maturity of a nation that is able to live in its own way, often regardless of opinions of the others, and to manifest the ideal of truth that lies in the basis of the whole system of vital activity of its national organism.'[17] So, to be an empire for Russia means to follow its own way without looking back at the reaction of 'the West'. As we will see later, this 'imperial' characteristic plays an important role not only in this segment of public discourse.

The approaches that were described above are more or less common for all projects of this group. But there are also some important differences between them.

'Imperial nationalists' differ in their interpretations of the 'mission' of Russia. Some of them (M. Smolin, M. Yuriev) follow the tradition of conservative nationalism and speak about the revival of the Orthodox Empire, while others (V. Zhirinovsky, A. Prokhanov, A. Dugin, N. Narochnitskaia) appeal to the logic of contemporary geopolitical oppositions and put forward the aim of the re-establishment of Eurasian unity and/or resistance to hegemony of the USA (the former position does not exclude the latter one). Sometimes 'the imperial idea' is defined rather vaguely. But one thing is clear enough: 'imperial nationalists' presuppose that Russia should keep its status of 'a great power'.

There are also different opinions about the borders of a future Russian empire. Most often, 'imperial nationalists' speak about restoration of the former Soviet borders (in this or that configuration). For example, A. Prokhanov puts it in the most straightforward way. According to his doctrine we are already witnessing the birth of the 'Fifth Empire' (four previous ones were: Kiev Rus', Moscow kingdom, Romanov's empire and USSR). There are many signs of the birth of the new empire that leave no doubt in restoration of the former boundaries. In Prokhanov's interpretation, 'countries of CIS are alienated extremities of empire that are doomed to decay outside of the imperial body. They are ... senseless set of wicked areas and divorced peoples among which the invalid molecules of false statehood cannot settle down.'[18]

But some 'imperial nationalists' dream of territorial expansion beyond the borders of the USSR. This was the point of the doctrine of 'the last spurt to the South' (*poslednij brosok na Yug*) that V. Zhirinovsky expressed in 1993. The idea of a 'spurt' to the Indian Ocean where the Russian soldier will be able 'to wash his dusted boots' was represented both as a preventive measure against the aggression of 'the South' and as 'a salvation of the Russian nation from the civil strife'. As far as these ideas are not appropriate for a parliamentary party, after 1993 Zhirinovsky stopped articulating them loudly but did not give them up. In the book published in 2006, he speculated about 'the right of the Russians for favourable life conditions' arguing for replacement of the most part of population to the Southern regions of Russia, 'former Kazakhstan', Dushanbe, Frunze and farther towards the Indian Ocean.[19]

A much more important variable is the ethno-nationalist component of these projects. All of them give to the ethnic Russians a special role in empire-building paying at the same time due regard to the rhetoric of 'equality of peoples'. But not all projects attached to this group see the interests of the 'humiliated and insulted' Russians as their primary concern. And there is an important difference between the concepts of Prokhanov and Zhirinovsky on the one hand and of Dugin and Yuriev on the other. The latter ground their projects on geopolitical and traditionalist reasons rather than on the welfare of the ethnic Russians.

To give a fuller notion about the range of interpretations of 'empire' to be found in the 'nationalist' segment of public discourse we should take a look at the writings of 'post-imperial nationalists' who treat imperial legacy more critically. For example, according to Valery and Tatiana Solovei, 'imperial state existed and developed exclusively at expense of exploitation of the Russian ethnic resources.'[20] So, the fact that ideologists and leaders of the Russian nationalism till recent times strived to retain the empire, looks like a paradox. There was 'a zero-sum game: the empire could exist only at expense of exploitation of the Russian ethnical substance, while the Russians could get freedom for the national development only having sacrificed the empire'. So the collapse of the USSR creates a unique chance for the project of the Russian national state. Actually it is the only way that is available insofar as the revival of empire is impossible: the Soviet experience 'discredited the Russian messianic myth' and in the post-Soviet context any 'large-scale integrative projects' look 'unacceptable to mass opinion.'[21]

There is an important difference between the 'imperial' and the 'post-imperial' nationalists: the former are much more bound by rhetoric of 'equality of peoples' than the latter. Though V. Solovei calls the proposed 'state of the Russian people' democratic and liberal, his notion of democracy is limited by majority (i.e. ethnic majority) rule. The only thing he is ready to cede to mitigate displeasure of minorities with the withdrawal of their 'preferences' is creation of career lifts for ethnic elites.[22] Solovei is sure that as far as realization of this programme is impossible under the rule of the present elite that is 'hostile to the interests of the Russian people', the country sooner or later will enter a national liberation revolution. And he is ready to admit that 'in the most unfavourable course Russia will remain a unitary state only within its European borders.'[23]

So, actually the projects that were included in this group have significant differences: while at the one pole we have those for whom 'imperial' claims are more important than 'nationalist' ones, at the other pole there are adherents of the Russian national state who are ready to resile not only from the dreams of empire but also from part of the present territory. But though the authors of these projects have different opinions about correlation between 'the revival of the Russian nation' and perspectives of empire, they speak the same language, share common cognitive frames and it seems appropriate to argue that they belong to a common discursive space.

The issue of empire in liberal discourse

In a very different way the topic of 'imperial legacy' is discussed by politicians and intellectuals from the 'liberal' camp. Here we also find both adherents and opponents of an imperial future for Russia: in 2003–4 there was a discussion about the project of 'liberal empire' that in September 2003 at the start of the electoral campaign for the State Duma was articulated by Anatoly Chubais.[24] In December 2004, a renewed version of this project was introduced in the Moscow office of the Rosbalt News Agency, by Leonid Gozman.[25] But the concept of 'liberal empire' was not included in official documents of their party, Union of the Right Forces (SPS).

It is important to note that both authors of the project of a 'liberal empire' interpret this term in a very specific way. For Chubais and Gozman, empire means, first of all, *capability of exercising international influence*. Empire is a state that can influence the politics of other, formally independent, states. Chubais's speech about 'liberal empire' was full of nostalgia about 'the unique Russian leadership' that existed in the twentieth century; he remembered 'the empire of unprecedented scale' that extended 'from China to Finland, from Vietnam to Cuba, from India to Ethiopia'.[26] So, for the leaders of SPS, 'imperial' status is the status of the great power that takes 'responsibility for the course of events in the other countries.'[27]

Their interpretation also relies on the other meaning of the term: the concept of empire for Chubais and Gozman is connected with some *universal idea* (though the latter still is to be invented). Chubais admitted that 'the idea' that Russia brought to the world in the twentieth century had failed, 'and we probably were doomed to this defeat as far as its values were false'. But during the last ten years Russia, according to his account, has successfully assimilated 'the right', liberal values that must become the basis for the new project that will give us a chance to unite with the other liberal and democratic states on equal terms.[28] So, in the liberal version 'an imperial idea' is not anti-Western, it calls for inclusion in the club of 'democratic world powers' on equal terms and with common aims. Actually the very fact of such inclusion is seen as a pledge of a firm will for democratic transition. However, this plan hardly could be regarded as realistic, if we take into consideration the domestic political situation in Russia and its image among 'democratic world powers'.

The practical part of the project included two points. First, Russia should retain its 'natural' leadership in the post-Soviet space, so the state should help the expansion of Russian business. Second, the Russian state 'should directly and with legal means do everything it can to support the basic values of freedom and democracy not only in Russia but also in the neighbouring states.'[29] Solving these tasks Russia will build on 'the newly shaping world of the twenty-first century'. According to Chubais and Gozman, Russia should enclose 'the northern chain' of civilized countries and together with Western Europe, USA and Japan take responsibility for the whole planet. This interpretation of 'empire' is rather metaphorical; it differs greatly from the way this term is treated in the nationalist segment of public discourse. Actually it did not become dominant in the liberal camp.

Though the interest of the 'liberal' politicians and intellectuals in the issue of empire is really significant, most of them follow a *post-imperial* approach that starts from the premise that 'the age of empires is in the past.'[30] According to Emil Pain, the transition from empires to the civic nations 'most likely has a universal character, though the route of this movement may vary'.[31] From this perspective, 'empire' is something that Russia should overcome; 'imperial legacy' seems an impediment for development in the direction that liberals consider as desirable.

What kind of interpretations of the concept of 'empire' can we find in 'post-imperial' liberal projects?

For most of the 'post-imperial liberals', the determinant feature of 'empire' is *hierarchy of Centre and Periphery (metropolis and colonies)* as well as *unequal exchange of resources to the benefit of the Centre and coercive methods of keeping Periphery in.*[32]

But some of them also consider as important the other characteristic of 'empire' – *autocratic way of integrating territories and society 'from above'* and the fact that subjects of empire both in the centre and in the periphery have no firm rights. According to the definition of E. Pain, empire is 'based on the principles of autocratic rule. Not every state that pursues expansionist politics and has colonies should be called an empire.'[33] In this sense, empire is contrasted to the nation state. Russian liberals give a specific interpretation of this opposition. In the words of Alexej Kara-Murza, 'an empire integrates people by service to itself.'[34] It is a type of political regime that integrates society mostly by coercive means, 'from above'. 'Nation' is principally a different type of organization not only of society but also of power. The term 'nation' is used as a synonym to 'nation-state' and is loaded with some additional senses derived from the theory of modernization.[35] Nation forms along with development in tandem with civic society (as 'cohesion of everybody with everybody else') and democratic state (as the mechanism of realization of public interests).[36] Following this interpretation it seems relevant to claim that 'Russia today is still empire, though a hybrid one ... i.e. empire with liberal façade, decorated to look like a federative republic. It has formal elements of democratic rule ... but it retains the essence of imperial political regime – a power that does not rest upon the consent of the peoples, upon their will.'[37] So, as long as the authoritarian political regime will not be transformed, Russia holds the shape of empire, hence the development of the 'civic nation' is blocked. Thus, in the fashion of official Soviet ideology, only the solution of 'the key question' – in this case, successful democratic transition – opens the way for development in the proper direction. The specific logic of this interpretation is based on opposition not only of the ideal types of 'empire' and 'nation-state', but also of 'empire' and 'nation' as historical phenomena which is hardly correct: on the one hand, there were a lot of polities that combined features of both ideal types, on the other hand, most of the contemporary large nations from the nineteenth century developed in the cores of prosperous empires.

From the 'liberal' point of view, the most preferable perspective is the development of the multiethnic 'civic' Russian nation (*rossijskaia natciia*) though many liberal intellectuals suppose its realization problematic. According to E. Pain, 'the civic nation has not formed in Russia yet.... There are even no signs of the basic factor of development in this direction – no stable predominance of the Russian civic identity over ethnic, regional, confessional ones.'[38]

The other point of view on the perspective of development of 'civic' nation is expressed by Valery Tishkov. In his opinion, 'the Rossian [*sic*] nation is definitely a valid project that is legalized by the statehood of Russian Federation and determined by historical, cultural, social, political commonality of the population of the country.'[39] The problem is in our discursive practices: due to the legacy of Soviet ideology and politics, the notions of nation and ethnic group are confused. Tishkov supposes that nation-building 'is first of all a practice of establishment of the nation that reflects and accentuates common features and values, including civic nationalism and Russian patriotism'. All that is needed is purposeful politics to establish the Rossian nation that can shift perception of the multi-level system of identities and bring it into correlation with the real measure of cultural and political unity that in Russia is not less than in many undoubted nation states.[40]

'Imperial' and 'Post-Imperial' meanings in the discourse of Russian power

So, the issue of 'empire' is actively discussed not only in the 'nationalist', but also in the 'liberal' segment of the Russian public space, though in radically different terms. It is much more difficult to give an account of the discourse of the part of the political and intellectual elite that elaborates an ideology legitimizing the politics of Presidents V. Putin and D. Medvedev. Though neither uses the term 'empire' to justify their actions, it is evident that many of their arguments resemble ideas that we have found in the texts of adherents and opponents of an imperial future for Russia from both 'nationalist' and 'liberal' wings. Taking into account the specific structure of the Russian public sphere that will be described in the last section of this chapter, these 'resemblances' are important insofar as they are recognized by people with different political positions as signs of partial 'consent' with their views. So, meanings articulated in official discourse might be 'read' in different ways.

In this section of the chapter, we will give some examples of 'imperial' and 'post-imperial' meanings derived from annual addresses of President Putin and President Medvedev to the Federal Assembly[41] and add to them some remarks from documents of the party, United Russia (*Edinaia Rossia* – ER) and texts of ideologists for the Kremlin administration. It would be an exaggeration to speak about development of *the issue of empire* in these texts. Rather we will try to distinguish some *meanings* that regardless of intentions of the speakers are analogous with interpretations of the symbol of 'empire' discussed above.

One of the central issues of all of Putin's addresses to the Federal Assembly is the thesis about self-dependence of Russia, its ability to determine its own politics independently, without looking back to opinions of 'the West'. As we have mentioned earlier, in the discourse of 'imperial nationalism' this thesis is interpreted as one of the important features of 'empire' – the latter is seen as a polity with its own 'truth' that should follow its own way. In 2005, for example, Putin declared: 'Russia is a country that has chosen democracy by the will of its own people. It took this way independently and it will decide independently how to realize the principles of freedom and democracy in accordance with its historical, geopolitical and other special circumstances though following all conventional democratic norms.'[42] Putin never raises this thesis to advance anti-Westernism – quite the contrary, he usually stresses that Russia is a European country that strives to be integrated into world structures on equal terms. The thesis of independent democratic choice of Russia is used as an argument against the Western critique of the country's authoritarian tendencies. Thus, Putin's interpretation is able to support aspirations of both 'conservative-nationalists' and 'liberals', though both have serious reservations about his position.

There is a clear link between Putin's statements of the thesis of 'self-dependence' and the doctrine of 'sovereign democracy' that was coined by the deputy head of Administration and President Putin's aide, Vladislav Surkov. However, in the interpretation of the latter, the idea of sovereignty/independence gets additional nuances. In particular, Surkov contends that 'the political creativity of every nation does not result in the acquirement of real sovereignty. Many countries do not even attempt this task and traditionally exist under patronage of other peoples, at times changing their patrons.' And he explains further: 'To be subject to "revolutions" and democracies governed from outside is actually quite natural for such countries.'[43] According to this logic, democracies can be 'sovereign' and 'non-sovereign', led from outside centres. So it is natural to suppose a struggle for influence between such centres. The doctrine of Surkov asserts a certain position in this struggle: 'Through keeping democratic order (integrity of diversity) in our country, its citizens are able … to take part in maintenance of balance of diversity in the world. Giving up hegemonic aspirations for ever, they do not let anybody else to take them.'[44]

Putin's presidency was marked by a series of political reforms that were justified to create 'the strong state'. An analysis of the parts of his addresses legitimizing these reforms shows many residues of 'imperial archetypes'. For example, in 2003, Putin said: 'The whole historical experience demonstrates that a country like Russia can live and develop in existing borders only if it remains a strong power'; he called his countrymen to consolidate 'around the principal national values and tasks' to be able to meet present challenges.[45] The link between 'keeping existing territory', 'strong power' and mobilization 'around national values and tasks' points to certain speech practices, though it would be clear exaggeration to interpret Putin's words as a call for the adoption of a messianic 'imperial idea'. In the same text, Putin called 'maintenance of the state on the great space, keeping a unique community of peoples and establishing strong positions of the country in the world "a historical deed" of Russia and its citizens.'[46] His own politics aimed at centralization (according to his address of 2005 – 'at the building of an effective state within existing borders'[47]) appeared as a part of this long tradition of resistance to the disintegration of the country.

A perennial issue of presidential addresses is the development of relationships with former Soviet republics. In all his addresses Putin politically correctly demonstrated respect for the independence of the new states, whenever he spoke about the importance of integrative processes and supporting former countrymen. He never gave any sign of readiness for territorial expansion (which is so important to 'imperial nationalists'). President Medvedev's position has been more complicated. The war with Georgia in August of 2008 which led to recognition of independence of Abkhazia and South Ossetia seemed to put in question the principle of inviolability of borders of the newly independent countries. At the same time, President Medvedev has hitherto avoided discussing the situation in terms of territorial expansion. In his presidential address he described 'the August crisis' as 'the moment of truth', demonstration of the fact of 'formation of a qualitatively new geopolitical situation' and of 'our ability actually to defend our national interests.'[48] While his comments cannot be interpreted as definitely 'pro-imperial', they were highly appreciated by 'nationalists'.

Conclusion: A patchwork of discourses

As we can see 'imperial' rhetoric of this or that kind is found in all segments of Russian political discourse – and this widespread interest points to certain shifts in the consciousness of the public. It is evident that the desire of politicians and public intellectuals with different political orientations to discuss the topic of 'empire' has different reasons. For some of them, 'empire' is the desired aim, for others, it is a part of reality that they suppose important to take into account.

Does the wide interest in the issue of empire mean an appearance of some common discursive space where different 'imperial' and 'post-imperial' projects could be justified, challenged and discussed? In our opinion, the answer must be 'no'. The discourses of 'nationalists', 'liberals' and 'power' are isolated from each other and highly mythologized. Neither of them takes into account a broad academic literature devoted to the historical phenomenon and theoretical concept of empire. The fact that the term 'empire' has different meanings is not accidental: the debates about the 'imperial' or 'post-imperial' future of Russia are held not only in different auditoriums but also 'in different terms'. In every segment of public discourse, it gets some particular meaning that corresponds to some basic values and ideas that it drives in this particular discourse. 'Empire' becomes not as much a concept that is used for discussion of the real problems that are to be solved in the process of construction of a new identity 'on the ruins', but mostly as a symbol that is differently interpreted and used for the construction of competing models of collective identity.

This situation is facilitated by the configuration of the public sphere that took shape during the years of Putin's presidency. It consists of 'the core' that includes the mass channels of communication (first of all – the federal TV channels) – and 'the periphery' represented by a multitude of 'alternative' public spheres that unite the publics of common-minded people. The events that happen in 'the core' are commented on and discussed in the spaces of 'the periphery', but insignificance of communication between them as well as the absence of a back relationship with 'the core' stimulates fragmentation of the public. This configuration of the public sphere impedes effective discussion of socially important issues and stimulates political fragmentation that actually invalidates the integrative efforts of those in power. So, we can find a patchwork of different discourses about collective identity that are neither authoritatively subjected to the official discourse (as it was in the USSR) nor are engaged in the dialogue that can bring a consensus.

Notes

The first draft of this chapter was presented at the seminar of the project 'The Legacy of Empire and the Future of Russia', supported by the Foundation 'The Liberal Mission'. I am indebted to the participants of the seminar whose questions, suggestions and remarks were very useful for my work.

1. Although there are good grounds for the arguments of imperial nature of the USSR, it was an empire of a very specific kind. See T. Martin, *The Affirmative Action Empire*, Cornell University Press, Ithaca, 2001; Yu.Slezkine, 'The USSR as a Communal Apartment, or How a Socialist State Promoted Ethnic Particularism', *Slavic Review*, Vol. 53, No. 2, 1994, pp. 414–52. It means some scholars argue that an imperial approach gives a wrong explanation of the causes of collapse of the USSR (V. Tishkov, 'Rossijskaia natciia i ee kritiki' in V. Tishkov and V. Shnirel'man (eds), *Nationalism v mirovoj istorii*, Nauka, Moscow, 2007, p. 582). At the same time some experts argue that Russia is still 'between' an empire and a nation state, so the imperial experience is

not only in the past (E. Pain, *Mezhdu imperiej i natciej*, Moscow: Novoe izdatel'stvo, 2004).

2. A. Miller (ed.), *Nasledie Imperij i Buduschee Rossii*, Liberal'naia Missija, Moscow: Novoe Literaturnoe Obozrenie, 2008.
3. V. Zhirinovsky, *Poslednij brosok na Yug*, TOO 'Bukvitca', Moscow 1993.
4. In the article that had a significant resonance, Shleifer and Treisman argued that the claims raised to Russia by the West derive from false estimations of its positions in the world. Russia nowadays is 'a normal country' with the average level of income and it fully corresponds to parameters of the other countries with the same level of economical development (A. Shleifer and D. Treisman, 'A Normal Country', *Foreign Affairs*, March/April, 2004).
5. A. Dugin, 'Rossiia kak demokraticheskaia imperiia', *Izvestiia*, 5 May 2006, http://www.izvestia.ru/politic/article34282/.
6. V. Alksnis (2006) 'Proschaj, Imperia (nakanune russkoj Rossii)', http://www. apn.ru/publications/article10796.htm.
7. Alksnis, 2006.
8. Alksnis, 2006. The same arguments might be found in texts of 'post-imperial nationalists', see V. Solovei, 'Ot imperii – k russkomu natcional'nomu democraticheskomu gosudarstvu', in I. Kliamkin (ed.), *Rossijskoe gosudarstvo: Vchera, segodnia, zavtra*, Moscow: Novoe Izdatel'stvo., 2007, pp. 206–8.
9. A. Dugin, *Evrazijskij put' kak natcional'naia ideia*, Arktogeia-Press, Moscow, 2002, p. 47.
10. M. Yuriev, 'Estesvennym dlia russkih variantom gosudarstvennogo ustrojstva iavliaetsia smes' ideokratii i imperskogo paternalizma' in I. Kliamkin (ed.), *Rossijskoe gosudarstvo: Vchera, segodnia, zavtra*, Moscow: Novoe Izdatel'stvo., 2007, p. 170.
11. Solovei, 2007, pp. 203–4.
12. The proposal to create 'the vertical exercise of executive power down to local places' was put forward by Zhirinovsky, long before it was realized by President Putin.
13. M. Smolin, 'Imperskoe myshlenie i imperskij natcionalism M. O. Menshikova' in M. O. Menshikov, *Pis'ma k russkoj natcii*, Moskva, Moscow, 1999, p. 7.
14. LDPR, *LDPR: vse pozitcii*, Izdatel'stvo LDPR, Moscow, 2007, pp. 10–11.
15. A. Dugin, 'Rossiia vsegda byla imperiej', *Belgorodskaia Pravda*, 19 August 2006, http://www.evrazia.org/modules.php?name=News&file=article&sid=3371.
16. Yuriev, 2007, pp. 173–4.
17. Smolin, 1999, p. 7.
18. A. Prokhanov (2006b) 'Gorchakovy "Piatoj imperii"', http://www.zavtra. ru/zavtra/5imperia/gorchakovy_5_imperii.html.
19. V. Zhirinovsky, *Rossiia pobedit!* Izdatel'stvo LDPR, Moscow, 2006, pp. 170–1.
20. V. Solovei and T. Solovei, 'Apologiia russkogo natcionalizma', *Politicheskij klass*, Vol. 11, No. 23, 2006, p. 35.
21. Solovei and Solovei, 2006, p. 38.
22. Solovei, 2007, p. 207.
23. Solovei, 2007, p. 209.
24. A. Chubais (2003) 'Rossiia kak liberal'naia imperiia', http://www.prpc.ru/ library/civ_09/01.shtml.
25. L. Gozman (2004) 'Rossiia dolzhna stat' imperiej', http://www.rosbalt.ru/ 2004/12/16/189420.html.

26. Chubais, 2003.
27. Gozman, 2004.
28. Chubais, 2003.
29. Chubais, 2003.
30. E. Gaidar, *Gibel' imperii. Uroki dlia sovremennoj Rossii*, Moscow: ROSSPEN, 2006, p. 7.
31. Pain, 2004, p. 17.
32. According to the definition of Egor Gaidar, empire 'is a strong state body in which the functions of power are concentrated in the metropolis and democratic institutions (if they exist) do not extend to the whole territory under control' (Gaidar, 2006, p. 8). A similar definition is given by E. Yasin: empire is a state 'in which one people (state-holding) dominates over the other people or peoples ... and keep them under its power by coercion or threat of coercion' (E. Yasin, 'Fantomnye boli ushedshej imperii' in I. M. Kliankin (ed.), *Posle imperii* (Moscow: Novoe izdatel'stvo, Moscow, 2007, p. 7). E. Pain also defines as specific features of empire: hierarchical character of relationships between centre and periphery, coercive methods of keeping the latter in and existence of a special source of state sovereignty in the figure of emperor (that could be represented by different actors – monarchs, dictators, oligarchic groups. etc.) (E. Pain, 'Imperiia v sebe. O vozrozdenii imperslogo sindroma v Rossii' in I. M. Kliankin (ed.), *Posle imperii*, 2007, p. 104).
33. Pain, 2004, p. 12.
34. A. Kara-Murza, 'Mezhdu imperiej i smutoj', *Polis*, No. 1, 1995, p. 96.
35. For example, Igor Yakovenko defines nation as 'a stage of development of ethnos that is characterized by a wide spread of autonomous individuals, by secularization of consciousness and culture' (I. Yakovenko, 'Ot imperii k natcional'nomu gosudarstvu (popytka konceptualizatcii processa)', *Polis*, No. 6, 1996, p. 118). According to Pain, nation states are 'states of citizens', in which 'horizontal, network relationships' play a decisive role; in spite of empires they are 'non-coercive, voluntary unions of citizens as well as territorial communities' (Pain, 2004, p. 104).
36. Kara-Murza, 1996, p. 96.
37. E. Pain, 'Sumerki liberal'noj imperii', *Nezavisimaia gazeta*, 15 June 2007, p. 10.
38. Pain, 2004, p. 18; cf. E. Yasin (2006) 'Tezisy k konferencii "Posle imperii"', http://www.liberal.ru/sitan.asp?Num=567.
39. V. Tishkov, 'Samoopredelenie rossijskoj natcii', *Mezhdunarodnye processy*, Vol. 3, No. 2, 2005, http://www.intertrends.ru/seven/002.htm. Tishkov argues that even the modification of spelling of the name of the country and its citizens in foreign languages could be one of the important steps towards the establishment of the Russian civic nation.
40. Tishkov, 2005.
41. The annual addresses are official documents summarizing the most important middle-range tasks of current politics. They are much more 'balanced' than occasional speeches and declarations.
42. V. Putin, *Address to the Federal Assembly of the Russian Federation*, 25 April 2005, http://www.kremlin.ru/appears/2005/04/25/1223_type63372type63374type82634_87049.shtml.

43. V. Surkov, 'Natcionalizatciia buduschego (paragrafy pro suverennuiu demokratiiu)', in *Suverennaia demokratiia: Ot idei k doctrine*, Moscow: Evropa, Moscow, 2006, p. 34.
44. Surkov, 2006, p. 31.
45. Vladimir Putin, Address to the Federal Assembly of the Russian Federation, 16 May 2003, http://www.kremlin.ru/appears/2003/05/16/1259_type63372 type63374_44623.shtml. D. Medvedev in his first address in 2008 also praised 'the people with thousand-years long history that have mastered and civilized the great territory' (D. Medvedev, Address to the Federal Assembly of the Russian Federation, 5 November 2008, http://www.kremlin. ru/appears/2008/11/05/1349_type63372type63374type63381type82634_ 208749.shtml.
46. Putin, 2003.
47. Putin, 2005.
48. Medvedev, 2008.

5

Picturing a Revolution – Photographic Representation of the Orange Revolution in the Ukrainian Newspapers

Ksenia Gorbenko

Introduction

The Brezhnev–Honecker kiss on a remnant of the Berlin Wall, Lenin on an armoured car, a female protester inserting a flower into the rifle of a National Guardsman, children fleeing a South Vietnamese napalm strike, planes crashing into the World Trade Center. Although differently potent for people from different cultures, each of these images has come to represent a turning point in national histories and has an immediate emotional impact. These iconic images are used not only to make sense of history, but also to justify policy decisions and mobilize social movements.

At recognized historical moments, thousands of photographs are taken; few of them become iconic. My research compares routine news images, the great majority of which are not etched in our memory, but which nonetheless played a crucial role in the formation of the 'critical mass' that helped determine the outcome of a stand-off. This study is about the visual aspect of the mass mobilization process that came to be known as the Orange Revolution, which amassed over one million people in the streets of Kyiv and led to a transfer of government power in late 2004 with the help of non-violent tactics. Although those events briefly propelled Ukraine onto the front pages around the world, this study focuses on the local, more detailed, representation of the protests. Presumably, the pictures accompanying the news helped the readers imagine the scope of the event, instil hope, and encouraged them to join the protests on one or the other side of the 'barricades'. By analysing the photographic coverage of the Orange Revolution by three Ukrainian dailies and an online newspaper, this chapter highlights the differences in the population's exposure to this historic moment depending on the region.

One of the milestones of Ukrainian national history, the Ukrainian presidential elections of 2004 both involved the unprecedented participation of the population and provoked a major crisis of political legitimacy after the second round of elections. The historical significance of these events was first articulated and reiterated by the media, without whose participation the outcome might have been quite different. To understand how a public consensus formed on the 'meaning' of the Orange Revolution requires scrutiny of the media's role first in which features of unfolding events were documented and next how those events that were singled out were interpreted. Drawing from the fields of communications, political science, and sociology, this chapter contributes to our understanding of the media's role in framing a social movement.

Background

For citizens of former Soviet countries, electing one presidential candidate over another may seem fairly limited in its consequences. As such, cynicism and scepticism are not unexpected. However, these elections were perceived as significant months before the fateful date. As their political campaigns unravelled, the two candidates – Viktor Yushchenko and Viktor Yanukovich – came to symbolize not only their political parties, but also the external forces interested in influencing Ukrainian politics as well. They were like a natural experiment to test the propositions of structuralism.

Victor Yushchenko, a Westernizer whose wife is Ukrainian American, was seen as a leader who had good relations with the Bush administration and who would help Ukraine develop closer ties with the EU, with hopes of joining it in the future. The other candidate, Victor Yanukovich, supported by the unpopular outgoing President Kuchma and the Kremlin, found his voters mainly in his home, the Russian-speaking Eastern part of Ukraine. He came to symbolize political proximity to Russia. Yushchenko spoke to his supporters in Ukrainian and Yanukovich in Russian, which reflects the country's linguistic divide between the West and the East. Although the two languages are mutually comprehensible and most Ukrainians know both, the language preference is sometimes used as a political statement. Yushchenko chose the orange colour for his campaign, hence the name of the uprising. Yanukovich's supporters used blue and white symbols.

In the months preceding the elections, the mass civic campaign organized by a number of youth organizations had prepared for possible electoral fraud. Exit polls were used to highlight discrepancies between the self-reported voting patterns and the results announced by the Central Elections Committee. The race was very close. In the first round on 31 October 2004, Yanukovich's lead was initially announced. Later, the votes were recalculated and the result reversed in favour of Yushchenko.

The run-off elections on 21 November brought the tension to its climax. Again, the exit polls and the preliminary results of the Central Elections Committee did not match. Exit polls and reports of mass electoral fraud became the rallying point of Yushchenko's supporters who claimed that their votes had been stolen.

The protests were spearheaded by a youth organization *Pora* (which means literally 'It's time!') modelled on the youth movement in Serbia *Otpor* (Resistance), which helped oust Slobodan Milosevic in 2000, and the student movement *Kmara* (Enough!), which was instrumental in lustrating the post-Soviet government headed by Eduard Shevarnadze in Georgia in 2003. The striking similarities among these three revolutions have been noted and highlighted by the media. Collectively, they are often referred to as 'colour revolutions'. Besides the strong two-syllable name for the leading youth organizations, other key characteristics underscored the movements' affinities: emphasis on non-violence, opposition to corrupt post-Communist powers, use of the rigged presidential elections as a rallying point, and unequivocal support by the West. In each of the three cases, police and the military did not use violence in repressing or dispersing the uprising, while the media sided with the opposition; all this yielded a victory for the opposition without any bloodshed.

International reaction to protests was controversial, if predictable. Russian President Putin threw his weight behind Yanukovich when he rushed to congratulate him on 'a landslide victory'. The Organization for Security and Co-Operation in Europe (OSCE) reported that the media coverage of the two candidates had been biased in favour of Yanukovich. The morning following the elections, Yushchenko's supporters flooded the Independence Square (Maidan Nezalezhnosti, or simply Maidan) in Kyiv demanding a revote.

Within the next few days, Yushchenko's supporters kept streaming into the capital from different parts of Ukraine to join the protests, reaching an estimated one million at the height of the crisis. Participants report immense feeling of solidarity and trust in those few days. Many Kyiv residents brought food to the square for the activists and opened their homes to strangers to take a shower or stay overnight. On 3 December, the Supreme Court of Ukraine invalidated the results of 21 November run-off election, and a revote was scheduled for 26 December 2004. By 8 December, when Parliament amended laws to make this new electoral round legitimate, the media proclaimed victory of the Orange Revolution and people started leaving the square, visible and photographable collective effervescence being difficult to maintain over an extended duration.

Although the revote of run-off elections on 26 December did bring victory to Yushchenko, the nation remained divided. Even then, over 40 per cent cast their votes for Kremlin-backed Yanukovich. The moment of victory for the Orange supporters was brief. Upsurge of national pride and a feeling of solidarity produced by the Orange Revolution gradually subsided and routine settled in. The schism between the President and his 'sister-in-arms' from the revolutionary days, Yulia Tymoshenko, whose fiery speeches on the Independence Square were critical to the Revolution's success, led to disappointment among the electorate who saw the Orange camp falling apart. Unable to work with ambitious Tymoshenko as prime minister, Yushchenko dismissed her from the post in September 2005.

In the next parliamentary elections of 2006, Yanukovich's Party of Regions received most votes (32%), followed by Yulia Tymoshenko Bloc (BYUT) (22%) and Yushchenko's Our Ukraine (14%). The negotiations about the post of prime minister lasted almost the whole summer, initially with the promise of Tymoshenko's return. After long negotiations, Yushchenko was forced to appoint his former rival as prime minister, which was perceived by the participants of the Orange Revolution as a betrayal of the revolutionary ideals.

Following a continuous struggle over political power with Yanukovich the prime minister, Yushchenko, dissolved the parliament on 2 April 2007, plunging the country into a new political crisis and giving Tymoshenko a chance for a new comeback as prime minister. A few months later, the two leaders of the Orange Revolution were to disappoint their followers once again, falling out over a number of issues, among them the Ukrainian stand on the Russian-Georgian war of August 2008.

Visualization of the national idea: Theoretical framework

In 2003, Ukrainian President Leonid Kuchma wrote a book with a provoking title *Ukraine is Not Russia*. Not surprisingly, the fact that he needed 513 pages to prove this point became the butt of numerous jokes. When presenting his book in Russia, Kuchma famously said that he was jealous of the Russians, who had both a state and a nation, whereas the Ukrainians only had a state but no nation.[1] This quote was invoked on several occasions during the Orange Revolution the following year, to indicate that now the nation was finally born.

Given that even the long-awaited revote of the second round of the presidential elections in 2004, which were reported to be free of fraud and falsifications, conspicuously lacked unanimity (with 44% still voting for Kremlin-supported Yanukovich), labelling the Orange Revolution a nation-building event seems at odds with Ernest Gellner's famous definition of nationalism, which, according to him, 'is a political principle that holds that the political and the national unit should be congruent.'[2] Clearly the whole nation was not represented on Independence Square in late 2004. A closer look at the visual side of the media coverage will help determine how the Orange protesters and the liberal media working in tandem convincingly presented the protesters as 'the nation', as well as how the Eastern region of the country might have been deprived of such visual representation. This study employs a theoretical framework of nationalism studies and social movements, aided by a visual sociological approach, to interpret the mediated experience of the Orange Revolution.

Spearheaded by the youth organization *Pora*, the Orange Revolution started off as a social movement. Literature on social movements has been largely focusing on their inception, tactics, structure, and ideology. Relevant to this chapter is Charles Tilly's idea of 'WUNC display' – an acronym for the four criteria that social movement activists use in their self-presentation:

> [W]*orthiness*: sober demeanor; neat clothing; presence of clergy; dignitaries, and mothers with children; *unity*: matching badges, headbands, banners, or costumes; marching in ranks; singing and chanting; *numbers*: headcounts, signatures on petitions, messages from constituencies, filling streets; *commitment*: braving bad weather; visible participation by the old and handicapped; resistance to oppression; ostentatious sacrifice, subscription, and/or benefaction.[3]

As the analysis of the photographs will demonstrate, the Orange protestors and their opponents acted in full compliance with Tilly's WUNC principles, portraying themselves as worthy, unified, committed, and numerous, and their counterparts – as the complete opposite. Ukrainian newspapers, being legitimate political actors, organized their photo display of the protests accordingly, in support of one of the political camps. By looking at what kind of visual narratives are presented in the newspapers, this study supplements existing social movement theories with an additional aspect – their visual representation.

A combination of efficient management of the campaign and its capacity to rely on vernacular mobilization of the masses, thanks to pre-existing national sentiment, is what helped determine the outcome of the Orange Revolution. In the months preceding the memorable presidential elections, the country was polarized between supporters of Yushchenko and Yanukovich. Despite the Blue camp's attempts to depict Yushchenko as a puppet of the West, they failed to propose a viable *national* display of their own cause. The Orange camp, on the other hand, drew inspiration from national liberation movements, which eventually brought Yushchenko to presidency.

As Benedict Anderson famously observed, the emergence of nations was conterminous with the decline of world religions and the rise of print capitalism, which not only made it possible to codify and normal-ize the previously existing vernaculars into print-languages, but also for the individuals to

> gradually [become] aware of the hundreds of thousands, even mil-lions, of people in their particular language-field, and at the same time that *only those* hundreds of thousands, or millions, so belonged. These fellow-readers ... formed, in their secular, particular, visible invisibility, the embryo of the nationally imagined community.[4]

With the advance of photography, and photojournalism in particular, the 'visible invisibility' of fellow-nationals has become obsolete. Thanks to photographs, the processes by which these co-nationals are imagined *and mobilized* can be quantified, analysed, and deconstructed. This is the objective of this chapter.

How did the Ukrainians see their world in those two weeks? What did the mirror of society, photojournalist, preserve for posterity from those heady days of the protests? How did the visual stories differ across the regions and political affiliations?

Data and methodology

This chapter analyses all photos pertinent to the Orange Revolution published in three Ukrainian dailies and one online newspaper between 22 November 2004 (election day) and 9 December 2004, when the most active street protests took place. Each of the three dailies is published in a different region of Ukraine: West, Centre, and East, which reflects the country's linguistic and cultural divides. Local newspapers from the largely Russian-speaking South ignored the protests in Kyiv, which, though a significant finding in itself, makes the data set inherently skewed. Predictably, the story of the Orange Revolution was experienced and interpreted – in both word and image – more heavily in those parts of the country where the majority of readers sympathized with the protesters. Although survey and interview data would be necessary to conclude that the Ukrainians in the East and South were less exposed to the media coverage of the Orange Revolution, one could guess that this was indeed so. One important implication of this is that while the Orange Revolution was widely proclaimed the victory of democracy by the Western media, half of the Ukrainian population did not and still do not feel that way about what has happened. Although the protests were portrayed as 'the people's revolution' in the West of Ukraine and in Kyiv, the sentiment was not shared by the Eastern part of the country. A glimpse at the visual coverage in different regions will help shed some light on dwindling support for Yushchenko a few years down the road, as well as widespread disillusionment with the revolution's results.

The three dailies analysed in this chapter are *Vysokyi Zamok*[5] (West), *Donbass*[6] (East), and *Den*[7] (Center/Kyiv). For all three newspapers, online archives were used. To make the analysis more comprehensive, a popular online newspaper *Ukrainska Pravda*[8] was added as the fourth source of images. Both the centrist *Den* and the pro-Orange *Ukrainska Pravda* published 132 photos each over the two-and-a-half-week period. *Vysokyi Zamok* located in the stronghold of Ukrainian nationalism Lviv published a comparable number of such photos: 106. The lack of visibility of the Orange Revolution in *Donbass* ($n = 25$) is predictable: in the home region of Viktor Yanukovich, Donetsk, there were few supporters of his opponent.[9] The newspaper reflected the dominant narrative in the region and downplayed the events in Kyiv, portraying them as parochial and negative, more often, not portraying them at all.

Although the number of newspapers used in this chapter is admittedly small, the astounding number of photographs published by them ($n = 395$, and more than 50 per cent of the total number of images published in these newspapers) is an indication of their importance (Graph 5.1). The contrasts among the four visual stories are striking and will be discussed in more detail below. The following section focuses on several overarching themes, such as Tilly's WUNC presentations, that lent – or denied – legitimacy to the Orange Revolution.

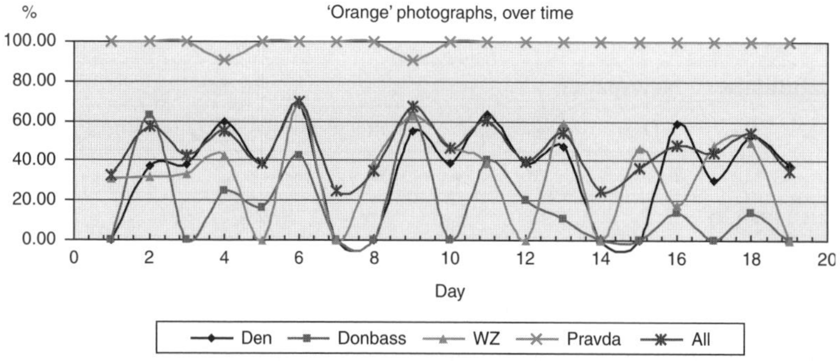

Graph 5.1 Photographs depicting the Orange Revolution in the four newspapers

Picturing a nation in revolution: Analysis

Presidential elections tend to focus singularly on the candidates and their immediate circle. Therefore, the fact that the Ukrainian dailies focused overwhelmingly on the demonstrators during the post-elections standoff may seem counter-intuitive.

The protesters' visual presence made them very real, whereas their recognizable anonymity allowed them to symbolically stand for the whole imagined community of Ukrainians. Typically, elections coverage portraits of politicians drowned in the torrent of citizens' portraits: less than 10–20 per cent of images in each paper featured Yushchenko or Yanukovich. The numerical breakdown of the two presidential candidates' portraits is displayed in Table 5.1.

As is seen from Table 5.1, the centrist-oriented *Den* had the most balanced coverage of the two candidates during the standoff, while at the same time paying comparatively little attention to them (publishing three photos of each, or 2.3%). Both Orange-leaning *Vysokyi Zamok* and *Ukrainska Pravda*, naturally, heavily over-represented Yushchenko (15 and 19 photos of him in the two newspapers, respectively, or about 14%) at Yanukovich's expense (5 and 11 images, or 5–8%). It is hard to speak of the evenness of representation in *Donbass* because of the small size of the sample.

There are several principles of self-display that social movements adopt to attract supporters for their cause and have their demands met. According to Charles Tilly, these can be loosely described as WUNC: portraying themselves as worthy, united, numerous, and committed.[10] As the analysis below demonstrates, these characteristics can be rendered visually.

Table 5.1 Numerical breakdown of the presidential candidates' portraits, by newspaper

Candidate	Newspaper							
	Den		Donbass		Vysokyi Zamok		Ukrainska Pravda	
	n	%	*n*	%	*n*	%	*n*	%
Yushchenko	3	2.3	2	8	15	14.2	19	14.4
Yanukovich	3	2.3	1	4	5	4.7	11	8.3

Aerial shots of crowds show the great numbers of protesters. Depiction of opponents in the same frame makes the visual story more inclusive and presents a united front of the protest. Utilizing iconic images of sacrifice and national belonging shows commitment of the Yushchenko's supporters. Pictures of children, women, and the elderly can be interpreted as an appeal to a worthy cause. Portraying the opponents as anti-WUNC is a popular tactic, I will briefly discuss examples of that as they arise.

Crowds

Imagine a blurry orange mass of people filling the square and spilling over to the adjacent streets and avenue. To make the story complete, a recognizable city landmark – a tall, white column with a female figure statue on its top, the Independence monument – is prominently featured in the background. This picture has become the iconic image of the revolution, which is clear from its wide replication on blogs, film reviews, and other websites, including Wikipedia (Figure 5.1).[11] This image succinctly tells a story of a popular uprising that seems so large that it almost equals the nation itself. In Tilly's terminology, such images stand for the numbers of the protesters.

Images like this were popular with the Kyiv newspapers, *Pravda* (*n* = 14) and *Den* (*n* = 6), perhaps due to the salience and proximity of the event to the paper's main office. At the same time, such pictures are lacking from the Lviv paper coverage. Lviv, which is known as the centre of Ukrainian nationalism, had their own 'Maidan' which drew some of the collective attention to itself and away from Kyiv. *Donbass*, by contrast, did include two aerial shots of the square on 25 and 27 November, recycling the same images that had appeared in the Kyiv press a few days earlier. Interestingly, the iconic image described above was published by *Donbass* on 25 November as part of the collage, the second half of which is a close-up of Yanukovich's supporters ('With Yanukovich in heart' reads the centrally located poster, and the

Figure 5.1   Orange Revolution

candidate's larger than life portrait is positioned right behind it). The proximity of these two images suggests an attempt on the part of the paper to hijack the popularity of the Orange movement, implying that at least some of those on the Independence Square in Kyiv are there to express their support for Yanukovich.

'Backstage' images

A number of pictures depicted the routine of being on Maidan for a long haul. With their emphasis on the hardships that people have to go through, they convey the commitment of the protesters who are determined to stand their ground even in such unfavourable conditions. There is a clear disconnect between the intimacy of these images – people sleeping or sharing food – and their political significance. The omnipresent orange in these, at first sight apolitical pictures, conveys the importance of the protests for the people, the pervasiveness of political ideas in everyday life. For example, a young man sat down to catch a bite during a break in his busy organizational schedule.[12] He is wearing an orange raincoat on top of a puffy winter jacket. In his right arm he's holding a fork with a hot dog propped on it, his modest lunch, his gaze is directed at the camera. If not for the orange raincoat, one could think this is a construction worker getting his lunch. The everyman-ness of the man is astounding. He could easily be a brother, friend, or neighbour.

In another picture, a woman in her fifties is sitting on the hard marble floor, her back against the wall, in what appears to be an official building.[13] Her eyes are closed; she is sleeping or trying to sleep. Next to her on the floor a man is sound asleep, his hand under his head. Both are wearing several layers of sweaters and have their legs covered with blankets, suggesting it is cold in the building. A little piece of orange fabric at the woman's feet clues the viewers in that these people are not homeless: rather, they are the anonymous Ukrainians who are suffering a great deal for the sake of their nation's future.

Another image published in *Den* portrays two fully clothed men sleeping on thin blankets in the middle of the floor of what looks like a post office.[14] In the background, people are going about their business as usual and no one seems to notice them. What makes this image political is an orange Christmas tree off centre, which clues the viewer into this holiday season turned political. This image captures life 'as is', while simultaneously pointing out at the hardships the protesters have to endure.

Such pictures work as a consolidating force for the national idea, in essence equalizing the ideas of the nation and the family. In images like these, the private and the public spheres conflate and create a powerful visual resonance, permitting to metaphorically imagine the nation as a family of blood-related individuals. The fact that this theme runs through the visual narratives of the two Orange-sympathizing newspapers (*Vysokyi Zamok* and *Ukrainska Pravda*) and the centrist *Den* in which it comprises between 7 and 12 per cent of all Orange photos, suggests that it is an emphatically pro-Orange approach to narrating the revolution.

Although focus on suffering and implied determination of the protesters make these pictures emotionally poignant, an additional cognitive jump is necessary to realize that these people's sacrifice is being laid to the national altar. As a rule, this connection is introduced in the accompanying article or caption. Once this connection is made, images of this category reinforce the feelings of sympathy with selfless individuals on Maidan and national pride they instil. The fact that such imagery is missing from the pro-Yanukovich press coverage suggests that residents of the East and South were not exposed to the same level of patriotic rhetoric associated with the Orange Revolution and might be unable to relate to it years later.

Inclusive vs exclusive representation

How does one picture unite? One way is to capture a Benetton-type diverse group struggling for the same goal. When one looks at the images in all the papers that did cover the Orange Revolution extensively (all except *Donbass*), old and young, male and female, rich and poor – literally everybody appears to be out on the Independence Square in Kyiv, having their voice heard (and their face seen) by millions of their compatriots across the country. In the centrist *Den*, representatives of both camps often end up in the same picture frame, to imply that no matter what one's individual political choice may be, 'East and West [are] together', as one of the popular revolutionary chants proclaimed. *Den* published six photographs depicting dialogue between the opposing camps. Both *Pravda* and *Vysokyi Zamok*, which happened to be more unequivocal about their Orange leanings than *Den*, did not pay as much photojournalistic heed to the confrontation and dialogue 'across the barricades'.

Understandably, diversity of representation is dependent on the overall numbers of demonstrators. With a clear majority of protesters on the Orange side, it would be difficult to depict supporters of Yanukovich as widely representative of the nation at large.[15] Nor did *Donbass* really try to do that. On the contrary, the paper's goal seems to have been to discredit the successful Orange protesters in Kyiv. First of all, a black-and-white picture of empty Maidan with a few tents and no people around them, published on 23 November, that is, the day after the elections, suggests that the news of a large popular uprising was overstated if not a straight-out lie. It is only on 25 November, when the images from Maidan had been flooding the Internet for several days that the paper publishes an iconic aerial shot of the crowds, with the qualifying addition I have discussed above.

A less subtle depiction of the opposition was offered by the paper on 2 December. In a collage of two images published together, the top picture labelled 'Kiev' is a close-up of a rowdy aggressive-looking crowd: somebody's fur hat is flying in the air, two extremely red-faced men in the foreground have their mouths open shouting. The bottom picture labelled 'Donetsk' portrays a peaceful gathering of people adorned in blue, unmistakably Yanukovich's supporters. Although the authenticity of this plate is somewhat dubious, and the juxtaposition of the two images comes across as rather propagandistic, this is an excellent example of an alternative visual presentation of the Orange Revolution. The interesting fact is that the top image seems to have been retouched. In the original picture that was made available to newspapers by the information agency *Unian* in Kyiv on November 28, the same people

Figure 5.2   Angry faces

have a more natural skin colour (Figure 5.2).[16] In Tilly's terminology, the Eastern newspaper used anti-WUNC tactics to describe the Orange protesters as unworthy and numerically insignificant.

To be fair, I must add that the very pro-Orange *Pravda* also included less than complimentary images of Yanukovich's supporters. Judging by the ten pictures the newspaper published on 25–26 November, the white-and-blue camp comprises only men, some of whom have their teeth missing, look somewhat anti-social and delinquent, corroborating the stereotype that Donetsk residents are mostly criminals or ex-convicts.[17] Although the image could be interpreted in a number of ways depending on the previously available information, this interpretation holds because of the famous argument against Yanukovich during the presidential campaign. His history of having been convicted and imprisoned twice, in 1968 and 1970, for robbery and bodily injury, had been thoroughly discussed in the media.

Children, women, and the elderly

There is no better way to present a social movement's worthiness than through participation of children and the elderly. Images of children, which comprise about 2–4 per cent of each set, function as a reminder that the political decisions of today will influence the nation's future.

In one image in *Den*, a seven- or eight-year-old boy is seen distributing newspapers on Maidan. In another, a little girl is seen sitting on her father's shoulders, waving a small orange flag, her mouth open singing. In a third one, a child wrapped in the Ukrainian flag is holding up a big orange sun-shaped smiley.

Children represent the general mood of the protesters, the perpetual celebration, with music, dancing, balloons, and happy orange colour all around. As one of *Den*'s journalists pointed out, the Orange Revolution – and its visual representation just as well – was balancing on the spectacle, the performance, the unrealness of reality, setting people free to be children again. 'Our orange rainbow is not as much a political action ... as our common childhood, which we, in our too-adult history, have not had in a long time. That is why everyone looks so young in Kyiv today, even the old folks.'[18]

At the same time, an image of an elderly lady in a kerchief, clutching her fists apprehensively, might remind one of his or her mother or grandmother that they visit less often than they should in the village, who always tries to save up a little money from her meagre pension for small presents for her grandchildren.

Presence of such images underscores the totality of the event, the fact that the whole of society is engaged in it. Pictures of the children and the elderly are so emotionally charged because these people are not supposed to 'do politics'. After all, the political domain remains dominated by men over 30. However, bringing these nominally less political groups into the picture (quite literally!) induces very personal, familial associations, portraying the nation as a family-type community existing from time immemorial: generations change, the nation remains.

Conclusions

Nations imagine themselves not only with the help of the press, but also through the imagery that accompanies the written word. Not only communities of press, but also communities of photography allow people to experience and keep for posterity important moments in their national histories. While the Ukrainian Orange Revolution was almost universally celebrated as the victory of democracy outside the country, its visual presentation within Ukraine was far from uniform. The Southern newspapers largely ignored the demonstrations in Kyiv, and a daily from the East portrayed the protests rather negatively.

The press that did support the Orange candidate, by contrast, published his portrait more often than his opponent's, but generally focused on the demonstrators; showed the protesters' hardships, unity, and solidarity; and emphasized the great numbers of people who had taken to the streets. The centrist newspaper from Kyiv tried to bring the nation together by placing members of opposing camps in the same frame. Finally, though specific tactics differed from paper to paper, visual opponent-bashing tricks and appeals to family life through pictures of children and the elderly were used by both sides.

To sum it up, though the Orange Revolution was perceived as a nation-founding event by its participants, a large portion of Ukraine's population was left unexposed to the same visual and verbal rhetoric. This study is an initial attempt to examine the differences in the visual media coverage of the Orange Revolution in different regions of Ukraine, and what these might entail for the consolidation of a nation.

Notes

I am grateful to Chuck Bosk, Randall Collins, Tukufu Zuberi, Barbie Zelizer, Orysia Kulick, and Margaret Hagan, as well as participants of the graduate student conference 'Idea Exchange: Mediums and Methods of Communication in Eastern Europe, Russia, and Central Asia' at the University of Pittsburgh and the pre-conference workshop 'Beyond the Nation: Critical Reflections on Nations and Nationalism in Uncertain Times' at the School of Politics, International Studies & Philosophy, Queen's University for their valuable comments on different versions of this chapter. Of course any errors are solely mine.

1. A. Fedynsky, 'Ukraine is not Russia: The Latest Version', *The Ukrainian Weekly*, No. 38, Vol. LXXI, 21 September 2003, http://www.ukrweekly.com/Archive/2003/380316.shtml.
2. E. Gellner, *Nations and Nationalism*, Ithaca: Cornell University Press, 1983, pp. 6–7.
3. C. Tilly, *Social Movements, 1768–2004*, Boulder and London: Paradigm Publishers, 2004, p. 4.
4. B. Anderson, *Imagined Communities: Reflections on the Origin and Spread of Nationalism*, London and New York: Verso, 2005 [1983], p. 44, italics in the original.
5. *Vysokyi Zamok* is a Ukrainian-language daily published every day except Fridays and Sundays in Lviv, the main city of Western Ukraine known as the citadel of Ukrainian nationalism. Online version is available at www.wz.lviv.ua.
6. *Donbass* is a Russian-language daily published every day except Mondays and Sundays in Donetsk region, home of Victor Yanukovich. The newspaper is available online at www.donbass.ua.
7. *Den* is a Kyiv-based newspaper published in both Ukrainian and Russian that is associated with the former Prime Minister Yevhen Marchuk, whose wife is *Den*'s editor-in-chief. The newspaper is regarded in general as a centrist pro-establishment medium. *Den*'s annual competition on photography is well known in the country. The current issue can be found at www.day.kiev.ua.

8. *Ukrainska Pravda* (www.pravda.com.ua) is a widely recognized and acclaimed Internet newspaper founded by Georgi Gongadze, a journalist whose kidnapping and murder in 2000 led to a wave of protests against President Kuchma, thus decisively liberal.

9. Yet even in *Donbass*, revolutionary imagery comprises up to 60 per cent of the total pictures published per issue (see Figure 5.1).

10. Tilly 2004.

11. For example, this image is part of the 'Orange Revolution' article at Wikipedia http://en.wikipedia.org/wiki/Orange_Revolution (accessed 3 December 2007). It was also published in *Den* on 25 November 2004 and posted on numerous personal blogs, to name just a few. See original at the Ukrainian Information Agency 'Unian' website (www.unian.net) under number 10592.

12. O. Harchenko, 'Na Maidan tyahne yak mahnitom (Maidan is attracting like a magnet)', *Vysokyi Zamok*, 1 December 2004 (available online at http://www .wz.lviv.ua/pages.php?ac=arch&atid=35549).

13. A. Kovalenko, 'Vpechatleniya boitsa palatochnogo gorodka (Tent Town Soldier's Impressions)', *Ukrainska Pravda*, 25 November 2004, available at http://pravda.com.ua/news/2004/11/25/14140.htm.

14. V. Gerasimchuk, 'Dim stav ukrainskim (The House Became Ukrainian)', *Den*, 9 December 2004, Issue 225 (http://www.day.kiev.ua/128951). Photo in this article is photo by M. Markiv.

15. Incongruity between word and image in one instance highlights this problem. In a picture published by *Donbass* on 30 November 2004, several elderly ladies are holding posters with Yanukovich's portraits, one of them reading 'Youth for Yanukovich!'

16. This image is available at www.unian.net, under picture number 10820.

17. O. Plastovets, 'Storonniki Yanukovicha v Kieve (Yanukovich's Supporters in Kiev)', *Ukrainska Pravda*, 24 November 2004. The article with images is available online at http://pravda.com.ua/news/2004/11/24/14074.htm.

18. D. Desyaterik, 'Oranzhevaya raduga (Orange Rainbow)', *Den*, 2 December 2004.

6
Nationalism and the Market Economy – Challenges to Hindu Nationalism in India

Sangit Kumar Ragi

Introduction

In post-independent India the ideology of Hindu nationalism (and *Hindutva* predominantly) has come to be identified with the ideas and acts of organizations like the Rashtriya Swayamsevak Sangh (RSS); Vishwa Hindu Parishad (VHP); Bharatiya Jana Sangh, which now is known as Bharatiya Janata Party (BJP); Vanvasi Kalyan Ashram (VKA) and so on. Of these RSS is the mother organization because the rest of the organizations mentioned above have been the brainwork of the former and derive their ideological oxygen from the same. There are around 65 small and big organizations currently linked to the RSS, working in different fields of national life ranging from school education to higher education, community service to trade union, tribal welfare to consumer protection and so on. Taken together, they constitute the popular phrase Sangh Parivar (Sangh family).[1]

While the RSS is the main ideological mind behind the ideology of *Hindutva*, these organizations work in different fields of the society keeping the broader goals of *Hindutva*. Take for example, VKA. This organization works among the tribals. The purpose of working among the tribals is not only to improve the overall conditions of life of the forest-dwellers tribes but also to integrate them into the mainstream Hindu society on the one hand and to prevent their desertion to other faiths on the other. Similarly VHP works in the religious field. The prime objective of the organization is to 'create a sense of glory, devotion and dedication towards *Dharma* and *Sanskriti*' in India and abroad among the Hindus, but it also espouses to eliminate 'the differences sprouting on account of language, caste, creed and class' and to consolidate the Hindus by creating harmony among them.[2] Thus it works to serve, apart from the religious cause, the political, educational and social domain as well. The main purpose is to strengthen the Hindu society against political Islam and political Christianity in India which these organizations consider not only non-indigenous faiths but also ones which work on exclusivist premises. Over the years VHP has acquired the most prominent voice on *Hindutva*, especially after the Ayodhya movement, though the RSS still continues to be the guiding organization and the final voice for these organizations on controversial and contentious issues, be it related to organizational structure or to the ideological dimension.

The RSS was formed in 1924 by Keshav Baliram Hedgewar. Before launching this organization, Hedgewar was a prominent Congress functionary in the Vidarbha region of Maharashtra. He was actively involved in the Freedom movement. Over a period he realized that mere political emancipation of the nation from the British was not enough; its spiritual, cultural and civilizational resurrection was in fact equally or far more important. Secondly, cultural and religious awakening of the Hindus that this nation belongs to them and their working as a united force was a must not only for the freedom of the nation but also for taking it further to the pristine glory of the past. RSS calls it the stage of *Paramvaibhav* (the stage of supreme prosperity and glory). Its premise was that India is a Hindu nation.[3] Hindus constitute the indigenous and native stock of this land and their forefathers have predominantly shaped the Indian civilization and given it certain distinctiveness. Like J. G. V. Herder, Hedgewar propounded the personality theory of nation, that is, every nation has a distinct personality. And this distinctiveness of the Indian nation, he contended, lies in the fact of its being Hindu.

He concluded further that Hinduism has been the cementing force of the Indian nation and wherever and whenever it weakened, that part of the country got subsequently sliced off from the mainland. In fact, if this nation succumbed to colonial rule and foreign aggression it was only because the Hindus of this land did not act as a single, consolidated force against the aliens. A divided Hindu society thus had been the reason for falling to alien aggression and occupation of this land, be it Islamic or British. Two operative premises emerged from this; firstly, that the Hindus must be united and secondly that Hindu-ness must be propagated, promoted and strengthened in order to undo the cultural colonization thrown upon the nation during the alien rule.

This idea of the Indian nation was not something exclusive and originally contributed by Dr Hedgewar. It was merely a totalization of the ideas of saints and seers, writers and social reformers which crystallized over a century and a half, starting from the second half of the eighteenth century. It first appeared in the form of reaction, evolved through internal reforms and revivalism before finally arising in the form of total assertion. The phase of reaction and revivalism remained dominated by cultural and religious reforms and resurrection of the past, whereas the period of assertion which culminated after the partition of Bengal in 1905 has predominantly been political though none of the phases are completely delinked from each other.

Emergence

Hindu nationalism emerged in the form of reaction against the Christian missionaries' abuse of Hindu ethos and icons, their gods and goddesses.[4] The missionaries who came to India attacked Hinduism. Hindus' religious images were denigrated and idolatry was condemned in the filthiest terms imaginable. Religious pluralism and multiplicity of gods and goddesses were derided. The sacred Vedas were described in a poor light by declaring them to be the songs of shepherds. One of the most respected saints of India, Swami Vivekananda, later on encapsulated this attack on the Hindu religion by saying that if the entire mud of the Pacific was thrown upon the missionaries that would be less than the abuses hurled by them against Hinduism.[5] Hindu society reacted to such attacks and the first intellectual defence, at that point of time, came from Raja Ram Mohan Roy.

Roy defended polytheism in Hinduism by arguing that it too in essence supported monotheism. Roy acknowledged the penetration of social evils and entrenched forms of rituals and superstitions within the Hindu society but he refused to recognize the superiority of Christianity and asserted further the might of spiritual *Hindutva*, especially of the Vedas and its essence of universalism. This period is popularly known as the period of Indian renaissance. But on the whole it was a defensive response to the cultural and religious attack launched by one section of Orientalists against Hindu culture.[6] Secondly he attempted to define *Hindutva* in light of Western modernity and of gospels of Christianity suggesting that what was there in Christianity was also there in Hinduism.[7]

It would be pertinent to note that such abuses against Hindu scriptures were not uncommon or the first of this kind. They were there even during the rule of Delhi Sultanate and the Mughal period. In fact, then they were more harsh and humiliating. But then Hindus had no courage to protest because of fear of brutal suppression at the hands of Islamic rulers. Whenever and wherever it happened, it was brutally crushed. British rule in that sense came as a relief to the Hindus as its advent at least emancipated them from the religious totalitarianism they were subjected to during the Mughal period.[8]

The reforms and renaissance that started with Raja Ram Mohan Roy subsequently gave way to the revivalist movement led by Swami Dayanand Saraswati who established the Arya Samaj in 1875 at Bombay. Arya Samaj resisted idolatry and depicted it as an aberration and in contradiction to the basic tenets of Hindu Dharma (eternal religion). However it aggressively pushed forward the idea of Hindu revivalism by starting the Shudhi movement which put stress on the reconversion to Hinduism of those who had embraced either Christianity or Islam under allurement or force. Though Arya Samaj too in some ways tried to define Hinduism in reference to Western modernity by distancing itself from polytheism and idolatry it gave a considerable force to the revivalist movement by giving a call to return to the Vedas and according primacy to the idea of numerical and political Hinduism. Later on, Swami Shraddhanand, another leader of Arya Samaj, proposed to establish *Bharat Mata Mandir* throughout the country where Hindus could meet every day for prayer and deliberate upon issues of national and religious concern.[9] The purpose was to organize the Hindus on the pattern of Muslims and Christians.

In subsequent years, Swami Vivekananda and Sri Aurobindo gave an intellectual and spiritual firepower to the idea of Hindu nationalism. Aurobindo equated Hindu nationalism with *Sanatan Dharma* and argued that the rise and the fall of the Indian nation would depend on the rise and fall of Hindu Dharma.[10] He considered Hindu Dharma as the soul of the nation. Vivekananda, a legendary Hindu monk who rose to fame mainly because of his nationalist pronouncements, not only asserted the might of Vedanta but also exhorted that India had nothing to learn from the West except the scientific developments. He depicted the West as the embodiment of 'lust and luxury' and warned Indians that India would not remain India if it turned to Europe for inspiration and imitation. It would perish.[11] He considered India as the cradle of spirituality. He strongly recommended revitalizing Indian wisdom and philosophy in order to instil a sense of pride in being Hindu. The famous slogan of the Hindu nationalists *Garv se Kaho Ham Hindu Hain* (Spell out with pride, we are Hindu!) has been borrowed from his speeches. He did not condemn Christianity but essentially slammed the missionaries for hurling abuse on other religions and converting the people of other faith. He considered it dangerous for the country and for the Hindu society. He held that the outgoing of every individual from the Hindu fold to Christianity or Islam amounted not only to dismembering of the Hindu society but also meant an increase of one more enemy. He asked Hindu society to synthesize the Vedantic mind with physical solidarity like Islam. Needless to say, Vivekananda remains a reference point for Hindu nationalists.

Hindutva

The most articulate, systematic and jargon-free interpretations of political *Hindutva* and the Hindu identity came from Vinayak Damodar Savarkar. He conceptualized the very idea of Hindu Rastra in his famous and controversial book *Hindutva*.[12] He called India a Hindu Rastra (Hindu nation). And Hindu according to him was one who had attachment with the land extending from the holy Sindhu (a river) in the North West to the great sea in the South and who also considered this land both as the holy land and fatherland. Thus he defined the meaning and boundary of 'We' and 'They'. By this definition anyone whose religion had its origin outside India was not Hindu. The idea of Hindu Rastra thus excluded the people belonging to faiths of non-Indian origin. The basic premise was that these people cannot have true loyalty to the Hindu Rastra. Thus in regard to Muslims he said:

> [T]heir holy land is far off Arabia or Palestine. Their mythology and godmen, ideas and heroes are not the children of this soil. Consequently, their names and outlook smack of foreign origin.... Their love is divided.[13]

He did not ask them to reconvert themselves to Hinduism. He suggested that they should start treating this land as the land of their seers and prophets, godmen and gurus, a land of their pilgrimage.[14] Savarkar justified his premise on the ground that 90 per cent of those who had been converted to non-Hindu faiths had been Hindus few generations back and thus their forefathers too were Hindus. Savarkar unfolded the political implications of conversion further by arguing that conversion to non-Hindu faiths was denationalization of the nation.

These above-mentioned articulations developed over a century-and-a-half provided the substance, logic and rationale for the idea of Hindu Rastra. The only contribution of the RSS therefore to the whole idea of Hindu nationalism can be seen in active and systemic build-up in the form of *Shakhas*, a cadre-building and networking mechanism, for awakening the Hindus along these lines. The RSS thus outlined the mantra and the method of realizing a Hindu India.

A closer scrutiny of the *Hindutva* movement thus clearly reveals five basic principles on which it thrives. First, India is a Hindu nation. Second, it has been a nation since time immemorial, not in political terms but in cultural and civilizational terms.[15] Third, *Hindutva* has acted as the cementing force and therefore whenever a part is weakened in numerical terms, that part finally got cut off from the country. And therefore Hindu consolidation is a must in order to save this nation as well as Hindu society. Fourth, centuries-old foreign rule has done damage to native traditions and has deliberately inflicted a humiliating cultural amnesia on us. What therefore is needed ahead is to resurrect our golden past by Hinduization of every gamut of national life. The first three premises provide the foundations of Hindu nationalism whereas the last two guide the same towards action.

The first premise entails the entitlement theory and defines the boundary of 'we' and 'they', 'outsiders and insiders'. This theory has been the driving force behind the ideology of Hindu nationalism because it suggests that this nation (territory) primarily belongs to the Hindus because Hindus have been the native stock of this land and it is their forefathers who laid down the foundation and nourished a distinct culture and civilization over here. This theory rejects the Aryan Invasion Theory which proposes that the Hindus too, like the Muslims and the British, came from outside and pushed the native Dravidians towards the South. Though this theory is the subject of historical debate and falls outside the purview of this chapter, a few points deserve valid attention. First, the Aryan Invasion Theory has been propounded not on the basis of any substantial archaeological facts or historical narratives but on speculative linguistic affinities discovered between the Indian language Sanskrit and European languages. Even the proponents of the theory now acknowledge that the theory lacks substantial historical facts. Secondly, that such a great conflict could not find appearance in the oral or written tradition of both the conqueror and the conquered is something that is unbelievable.[16] Ambedkar, who had no great love for Hinduism, also pointed out that prior to the coming of the British this theory was alien to India. Critics' argument that this theory was deliberately conceived to legitimize the British rule in India is not without merit. Winston Churchill's speech on the Government of India Act 1935 in the British parliament to some extent proves that point. Churchill thus said: 'we have as much right to be in India as anyone except perhaps for the depressed classes who are the native stock'.

The second premise whether India is an ancient nation or not, is again a matter of competing historical narratives and ideological formulations and therefore falls outside the discussion of this topic. In the nationalist discourses again it has been a common narrative as every nation claims itself as the ancient one and attaches superlative adjectives to glorify it. Whether that claim is true or false is an inconclusive debate, and historians of nationalism are yet to reach the consensus. The working premises, therefore, that the Hindus should be united and turned into a monolithic, cultural and political unit and that every gamut of the national life should be *Indianized* or *Hinduized* became important for further discussion.

The operating aspects of Hindu nationalism can be safely placed in four broad categories. First, containing the numerical strength of political Islam and political Christianity as that has a potential to increase their say and bargaining position in the system. Any policy or practice therefore that favours increase in the numerical strength of these cultural and religious denominations encounters opposition from Hindu nationalists. Opposition to allowing multiple marriages for the Muslims, supporting sterilization programmes, two-children norms have therefore always been favourite subjects of Hindu nationalists. It is also the reason that the BJP and other Hindu nationalist organizations have been asking for a ban on religious conversion through deceit and allurement, because these conversions have little to do with spirituality and ultimately reduce the relative numerical strength of Hindus, contributing finally to de-Hinduization of the nation.

Secondly, Hinduization of every aspect of the national life on the one hand and reducing or erasing the non-Hindu impacts which came with and crystallized due to Islamic and British rule in India, on the other. Some also call it inculcating Hindu-ness. Bhartiya Jan Sangh called it *Indianization*.[17] In other words Hindu nationalism intends to erase the symbols and impacts of the alien rule replacing them by Indian ones. It thus aims to propagate the indigenous culture on the one hand and insulates the same against possible threats from outside on the other. This leads the Hindu nationalists to oppose Western influences, such as celebrating New Year as per the Christian calendar, Valentine's Day, Western music and dance forms, and so on, as well as Islamic influences. The West in their opinion represents the epitome of consumerism and sexual nudity contrary to spirituality-centred India[18] and therefore is un-Hindu, if not anti-Hindu in nature. They do not want the cultural, religious, political and social spaces of the nation to be dominated or equally shared by non-Indian religious faiths.

Thirdly, Hindu nationalism involves opposing any such move which carries the potential of strengthening the identity politics of minorities and their further consolidation, be it the issue of personal laws, Haj subsidy, issue of Urdu, and so on. Accordingly, Jan Sangh opposed the privileged status accorded to minorities, especially the Christian and Islamic denominations, and asked for their treatment as equal citizens. Fourthly and most important of all, it involves creating a monolithic *Hindutva*; a *Hindutva* not without diversity, but essentially not divided and fragmented from within. It was thought essential to arouse a composite Hindu consciousness, political in nature to tackle the political and exclusivist ideology of Islam and a section of Christianity. Thus the *Hindutva* of Jan Sangh and the RSS essentially is and was political in character, emanating from cultural and territorial insecurity of the native Hindu community.

Political mobilization

Since the 1920s, the RSS has gone from local to global in its reach and has diversified its work in manifold ways, but it has failed to create a monolithic Hindu category. Regional, caste and linguistic diversity and divides and the inherent cult of religious pluralism not only restricted its all-India growth, reducing its influence, for all practical purposes, to the Hindi belts but also acted as deterrent to the emergence of pan-Indian Hindu consciousness. Political expansion and influence of the BJP has by and large followed this pattern. The party has failed to expand significantly beyond the cow belt or the Hindi heartland, Karnataka being an exception. In fact the partition of the country followed by communal carnage throughout the country created a fertile ground for Hindu nationalists to push forward the idea and agenda of *Hindutva* but the murder of Gandhi sealed its political fate. This act, perpetrated by an activist of the Hindu Mahasabha, tarnished the image of Hindu nationalists of all variants. Jan Sangh, a Hindu nationalist party, became politically untouchable. Nehru used it successfully both to isolate the then Home Minister Sardar Patel, who happened to be sympathetic to the right-wing organizations and considered their people as misguided patriots, within the cabinet and outside by giving a bad name to all Hindu organizations.

This political isolation, to some extent, came to an end in the mid-1960s when Ram Manohar Lohia, a veteran socialist leader from Uttar Pradesh, invited the Jan Sangh to join hands against the Congress. The party entered into coalition and formed government in some of the central provinces. Its real isolation however came to an end in 1977 with the formation of the Janata Party of which it was one of the most important constituents. This experiment failed due to inner ideological contradictions, clash of personal egos, and most importantly, the power conflicts within the new formation. The BJS component of the Janata Party exited and formed a new party, now known as Bharatiya Janata Party, in 1980. The BJP in its first meeting committed to the broad ideological components of the Jan Sangh but at the same time also tried to be more inclusive by adopting some Gandhian premises such as Gandhian socialism[19] in place of the integral humanism of Deen Dayal Upadhyay which had been the guiding principles of the party so far. Though the party expected a big electoral growth in the post-Janata fiasco, the murder of Indira Gandhi in 1984 damaged its electoral prospects, reducing its parliamentary strength to two members in the Lok Sabha in the general elections held in 1985. The success of the Congress was a result of polarization of the Hindu community against Sikh extremism. Though the RSS and its ancillaries came out to save the Sikhs throughout the country, the election results showed that a wider political Hindu consolidation was possible.

Rajiv Gandhi's pandering to Islamic clergy and their aggressive postures on the infamous Shahbano case,[20] in which his government changed the Constitution to undo the Supreme Court verdict, made the Hindus in general and Hindu organizations fume in anger. The unlocking of the disputed shrine at Ayodhya for the Hindus as a balancing act and the opposition to the same by the Muslims provided a long-desired opportunity for Hindu nationalist forces. The RSS, VHP and BJP succeeded in convincing people to a great extent that Congress's stance on the whole issue of secularism was duplicitous and dubious. Pseudo-secularism, as a term, acquired a real legitimacy during this period and put non-BJP formations on the defensive on this count. The Ayodhya movement which started in early 1990s proved to be historic in many senses. First, it polarized the fractured and fragmented Hindu society 'as Hindu', for the first time on a large scale. Its impact was indeed felt throughout India, though this was not reflected everywhere evenly in electoral terms. Its influence reached well to the South where the large state of Karnataka emerged as a bastion of the BJP. In Uttar Pradesh, where the BJP had been a marginal player, it became the ruling power. The state provided the largest number of members to the Lok Sabha for three successive terms. In many of the central provinces, the BJP formed the government on its own. The BJP made an impressive foothold in the North-East, especially in the state of Assam. In brief, the Ayodhya movement enabled the party to come closer to the numbers required for forming a government at the centre. Secondly, it changed the entire discourse of Indian politics by replacing the anti-Congressism of yesteryears by anti-BJPism. It bipolarized Indian politics to a great extent. Thirdly, it bridged the regional and caste rifts that had emerged from the implementation of the report of the Mandal Commission on job reservations.[21]

The last decade of the twentieth century thus can safely be described as the decade of *Hindutva*. *Hindutva* not only dominated the national discourse but also turned out to be a governing class, of course in coalition, at the centre. While the BJP saw a spiral upsurge, the Congress Party witnessed a commensurate downfall. The rise of the BJP to power at the centre had several meanings and indicated several factors in play. First, it endorsed the contention that non-BJP political formations were engaged in pseudo-secularism, a word popularized by L. K. Advani during the Ayodhya movement, and that secularism was more for political sloganeering for votes than anything else. Several champions of yesteryears joined hands with the BJP to be in government. Second, it underlined that secularism in India, for all practical purposes, was seen as nothing but a crude policy of appeasement towards the Muslim minority, in particular, keeping their numerical electoral strength in mind.

Though the BJP's rise to power undoubtedly owed much to the Ayodhya movement which projected it as a nationalist party, on the one hand, and brought it to villages remote from urban-centric fossilization, on the other, the economy played an equally important role. In fact, the introduction of the new market economy contributed immensely to the rise of the BJP as an alternative to the Congress. If the success of the Ayodhya movement exposed and discredited appeasement-centric Nehruvian secularism, the collapse of the controlled economy, borrowed under emotional impulse from the Soviet Union, provided further proof of the fallacy of the Nehruvian world view. At the same time, it also vindicated the position of the BJP, which since Jan Sangh days had been talking of freeing the domestic economy from the control regimes popularly known as the Licence-Quota-Permit system.[22] It also coincided with the fall of Communism (Marxism), which, along with the other two Ms, Macaulay and Madrassas, has always been in the firing line of Hindu nationalists.

The new market economy was introduced in the wake of the serious economic crisis the nation faced at the beginning of 1990s. In 1991 the government of India had to mortgage gold reserves with the World Bank to meet the country's weekly import needs. The new Congress government formed under the premiership of Narsimha Rao introduced the new economic policy which contained several economic reforms in tune with a free market economy. Privatization and liberalization became the new buzzwords in public discourse. At the same time, the government's negotiations to join the World Trade Organization (WTO) created panic and insecurity in different sectors of the economy. While issues like cuts in subsidies and the patenting of seeds by foreign multinational companies created fear among farmers and agricultural labourers, steps towards privatization of loss-making industrial units unleashed unrest among government and industrial employees.

The BJP grabbed this opportunity and cleverly fine-tuned its logic and slogan of *Swadeshi* to work in its favour. It now combined 'Roti with Ram', the former eulogizing the idea of economic nationalism, whereas the latter was a synonym for cultural nationalism. The then president of the party, Murli Manohar Joshi, in the national executive meeting at Jaipur called the battle against the multinationals the 'second freedom struggle'. The party projected itself as the only saviour in this crisis. Not to forget, it was the intermediary class in urban India, the *bania* (small shopkeepers) and the trading class, instead of big business houses, which formed the major support base of the party. This class liked the BJP's call for *Swadeshi* as it protected their business interests. Interestingly, BJP did not denounce globalization and liberalization per se. It merely opposed the timing, the nature and the method. Thus the famous slogan became 'computer chips yes, potato chips no', the former indicating high technology and the latter depicting normal consumer goods. It further argued that integration of the domestic economy with the world market was fine but it should be preceded by internal liberalization to stimulate, strengthen and enable the economy to sustain global competition. The campaign of *Swadeshi* brought the BJP closer not only to the urban middle class but also to the rural peasantry. The entire Sangh Parivar swung into action. The RSS launched a new organization, Swadeshi Jagran Manch, especially to carry forward this cause. Bharatiya Mazdoor Sangh, an organization working among the industrial workers, became the largest trade union body in competition with Congress- and Communist-supported trade unions. All this created a new electoral support base for the BJP which finally culminated in the party's acquiring power at the centre.

The success of the BJP was phenomenal. But so has been its subsequent numerical stagnation and ideological decline. It all happened within a decade. In fact, the conditions which created a wind in its favour in the initial years also became the reasons for its decline. Whereas the compulsions of coalition-building and managing it prevented it from pursuing the issues pertaining to cultural nationalism, such as the construction of the Ram Temple at Ayodhya, sending back

Bangladeshi Muslim infiltrators, introducing a uniform civil code and the abrogation of Article 370, the compulsions and dynamics of the market blunted its slogans of new economic nationalism articulated in the form of *Swadeshi*. Both created contradiction and conflict within the Sangh Parivar and many of the organizations which supported the party before it came to power became its strongest critics. VHP, Bajrang Dal, RSS, Bharatiya Mazdoor Sangh, Swadeshi Jagran Manch and so on took the cause to the streets and openly condemned the party for dumping its ideological positions for the sake of power. It weakened the BJP's projection of itself as a principled party.

Ideology in the newly emerging market economy

Amid these developments, the market, however, played an interesting role. It did two things. First, it blunted the ideology by pushing the cultural issues and *Swadeshi* agenda to the background. It made the economic agenda and the issue of governance the central point of national discourse. Second, it de-cadreized the party and tarnished the image of a disciplined party and the party with a difference. Third, it blunted the party's anti-Western rhetoric. Fourth, it fragmented Hindu solidarity which had emerged from the Ayodhya movement. Fifth, it created a rift within the Sangh Parivar.

Capitalist economy is not a fertile ground for the propagation of any ideology in a pure form. The practice of ideological purity (either right or left) and for that matter in any sphere of life requires few things. First, it requires a highly motivated group of cadres for whom the communitarian goal is always preferable to self-interest and self-aggrandizement. Second, there is a need for a well-knit organization providing the structural strength and network to accomplish these goals. The market destroys the first and consequently makes the second defunct. Organization without cadres becomes inert and immobile and this is what the market produces in the end. There is an essential conflict between market morality and communitarian ethics that governs any ideology. The market creates a man who is closer to Hobbes's description of possessive individualism. It produces a utility-maximizer always driven by his or her self-interests and self-fulfilment. This does not go with the communitarian ideology as they contradict each other. The market works through the premise of 'sacrifice of others for self', while communitarian ideology demands a person who is ready to sacrifice his or her 'self' for others.

Secondly, time is an important factor in the practice of ideology. Ideology demands time from its followers. Peasant economy provides more scope for it compared to the industrial economy. In peasant economy, the population is confined within a relatively small territorial radius, both for habitation and occupational purposes. There is not much occupational mobility. People further are reluctant to adopt new technology which could accelerate their mobility. The productive process is relatively slow and involves a long gestation period that stretches from the planting of seeds to harvesting. This provides time and opportunity to the people to participate in activities other than those related to production. Peasant economy is also relatively less exposed to the rules of economic Darwinism. That has two meanings. First, there is no cut-throat economic competitiveness. And second, the production process does not involve stakes on a daily basis. There is no big surplus but relatively more secure subsistence income accrues to those who are associated with it. All this enables the people to spare time for political and other social activities.

Contrary to the above, in the industrially dominant economy there is production on a daily basis. Economic competition among companies is cut throat and lethargy, inertia or work disruption for a day or two is unacceptable as these may expunge the company from the market place, damaging not only the interests of the owner but also of the employees. Industrial units therefore cannot afford to have violent trade unions on their premises. These units therefore not only formally discourage trade unionism but also create conditions that tend to deter workers from joining in such activities. First, the market not only fulfils our existing needs but also creates new needs and instils the impulse to accomplish them. It keeps raising the cost of living and forces us to shrink our activities to remunerative work to meet the expanded expenditure. Workers, therefore, think twice before joining in trade union activities. A worker knows that a strike might cost his job and might consequently leave him unable to meet even his basic needs. The market economy thus deters and discourages a non-productive, rigid and violent man and absorbs him in the productive process, emasculating his revolutionary zeal.

There is also another dimension to this aspect. Contrary to the much talked about bipolar class formation according to Marxian premises, the market economy not only creates possessive individuals but also breeds not one or two but multiple classes of varied occupational and other interests. These classes instead of converging further to crystallize into two classes on the classical lines of Marxism stand and work against each other. They are critical of each other's revolutionary activities and trade unionism. For example, when the bank union goes on strike, teachers come out to condemn it. Similarly when the teachers go on strike bank employees do not like it. Class-based revolution therefore becomes impossible in a market economy. No wonder, radical socialism in the West lost its identity in the whirlpool of the market!

The practice of ideology requires a certain degree of rigid principled conduct from its adherents. Peasant economy produces a more rigid and aggressive man compared to the industrial and urban counterparts. On the other hand market economy produces a flexible person. In fact flexibility is very much inherent in the market. Rigidity has no place in it. It happens something like this: market is governed by the rules of bargain and compromise. Neither the seller nor the buyer can afford to stick to his position while deciding the price of a commodity. Rigidity and obstinacy on either part in their respective positions may result in losses for both. That necessitates compromise. This is conditioning of mind and attitude. The market economy facilitates the compromising man and minimizes aggression in conduct.

This is not to suggest that the market alone brought the decline in the ideology and that other factors had no role to play. There were several factors but the economy created new challenges which the Hindu organizations failed to resolve in tune with their ideological commitments. The biggest deviation first appeared in economic policy. It was shocking for the nation to see that the same Enron project, to be located in the state of Maharashtra, which had been pending central government clearance due to opposition from the BJP and the Shiv Sena, was signed within a week of the party's assuming power at the centre for the first time in 1998. Negotiations with the WTO had been an election issue, with the BJP highly critical of India's joining the WTO on existing terms related to patent clauses and some other provisions. It also promised the electorate to reverse the process of globalization to suit Indian interests. *Swadeshi* was the cherished word that attracted the electorate. But instead of applying it, the BJP-led National Democratic Alliance emerged as the new champion of market reforms. This was a definite and visible deviation from its economic ideology. It created fissures within the Sangh Parivar. Many of the front organizations of the Parivar opposed government policy, took to the streets and organized public protests.[23] But this did not deter the BJP from going ahead with the opening up of several sectors of the economy such as banking and insurance to foreign companies. By the time it completed its first full term in power, the word *Swadeshi* became alien to its dictionary. The 'Vision Document'[24] released on the eve of the Lok Sabha election of 2004 dumped *Swadeshi*. It was argued that there was no need to be fearful of foreign multinationals and that Indian multinationals were capable of meeting the challenges of globalization.

Two factors contributed to this change in ideology: first, the powerful emergence of the market itself and, second, the overseas link of the BJP. The market orientation was introduced during the time of Rajiv Gandhi's government. It gained momentum during the Narsimha Rao government. By the time the BJP took over the reign of power it had deeply strengthened its roots in the system and had developed a clout. This increased relative strength enabled market forces not only to enjoy a certain degree of autonomy but also to influence the policymakers. Indian companies and businessmen who had been suspicious of liberalization and globalization were mesmerized by the opportunities and gains from market-driven policies and became advocates of the same. All the leading industrial and commercial chambers such as FICCI, ASSOCHAM, CII, and so on welcomed the government's approach.

Within the BJP too there emerged a contradiction which had hitherto remained dormant. Since Jan Sangh days there had been two viewpoints within the party on economic policy. One section of the party was staunch in its support of *Swadeshi* and the omnipresent role of the state whereas the second set of people was for a liberalized economy. The former controlled the policies while the BJP remained in opposition. This suited the party politically also and therefore, though there were those against state control of the economy, they were unable to become the predominant voice in the party. This equation within the party changed with the coming of the party into power. Market forces created a strong lobby within the party and succeeded in changing the age-old stance of the party on economic issues. The big business houses had already been hobnobbing with the party considering its phenomenal electoral rise since the Ayodhya movement. It was not without reason that people like Jaswant Singh, Arun Shourie and Pramod Mahajan were chosen to decide on key economic issues rather than hardliners like Murli Manohar Joshi, Kushabhau Thakre and Govindacharya who had played a key role on *Swadeshi* and were known for their allegiance to the basics of Deen Dayal Upadhyay's integral humanism.

The second influence came from the BJP overseas. Overseas friends of the party had extended support during the Ayodhya movement as well as in the period of post-Pokhran economic sanctions on the Indian government. The Indian Hindu diaspora wholeheartedly supported the nationalist premise of the BJP. And therefore when the party came to power people within the diaspora came forward to contribute towards the economic rebuilding of the nation. Of course, they also saw a business opportunity. At the same time they also genuinely wanted to help their homeland. They convinced the top brass within the party that market economy should not be looked upon with contempt and suspicion. Further, that nuclear nationalism and cultural nationalism were not enough by themselves or would be meaningless without the economic empowerment of the nation. Economic empowerment and good governance were equally important. The BJP finally acceded; the market made such a penetration within the party that many of the ministers earned bad reputations lobbying for corporate giants. Pramod Mahajan, a high profile minister, had to resign for supposedly favouring Reliance Industries. This not only created a rift between the party and the Sangh Parivar but also put common cadres in a dilemma as to whom to support. The cadres of the party did not readily take to these changes and the commitment to the market made it difficult for leaders to appeal to the cadres to make supreme sacrifices for the party and its ideology.

Communications revolution

The logic and philosophy of the market economy was not confined to the core areas of economy but pervaded other areas of national life as well. The communications field was one such area. Post-liberalization India witnessed a huge communications revolution. A controlled communication network any way is not good for the market. The market always therefore promotes a free and competitive press. The monopoly of the government in the field of radio and television came to an end. Private players jumped into the fray and within a few years several channels catering to the specific needs of different segments of society made their appearance. These channels responded to the new market opportunities and audience groups. The successful serialization of the epics like the Ramayana and the Mahabharata had already proved their worth, both in terms of viewers and business.

While religious channels like Astha, Sanskar, Sadhana and Jagran engaged the older generations and the people of religious bent, ITV, fashion TV and MTV attracted the attention of younger generations. Sony, Star group and Zee group launched serial-based channels that engaged the attention of housewives. These channels not only engaged their time but also exposed them to a new world altogether. These channels accelerated the process of de-cadreization as they seriously dented the recruitment of new cadres. The *Shakhas*[25] and get-together programmes on a daily and weekly basis were the main way that the RSS recruited new cadres. These *Shakhas* attracted young school- and college-goers because of the physical, intellectual and entertainment programmes organized at the *Shakha* place. Once they became regulars they were indoctrinated into the ideology. This worked well for over six decades after the birth of the RSS. The market economy disturbed and dented this process by drawing the young population into the production process and exposing them to new avenues of entertainment. The new communication channels disengaged them from the *Shakha* by providing alternatives at home. These channels consumed a big proportion of time of the individuals, probably next to sleeping[26] and kept them away from social engagements.[27] Moreover it disrupted the social space. Television entered the Indian home through the drawing room but soon became an essential gadget of the bedroom and confined the viewers to that space also. No wonder Raymond Williams called it an instrument of 'privatized mobilization.'[28]

It had serious implications for the ideology and structures of these organizations. Antipathy to the West has always been one of the important components of the Hindu nationalists' ideology. Hindu nationalists have been opposed to the cultural symbols of the West; be that dress or dance, language or music. They considered them as polluting and always advocated insulating the country against them. This so far had been dominating the cultural discourse in modern India. The new channels changed this mindset. They exposed the young generation to the new world of icons ranging from pop music to Western dance to new fashions in Bollywood and Hollywood. Television through live shows and performances brought film and music personalities close to the people. A new market developed in fields from fashion to health and in no time impinged on people's lifestyle.

Television made celebrities related to these fields household names and created a new reference group and role models for the younger people. Success in the international beauty contests created new role models for girls, while youngsters on campus and outside discovered the rock stars of Western music. Rapid inflow of foreign brands and fashion in the garment sectors attracted the young urban middle class. A new *Sanskritization* gained ground in forms of the young generation madly rushing towards new cultural icons and events like Valentine's Day, Friendship Day, Father's Day and so on. These 'days' were unknown and unheard of among Indian youth a few years back. The media made them popular and created a new market for them. The greeting cards business witnessed a massive boom. It also provided an intellectual cover to these developments against protests in this regard by initiating new debates on tradition, multiculturalism, modernity, freedom, social and cultural policing and so on.

The new cultural winds carrying Western icons and images into Indian homes via electronic channels brought Hindu nationalists into direct conflict with the urban middle class, which traditionally formed their electoral base. Hindu nationalists reacted to these new symbols with aggression and violent protests. The media and people from civil society termed it cultural policing and condemned it in the strongest terms. This tarnished the image of these organizations and made them appear a regressive and conservative force that did not value personal freedom. The new generation refused to accept that the new channels were instruments of cultural pollution and an assault on Indianness. They rather accepted and welcomed them without moral prejudice, considered them a symbol of modernity and found no harm in being exposed to them. This essentially blunted the attack of Hindu nationalists against Western modernity. Both the media and the market came together to fight the issue in the name of protecting individual freedom, extending choices and creating a more tolerant liberal society. In fact, the controversy benefited the market.

The ruckus over the question of English language met with the same fate. The English language which had been a symbol of colonialism acquired a new respectability and acceptance. The movement against the knowledge of English lost momentum and today it is not an issue at all. Whereas previously it was the language of bureaucracy, scientific society and the elite class, it has now become the language of the new professional class related to trade, commerce and management. It has become the source of new job opportunities. While travelling to the countryside one finds wall after wall covered with attractive advertisements to draw students to English medium schools and English teaching institutes. The notion of replacing English with Hindi, envisaged under the Constitution, is looked down upon with contempt.

The combination of the media and the market has also neutralized criticism of the Western developmental model. Hindu nationalists have long been critical of capitalism and the capitalist model of development.[29] An important dimension of the criticism has been that it promotes consumerism, materialism and therefore it is un-Indian, if not anti-Indian. This is quite apart from the argument that it is exploitative, would ruin indigenous enterprises and make life more miserable for the poor. From Vivekananda to Aurobindo to Gandhi, arguments along these lines presented a negative picture of capitalism. Success of the market economy in terms of expanding job opportunities, releasing productive capacity in all areas of life and raising living standards, has by and large nullified the apprehensions, as has the emergence of indigenous multinationals and the increasing purchasing power of the people at every level, including villages. The younger generation is no longer ready to be the captive of the confines of any kind of 'ism'. Insofar as the market appears to provide an answer to sulking eyes and empty stomachs, the slogans of the class war or developing a model beyond the market do not make sense to this generation.

In fact the market and the media, especially through the electronic channels, have brought the West closer to India and have succeeded in changing the notion of the West. The fact of the matter is that the material wealth and technological success of the West fascinates the young and they are not ready to buy the traditional criticism levelled against the market society. Prior to the television revolution people derived their idea of the West from secondary sources on the basis of spoken or written versions which in most cases contained vilification of the West due to the prevalence of anti-colonial narratives. Television has made everything available for visual evaluation. Consequently, urban youths are not ready to accept the premise that Westernization and the import of the West in the life of the nation entails cultural stress and spiritual contamination.

A generational divide within the party

In this regard there is an obvious generational divide within the BJP between the new leaders and the leaders of older generations. While the leaders of the older generations brought up on anti-colonial narratives continue to look upon the West with a sense of suspicion and imagine imperialist designs to be behind every Western initiative, this is not the attitude of leaders of the younger generation. They are ready to compete, contest and cooperate with the West. The market has widened this generational divide within the party. The former has supported and promoted leaders who are market friendly. This has brought good as well as bad for the party. While on the one hand it has given a new liberal face to the party, it has also created serious ideological conflicts within the organization.

Many of the young leaders of the BJP who now occupy important positions in the party and had earlier held important portfolios in the National Democratic Alliance (NDA) government at the centre are not hardcore cadres of the RSS. Figures such as Arun Jaitley, Ravi Shankar Prasad, Yashwant Sinha or Rajiv Pratap Rudi, who by and large now call the shots in the party, represent the younger generation in the party and they are all market friendly. They are not grass roots people. They have not come from below but have descended from above and are essentially the product of the 24×7 news channels which popularized their faces. These Delhi-based politicians reached such positions in the party not because of ideological training, grass roots work and mass followings, which were a must earlier either in Jan Sangh or in the BJP, but due to their intellectual calibre to defend the ideology and the party's positions on different issues, their techno-managerial skills, their capacity to understand the new political economy and formulate winning electoral coalitions. They convinced the party that ideological rigidity and principled political positioning were not essential in the road to power. These leaders are cut off from grass roots politics but devise strategies for the same and they were the ones who formulated the 'India Shining' campaign for the party which failed miserably in the general elections in 2004.

Prior to the defeat of the 'India Shining' campaign the top leadership in the BJP was so convinced and mesmerized by the calibre of these new young Turks in the party that it dared to ignore the grass roots leaders on key policies issues. In the tussle between these market-friendly leaders and the older or hardcore grass roots leaders the top brass in the party always appeared to be siding with the former. Important mass leaders like Uma Bharti in Madhya Pradesh, Madan Lal Khurana in Delhi and Kalyan Singh in Uttar Pradesh were either sidelined or were shown the door. Now that haunts the party, because it lost several popular faces in some key states and the new crop of media-made leaders are incapable of enthusing the BJP's cadres.

Another impact of the market on the ideology and ideology-based activism has come from the rising cost of practising the ideology. Economic liberalization brought in new technologies and gadgets which so far had not been in common use. These new networks speeded up communication but at the same time cut people off from face-to-face meeting. The mission of Hindu nationalists lost the individual touch which they used to generate by going from door to door to meet people. Now the way of informing the cadres for any programme or get-together has become relatively easier but it has lost the human touch. Equally important is the increased cost of communications in the wake of easy availability and access to new gadgets. The monthly bill on telephone or petrol for oneself is considerable but the same for ideology becomes burdensome. As a consequence there is lesser participation and activism on the part of the cadres unless these costs are borne by the organizations. Thus the cult of selfless dedication to the nation and the society has received a severe jolt.

Lesser activism has also been accentuated by two other developments, namely greater engagement of the people in the productive process and the emerging new lifestyle. Goods which were luxury items for most of the people few years ago are now easily available even to the common man. Even the slum dwellers now have access to colour TV and refrigerators which earlier were within the reach of only the rich class of people. The increased level of comfort has worked as a deterrent to street activism. In order to sustain this level of comfort they are forced to be more engaged in the productive process. They now cannot afford nor do they have time for social activities. This engagement which earlier was round the year in the industrial sector has now reached the rural hinterlands. The market has tremendously increased employment opportunities both in urban and rural India. Expansion of the retail markets, linking of the rural production centres to the urban markets, massive semi-urbanization in the past one-and-a-half decade has opened tremendous job opportunities in rural India. Public call outlets (PCOs), photocopy centres, fax facilities, diagnostic centres with latest machines have reached the semi-urban areas engaging previously underemployed youths.

The rising economy has reduced the numbers willing to respond to the call of Hindu nationalists to be part of ideological mobilization. The new lifestyle of the leadership has also not gone down well with the cadres. The leaders themselves are no longer the embodiment of self-sacrifice and dedication to the cause of the nation. People do not see any difference between the BJP and other political formations. The BJP seems as susceptible to corruption as anyone else, while they have proved to be as power hungry as any other party. The image of the BJP as a party with a difference has received a serious blow and it has now come to be known more as a party with differences.

India is a young country with 50–55 per cent of the population between the ages of 18 and 38 years. This age group is no longer interested in the ideological discourses of either left or right. It is more interested in a better economic life, employment, education, better health facilities and so on. High-rise shopping malls, multiplexes, new mobile sets, new cars and so on fascinate them irrespective of which part of the globe the products have come from. They are not interested in arguments of *Swadeshi*. The market has created a new cult of consumerism and young India is not at ease either with the Gandhian or any other idea of restrained consumerism.

The same applies to the *Dalits* and other downtrodden sections of society. The market for them has been an emancipator, not only in the sense that economic liberalization has opened new avenues of work for them, but also because it has liberated them from inhuman manual jobs they had to perform in the absence of technology. A new awareness has come to them. These people are now more concerned about the education and employment of their children. They are competing with and contesting the upper castes in the system on several issues. The issue of distributive justice primarily in the form of caste-based reservations has brought irreparable fissures within the Hindu society and has presented Hindu nationalists with a real dilemma. They fear being branded anti-*Dalit* if they oppose reservations, whereas supporting the policy results in further polarization and fragmentation of society on caste lines. This has seriously damaged their mission of achieving a monolithic *Hindutva*. Dalits who had sided with *Hindutva* forces during the Ayodhya movement have gradually distanced themselves and gravitated towards regional groups and parties such as the Bahujan Samaj Party.

History has shown us that the market has worked as a great ideological leveller in the past. It did so in Europe earlier. Now it is doing the same in the newly emerged market societies of the Third World. European societies too were subjected to ideological extremes during their transition to industrialization. The market either blunted or moderated the extremes. This is one of the reasons that one does not come across sharp ideological divides in a market society. There is elite consensus[30] which also facilitated the emergence and sustenance of the two-party system. In major democracies of the Western world political formations are rooted not in extreme ideological divides but commitment to delivery. Their election manifestoes are not sharply different from each other.

Conclusion

With the market economy strengthening its roots in India such ideological sublimation is all too apparent today. Bengal under the Communist Party of India (Marxist) (CPM) is aspiring to emulate the Gujarat model under the BJP. The Chief Minister of West Bengal condemned the protests of left intellectuals on the Singur and Nandigram episodes terming them 'bookish economists cut off from the ground realities' and the CPM in Kerala, another bastion of left politics, divided between the State Secretary, Pinarayi Vijayan and Chief Minister V. Achuthanandan, the former arguing for the market model and the latter still in favour of state capitalism. In December 2008 a CPM MP from Kerala, Abdullah Kutty, suggested that the state government should imitate the approach of Gujarat to attract investors.[31] The market has dented the revolutionary spirit of the comrades, just as it has undercut the *Swadeshi* variant of economic nationalism of Hindu nationalists. Narendra Modi's market model is the new mantra and a role model for development not only for the BJP-governed states but even for Congress and the Communist parties.

The market is fascinating young India and its electoral impact is evident. Delhi, which used to be a bastion of the RSS and the BJP, has denied them power for the third consecutive time. The Akhil Bhartiya Vidyarthi Parishad, which was once the most powerful student force on Delhi University campus, has been losing elections for the past ten years. Young voters who had brought about the decline of the Congress by moving towards the BJP for its nationalist stands and the cultural discourses initiated by the party are now gradually gravitating towards making economic and social issues their overriding priority.

Notes

1. For details about the work of RSS, see K. R. Malkani, *The RSS Story*, New Delhi: Impex India, 1980.
2. Raghunandan Prasad Sharma, *An Introduction to Vishwa Hindu Parishad* (5th edition), Delhi: Vishwa Hindu Publication, 2003, p. 8.
3. H. V. Seshadri, *RSS: A Vision in Action*, Bangalore: Jagran Prakashan, 1988, p. 14.
4. *Letters of Swami Vivekanand*, Calcutta: Advaita Ashrama, 1991, p. 162. He writes that if the book published in Madras against the Hindus had been written by Hindus against the Christians the latter would have cried fire and vengeance. See also Michel Danino and Sujata Nahar, *The Invasion that Never Was*, Delhi: The Mother's Research Institute, 1996, p. 38.
5. Sita Ram Goel, *Hindu Samaj: Sankaton Ke Ghere Mein* (2nd edition), Delhi: Bharat Bharti, 1993, p. 25.
6. All the Orientalists were not abusive towards Indian civilization. Contrarily there were several Orientalists who had nothing but praise for Indian civilization.
7. Shamita Basu, *Religious Revivalism as Nationalist Discourse: Swami Vivekanand and New Hinduism in 19th Century Bengal*, New Delhi: Oxford University Press, 2002.
8. Bankim Chandra quoted in Mushirul Hasan, *Islam in the Subcontinent: Muslims in the Pluralist Society*, Delhi: Manohar Publications, 2000, p. 47.
9. Shraddhanand Sanyasi, *Hindu Sangathan: Saviour of the Dying Race*, Delhi: Arjun Press, 1926, pp. 140–1.
10. Sri Aurobindo, *On Nationalism* (2nd edition), Pondicherry: Sri Aurobindo Ashram publication, 1996, p. 376. The RSS too calls its *Shakha* work as divine work as it works towards realizing the godly appointed mission of organizing and protecting the Hindu race (*Daiviya Karya*).
11. Swami Vivekananda, *Swami Vivekananda Lectures from Colombo to Almora*, Calcutta: Advaita Ashram, 1991, pp. 164–8.
12. It was first published in 1923 by V. V. Kelkar under the nom de plume, Maratha, because Savarkar at that time was in jail.
13. V. D. Savarkar, *Hindutva*, Poona: S. P. Gokhale Publications, 1949, p. 3.

14. Ibid., p. 94.
15. This point has been articulated by both Gandhi and Nehru. For details, see *Hind Swaraj* of Gandhi and *Discovery of India* by Nehru.
16. Ambedkar quoted in Danino and Nahar (1996), p. 46.
17. Indianization was the term first discussed by Balraj Madhoke, the president of the Bhartiya Jan Sangh. For details see Balraj Madhoke, *Indianization*, Delhi: Hind Pocket Books, 1981.
18. Vivekananda, Gandhi and Aurobindo all argue this point.
19. A. B. Vajpayee, *President's Addresses*, Delhi: BJP Publication, 2000, p. 4.
20. Shahbano was a Muslim divorcee who had approached the Supreme Court of India for her maintenance and had questioned the substance of *Talak*. The Court gave the verdict in her favour, which was opposed by the Ulemmas and the fanatic Muslim leaders forced the government of the day to amend the Constitution supposedly strengthening the fanatic elements within the Muslim community.
21. The Mandal Commission envisaged reservation of jobs for 'other backward classes' in the central government. It was implemented by the V. P. Singh government. This polarized the entire nation on caste lines which subsequently witnessed caste conflicts across the nation. The Ayodhya movement blurred this divide to an extent.
22. *Economic Resolutions of Bhartiya Jansangh: Volume II*, Delhi: BJP Publications, 1973.
23. Dattopant Thengadi, who happened to be one of the most prominent RSS leaders and the mind behind the creation of several organizations like the Akhil Bharatiya Vidyarthi Parishad, Bhartiya Mazdoor Sangh and so on called Vajpayee's finance minister an *Anarth Mantri* (a minister who is causing damage to the nation).
24. *Vision Document*, Delhi: BJP Publication, 2004.
25. *Shakha* is a system of meeting and networking the workers together every day at a definite place in front of the Saffron flag of the RSS. The workers gather there, work out, discuss issues which concern society and the nation and finally disperse after reciting prayers and saluting the flag.
26. Paul Ginsborg, *Politics of Everyday Life*, India: Penguin Books, 2005, p. 51.
27. Robert Putnam, *Bowling Alone*, New York: Simon & Schuster, 2000, pp. 224–5, 231.
28. Raymond Williams, *Television Technology and Cultural Form*, London: Fontana, 1974, p. 26.
29. Both the BJP and the RSS have been talking about the 'Third Way', that is, neither complete imitation of capitalism nor the socialist model of development.
30. The elite consensus is defined as the absence of extreme divergence in views and methods. In other words there are agreed limits to what is and what is not acceptable. For details see Andrew Beck, Peter Bennett and Peter Wall, *Communication Studies: The Essential Resource*, London: Routledge, 2004, p. 274.
31. *The Pioneer*, New Delhi, 5 January 2009.

7

How Parties of Stateless Nations adapt to Multi-Level Politics: Catalan Political Parties and their Concept of the State

Klaus-Jürgen Nagel

This chapter analyses the concept of state held by the relevant parties of Catalonia. It defends the thesis that these parties, to different extents, have accepted the State of the Autonomies as advocated by the Spanish Constitution, not just in their day-to-day behaviour and in the strategies they pursue, but even in their programmes. Instead of defending alternatives, the parties have adapted to the multi-level context offered to them. The Spanish Constitution of 1978 largely regulates matters of sovereignty, statehood, and nationality. The autonomy of the regions is also regulated by their respective Statutes of Autonomy, the Catalan one dating from 1979. During these years, the parties standing for election in Catalonia represented a very broad range of positions on the state. Such positions have come closer to each other now. With time, the Catalan parties have concentrated rather on reforms than on system alternatives.

If we talk of concepts of state, we refer, above all to the ideas about sovereignty, about the territory and its frontiers, about the *demos*, and democratic legitimacy. As Spain can arguably be considered a multi-ethnic and a multinational state, we also speak of nations. We do not insist on other aspects of the state, for example, its link to civil society.

Catalonia's particular party system emerged just before the 1979 Statute of Autonomy. With autonomy (and, later, with the state's integration into the European Union), parties had to compete for votes in different elections. The multi-level system ended up conditioning their vote-seeking strategies, including electoral programmes. In order to demonstrate the change in programmes more clearly, we contrast the years 1977–82, when the new State of the Autonomies was defined, with the most recent years, 2003–6, when attempts were made to reform it. For reasons of space we cannot follow the particular steps of adaptation that took place in each case. Our sources are basically the electoral programmes and the resolutions of party congresses. We also resort to the statements of leading politicians. Unfortunately, there are still only few monographs written about Catalan parties, many of which are somewhat antiquated. The Catalan party system differs from the Spanish as there are powerful non-statewide parties. In Catalonia, the usual left–right axis is completed by a second one that orders parties along their positions on the national question.

The parties and the development of the State of Autonomies

Spain's transition to democracy (1977–82) was successful in establishing a liberal democracy and a welfare state. It was less successful in solving the national question. What was established was a decentralised state, which grants a considerable degree of autonomy to its regions termed Autonomous Communities (AC). But if we understand that a federal state combines self-government with shared government, the logic of the State of the Autonomies was always more regionalising than federalising. The initially asymmetric process became generalised, achieving an initially unforeseen degree of symmetry in spite of the different character of the 17 autonomies. Three of them call themselves nations.

We can identify four stages of the development of the State of the Autonomies. The first stage saw its establishment (up to 1983) with the generalisation of the autonomy process (1981) and, afterwards, the attempt to harmonise the process via an organic law, the notorious Ley Organica de Armonizacion del Proceso Autonomico (Organic Law on the Harmonization of the Autonomy Process) (LOAPA), which the Constitutional Court found to be partially unconstitutional, and other basic laws. Such decisions were agreed between the two largest statewide parties (centre-right Unión de Centro Democrático (UCD) and socialist Partido Socialista Obrero Español (PSOE)). But in Catalonia, a coalition of two parties, Convergència i Unió (CiU), that is Convergència Democràtica (CDC) and Unió Democràtica (UDC), parties which had lost the general elections of 1977 and 1979, won the first elections in autonomous Catalonia (1980). The Catalan party system of 1980, with CiU and socialist PSC-PSOE as the largest parties, still exists, although the order of the minor parties has changed. During the second stage, while legislation on the autonomies was deployed (1984–92), CiU always won the elections to the Catalan *Parlament*, and polled ahead of the PSC-PSOE that remained in the second place. However, in Catalonia, the socialists used to win elections on all other levels. And in Spain, they governed.

In the third stage (1992–2001/3), the competencies of the AC were evened up as a consequence of the pact of the biggest statewide parties (PSOE and liberal-conservative PP). This time, homogenisation took place by raising the level of competencies of the slow procedure autonomies to that of the 'first division'. The financing system of the common regime AC was improved and levelled off, under governments of both the PSOE and the PP. It is true that we could distinguish between two sub-stages: from 1993 to 2000, the socialist and popular governments, which lacked absolute majorities, depended upon agreements with nationalist parties, in the first place, CiU. After 2000, the PP governed with an absolute majority. In Catalonia, in 1995, and between 1999 and 2003, CiU governed with the parliamentary support of the PP. A new stage began with the recovery of the socialists at the regional elections, the new tripartite government in Catalonia in 2003, and the victory of the PSOE in the general elections of 2004. The debates about national recognition and financial autonomy were reopened. A new Catalan Statute was proposed by an 80 per cent majority of the Catalan *Parlament*. A window of opportunity to recognise and to accommodate the minority nations asymmetrically seemed to have opened. It seemed possible that *la España plural* of Zapatero would also recognise and accept its plurinationality.

The Catalan sections of the statewide parties are more autonomous than those of the other AC. On matters that were essential to the Catalan identity (the Statute, the laws on linguistic normalisation), for many years, Catalonia maintained a political and social consensus that stemmed from the anti-Franco resistance and included the non-statewide parties. This led to agreements and situations of 'Catalan oasis'. It should be stressed, however, that neither the last law on linguistic normalisation nor the statute of 2006 obtained the degree of social approval enjoyed by their predecessors.

At the same time, no Catalan party stopped acting on the Spanish level, quite the contrary. Obviously, the actors have different preferences, but even the most nationalist Catalan parties participate devoutly at the Spanish *Cortes* and they even try to do so in Brussels, acting at all levels. As our analysis will demonstrate, such *de facto* integration was not limited to practical politics, but it also had its repercussions in the different ideological documents that parties usually produce. Topics of stateness and nationality are still most controversial, but at least in comparison with the initial stage, the gaps have narrowed.

The initial stage (1977–82)[1]

The socialists (PSC-PSOE)[2]

One of the most impressive processes of adaptation is certainly that of the Catalan socialist party. In its origins, Catalan socialism differed much from the Spanish. Whereas the latter was dominated by Jacobinism and statism, the former is founded on traditions of cooperativism, Austro-Marxist influences, federalism, and even Catalan nationalist claims.[3] The PSC-PSOE is the product of the fusion of three different parties (1978). Among the three, the Federación Catalana del PSOE was not even the strongest. While the two other parties wanted to be federated 'with' the PSOE, the PSOE understood the PSC as the Catalan federation 'of' the PSOE, and this position prevailed in the long run. The new PSC-PSOE party held its first congress only in 1980, following the good results in the first general elections of 1977 and 1979, but also after losing the first Catalan elections of 1980. The electoral results had their consequences. In 1976, slogans included the 'right to self-determination of all peoples', 'the right of Catalans to our nationality … linked to the rest of the Catalan Countries', although 'fraternally open to collaboration among all socialists of the Spanish State and decidedly launched into socialist internationalism.'[4] One of the founding parties, the PSC-C, at its congress of 1976, had considered 'Catalonia … a nation … oppressed by the Spanish state'[5] and, in 1978, had advocated 'an open process towards national liberation.'[6] Even the statewide PSOE, at its XXVII Congress of 1976, had recognised the 'right to self-determination of the peoples as a constitutional principle', but very clearly within a federal State. However, these claims gave way to an optimistic interpretation of the 1978 constitution, highlighting single sovereignty and territorial solidarity 'without any privileges of any kind' (XXVIII Congress). During this time, the Constitution was still considered as a starting point for the later federal development of the state. After the good results in Catalonia in the state elections and the poor results in the Catalan elections, however, and with CiU's long government, many socialists went on to criticise nationalism as such, also in Catalonia.

The PSUC

The historical Partit Socialista Unificat de Catalunya (1936) was the third Catalan political force during the transition. A reference point for anti-Francoist struggle, it is in this party that we find the most elaborate theoretical debates as to state and nation. Party theorist Rafael Ribó spoke clearly of the plurinationality of the Spanish state, consisting of four 'national areas'. He distinguished between these 'nationalities', and 'regions' like Andalucía. Although using the term 'nationalities', he expressly applied the Leninist criteria for a 'nation' to define the Catalan case. He also distinguished between oppressive nationalisms, and those 'in response, defensive, of the oppressed nationalities.'[7]

Far from 'inflating the balloon of separatism', the solution would hinge on recognising the right to self-determination, but choosing federalism as the solution – a federation between the four nationalities, rejecting all merely technocratic and decentralising proposals. He did not fear the usual accusations of being a Catalan egoist:

> [T]he surplus obtained by the state ... is not invested today in the industrialisation of the poor regions but in the enrichment of the dominant oligarchy ... those who suffer the deficiencies of the public administration in Catalonia (schools, hospitals, for example) are the popular classes, autochthonous or immigrant.[8]

Ribó found some difficulty in dealing with the question of the Catalan Countries (Catalonia plus all other territories where Catalan is spoken), which was widely discussed at that time. Our author sees them as 'a national area or as a nationality', but only in a 'sociological sense', with no common conscience or national project.[9]

The discussion in the PSUC contrasted with the Spanish Communist Party. The PCE laid great store on defending the Constitution and the unity of Spain. With the general crisis of Communism and the boom of new social movements, both PSUC and PCE submerged into a series of debates on the role of Marxism, the revolutionary subject, the relationship between liberal democracy and socialism.[10] From 1982 onwards, this tendency towards introspection led to a series of split-offs and recovering of unity which sapped the party's energy.

The Spanish right

The high degree of dependence of the Catalan sections of the Spanish right was always a brunt of jokes: 'Just to move a chair you need authorisation from Madrid.'[11] The Catalan section of Alianza Popular (AP), at the very start of the transition, already had a reputation of being succursal to the Madrid leaders. AP represented the continuity of Francoism, and that caused it problems in Catalonia. During the constitutional debate, AP clearly did not even wish to talk about 'nationalities', deeming the term incompatible with the principle of the unity of the Spanish nation. In its electoral programme of 1977, AP had only advocated a 'decentralisation of functions and competencies to the regions', but more in terms of technocratic efficiency than of democratic self-administration, not to mention national self-determination. It had clearly opposed both federalists and separatists. The nationalists in Catalonia were being branded 'tribal', the State of the Autonomies looked like the 'taifas kingdoms', the autonomy process 'a step backwards in history'. Until 1982, party leader Fraga still wanted to reform section VIII of the Constitution, obviously, in order to restrict autonomy.

AP stood for a 'risk-free change' of the regime, not losing 'the efficacy demonstrated in previous times'. Economic issues stood out in election platforms: 'With the centre-right you will have prosperity' (1979).[12] The fleeting success of 1982 (with eight Catalan seats) may be explained by the statewide degeneration of the centre-right UCD party. The UCD had been an ad hoc creation to counteract the left, an amalgam of conservatives, liberals, Christian Democrats, even social democrats. In Catalonia, its frail attempts to associate with Catalan Christian Democrats coming from anti-Francoism had failed, and many politicians of the centre finally strengthened the ranks of CiU, where even those that could not present Catalanist credentials were accepted. In Madrid, the UCD stood beside the socialists defending the LOAPA, but in Catalonia it fought against the law. This marked the end of a party which failed to take advantage of the multi-level system it had contributed so much to creating.

Convergència i Unió[13]

When CDC was founded in 1974, its vocation was to become a movement agglutinating the centre-left, only excluding Communists. In 1976, it was founded as a party, with a nationalist, social democratic programme.[14] With the adhesion of the liberal Esquerra Democràtica it opened to other positions, defending individual initiative in a market economy. With the 1978 pact with the Christian Democrats of historic Unió Democràtica (UDC, founded in 1931), it strengthened social Catholicism, although the pact left members of both parties a free hand when it came to policies on the family and some other questions that liberals and Catholics tend to see differently. Following the surprise victory in the first Catalan elections of 1980, the vote for CiU became 'strategic' for the voters of the centre. The VI Convergència Congress, held in 1981, relegated the reference to the centre-left to a second place, highlighting nationalism.[15] Jordi Pujol was to maintain the 'movementist' elements of the party, which served to keep up his personal leadership.

In the absence of a model of state of its own, CDC defended the State of the Autonomies.[16] In 1977, Pujol said:

> [W]e are nationalists, we believe that Catalonia is a nation. But we are not separatists. Not in any circumstances. Catalonia, therefore, within the Spanish State, but without losing a single one of its rights, the rights every nation should have.[17]

For years, little more became clear in the party programmes. Convergència avoided too complex and too specific doctrines. Being in government, 'building Catalonia', provided references for the electorate. The electoral programme of 1980 asserted that Catalonia is 'an open, integrating nation, that has always defended its personality and which, therefore, has welcomed with brotherly spirit all those who have wished to come to live here and work here and form a part of it.'[18] Instead of philosophising on the concept of state, the party preferred to talk about the nation. The CDC accepted the Constitution and the Statute, at least with the intention of exploiting its possibilities. On several occasions in 1980 and 1981, CiU members of the Spanish parliament assured the governability of Spain.

Unió Democràtica de Catalunya, the second party of the CiU coalition (today a federation), is proud of its past on the side of the Second Republic.[19] The manifesto of foundation, published by *El Matí* on 7 November 1931, had already defended Catholicism. The UDC had always maintained good relations with the Basque nationalist Partido Nacionalista Vasco (PNV), which was Catholic, and, during anti-Francoism, with European Christian Democrats. The founding manifesto had defended a confederal model of state. But at its Third Assembly of 1976, the first one as a party, the UDC only spoke of the right to self-determination of all the peoples of the Spanish state, putting federal agreements on hold.[20] After trying different outlines for coalitions with statewide Christian Democrats, in 1978, the UDC plumped for the pact with CDC. Nonetheless, on different occasions, whims of Spanish alliances appeared. Based on Catholic social doctrine and personalist philosophy, UCD's programmes always insist on the principle of subsidiarity. While Convergència, increasingly, developed the vision of being *the* nationalist catch-all party, UDC presented itself as *a* nationalist party, the Christian Democrat one, in a party system in which, in principle, all parties ought to be nationalist.

Esquerra Republicana de Catalunya

Another Catalan party that set great stake on its historic prestige was Esquerra Republicana de Catalunya (ERC). It was founded during the

Republic by left-wing Catalanist groups, some federalist, some separatist. The *declaració ideològica* promulgated at the extraordinary congress of 1980 copies the founding declaration of 1931. These 'principles' assert the national character of Catalonia, but they accept 'the federation' of Catalonia with the 'other Iberian peoples' for 'supreme interests of universal fraternity and historical-geographical reasons.'[21] Although the youth of the party pushed to highlight the right to self-determination, Heribert Barrera, the historical anti-Francoist leader, defended federalism. In the end, among the historic party leaders, neither Macià (1931) nor Companys (1934) had proclaimed secession, but the Catalan Republic in Spanish federations.

At the time of the 1977 electoral campaign, when due to its republicanism the party was still not legal, the re-establishment of the Statute of 1932 and the Generalitat government were the central claims. So was the return of Tarradellas, its president in exile, who was, after all, a party member. At the time of the constitutional debate, for Esquerra, Catalonia was a nation, but Spain was not. Not even as a nation of nationalities, or a nation of nations. This did not mean to claim Catalan independence as a state. For Heribert Barrera, Catalonia could fit within Spain, as long as Spain was just a political system, a state, and did not pretend to be a nation. It would even be desirable to keep the Spanish state, consolidated by history.[22] But it should be up to the Catalan nation to decide. ERC's declaration of principles of 1978 insisted on the 'right to the use of the self-determining faculty as a means to achieve national liberation'; on the Catalan Countries as a national space, but with the 'right to abandon the federal structure of the Catalan Countries that make up the Catalan nation', as well as the 'right to form a confederation with all ethnic nations and natural regions of Europe, governed democratically, for the supreme interests of universal fraternity.'[23] From this standpoint, logically, the party was against the Spanish Constitution, which, as is well known, is based on a sole pre-constitutional Spanish nation.

During the discussions on the Statute in 1979, Esquerra insisted that administrative decentralisation was not enough. The Statute would have to mean recognition by the state, a true Catalan autonomy, even sovereignty. As a consequence, the party's ideological declaration of 1980 also highlighted the right 'to full sovereignty and to self-determination', without being, as a result, separatist. One year later, Barrera summed up his concept of the Spanish state like this:

> [T]he only viable, peaceful, democratic solution would be that of Spain as a plurinational state .... Administrative autonomy, for the

regions that form a nation, should not be confused with the self-government of the sovereign nations, which would pact a federation or a confederation.[24]

Esquerra did not propose separation, but a plurinational and federal or confederal Spain. In spite of its programme, the party complied with the Constitution, voted for the Statute, and used the framework offered for its political activities. After 1980, with its systematic support for Jordi Pujol, the particularities of ERC's position became diluted and the party's popular support fell drastically.

The Catalan parties today

The PSC-PSOE

The trajectory of the PSOE and of the PSC, from defending the right to self-determination and the federalism they presented prior to the transition, passing through a stage of absolute rejection of self-determination and the abandonment of the federalist vision in the PSOE during the 1980s, to the official recovery of symmetrical (PSOE) or asymmetrical (part of the PSC) federalism, shows the particular adaptation of socialist projects of the state to the conditions and opportunities of the State of the Autonomies.

With the electoral victories of Pujol in Catalonia in 1980 and of Felipe González in Spain in 1982 the orientation of the PSC underwent a change, and the Spanish level dominated. In the interest of the statewide party, the PSC had to 'swallow' LOAPA and lost its own parliamentary group in the *Cortes*. The PSOE took little account of the interests of the PSC in Catalonia, following the maxim 'what's good for Spain will also be good for Catalonia.'[25] The PSOE, and also the PSC, relegated their self-determinist programmes to the archives. In the PSOE's programmes, constitutional reform was substituted by a mere reform of the Senate, and the establishment of multilateral bodies of meeting and cooperation with the state.

It is true, however, that in the PSC other claims 'survived'. It has been discussed whether, during this epoch, the PSC gave up disputing the Catalan national flag to Pujol, or whether it fought for it under the label of Catalanism, attempting to contrast this to nationalism. The PSC's 'federalist' proposal of 1987 seems to be an example to take into account, since it meant a considerable programmatic effort. It was presented as the surpassment of *loapism* and of *café para todos*, or 'one size fits all', assuming the plurinational reality of Spain, and combining it with the principle of subsidiarity which would leave a political space for the municipalities.[26] But the federalist development of the State of the Autonomies defended by the PSC at its congresses hardly influenced the electoral programmes, especially those of the PSOE.

The opinion of PSC minister Ernest Lluch, later killed by Basque terrorists, remained widely unheard. He had declared:

> I am not in favour of one people, the people of Castile, being more important within Spain than others. I am all for total equality. I am for a Spain like that of the Austrias and not the Spain of the past Bourbons.[27]

Equality of rights and opportunities for the members of all nations that live in the Spanish territory could either mean treating all Spanish peoples equally (considering Castilians as one such people), or a different treatment for the AC that are minority nations.

There is no space here to demonstrate how socialist programmes adapted to the political situation of the party. When depending on CiU votes in Madrid, the socialists included constitutional reform and even some asymmetrical elements. When the PP governed with CiU support, socialist manifestations were published against self-determination, against bilateral negotiations, reminding Aznar of interterritorial solidarity, and accusing the PP of departing from the common ground of the two major Spanish parties on the national question. In opposition, the official socialist model for the state became, once again, the symmetrical federal one, and the programmatic discourse was re-'federalised'.

With the PSOE out of Spanish government, the PSC had recovered some freedom of action. The programme for the 1999 Catalan elections under the slogan 'for a federal Catalanism' contained elements of asymmetry. It introduced the neologism of 'devolució', taken from the British context. Basically, the programme insists on federalising Spain, including 'fiscal federalism', in addition to 'judicial' and 'cultural federalism'. Spain is seen as 'plurinational', and for Catalonia 'it is fair to expect explicit recognition as a nation.'[28] In a reformed Senate, four languages would be spoken, and the symbols of the state would include the four, too. This could clearly lead to different roles for some AC, which would be represented in European and international bodies and even at the Ministry of Culture.

The PSOE, to win the Spanish elections, depended on votes at the periphery, too. In the declaration of Santillana del Mar on 30 August 2003, the PSOE asserted that 'A plural Spain is a united Spain.' Zapatero believed that 'Catalonia has a national identity', obviously one which he sees as being perfectly compatible with the contents of Article 2 of the

Constitution. In its 2004 Congress, again, the PSOE recovered its federalism from the archives. Nonetheless, it remained clearly opposed to sovereignty (other than Spanish), rejecting the right to self-determination and the notion of collective rights.

In Catalonia, the PSC, and especially its candidate, Maragall, went further, clearly in the direction of an asymmetric accommodation. And the terminology gives it away: 'Plural Spain' in the centre, whereas in Catalonia, 'plurinational Spain' was also used, and Maragall experimented with the formula of 'national communities', which the PSOE rejected (*Avui*, 28 January 2005) and often used 'nation'. There was even the odd Catalan socialist politician who broke with taboo and spoke, without authorisation, of the 'right to national self-determination' (examples in *Avui*, 27 October 2004 and 4 November 2004). In the discourse of the PSOE, everything breathed symmetry among the AC. Meanwhile, the PSC remembered that the Spanish Constitution allows the recognition of the difference between national and regional AC, and insisted on bilateral relations with the state. Maragall's proposal 'for a plural Spain', presented in Madrid in May 2004, made it clear that the main issue, however, was to regenerate Spain, and that the vision is federalist rather than nationalist. Rather than a 'nation of nations', the federal vision would be to organise Spain as a 'state of states'; not sovereign states, but inter-dependent ones.[29]

In the negotiations on the statute, the PSC had to wear two hats, one as part of the Catalan 'quadripartite coalition' that proposed the statute (governing and opposition parties of the Catalan *Parlament* with the only exception of the PP), and a second one as a part of the PSOE. In the cases of conflict between the PSOE and the PSC, normally the statewide party predominated.

Iniciativa per Catalunya

On the left of the PSOE, Iniciativa per Catalunya-Verds (ICV) is totally independent from what may be considered its statewide referent, Izquierda Unida (IU). IU also declared itself federal and anti-centralist. Federalisation was planned by stepping up the Statutes of the Autonomies, including constitutional reforms if possible. Even the right to self-determination of the peoples reappears sometimes, although clarifications are provided that this does not include the independentist option, but recognises historic sovereignties of the peoples prior to the Constitution.

Iniciativa per Catalunya (IC) was born in 1987, thanks to a pact between the PSUC, its more orthodox splinter groups (Partit dels Comunistes de Catalunya – PCC), some left-wing nationalists, and others. Ten years later, the PCC, together with other, small associations, left Iniciativa to found Esquerra Unida i Alternativa, the Catalan organisation of IU. Current ICV now deals more with ecology, peace and feminism. In 1997, IC leader Rafael Ribó summarised his concept of the Spanish state. For him, Spain's plurinationality required a series of 'federalising' reforms: all administration in one hand, recognition of the principle of subsidiarity. He even spoke of 'concerts econòmics', the type of fiscal autonomy the Basque Country and Navarre enjoy, but added that these agreements have to be 'solidary', re-equilibrating the federated units.

Symmetrical federalism, however, is not enough. To tackle the problem of plurinationality, asymmetrical federalism is needed, for example, in questions of language, culture, communication policy, or representation abroad.[30] For Miquel Caminal, federalism represents a chance to break the vicious circle of (Spanish and Catalan) national self-determination.[31] When a symmetrical federation of regions only reinforces inequality between nations, what is needed is to complete it with compensating asymmetrical elements, precisely to realise the goal of equality among people of different nationalities. However, ICV maintains the right to national self-determination in its programmes, but solutions are sought to avoid costly separations.

ICV backed the statute elaborated in the *Parlament* as well as the very different text that came out of the Zapatero-Mas pact. Also in the case of PSUC-ICV, and despite all changes in its programme, we find, in the long run, a tendency to adapt to the game proposed by the multi-level political system of the Spanish State of the Autonomies.

Partido Popular

One of the most significant processes of programme adaptation was that carried out by the Spanish right (AP/PP). From being the foremost critics of the Constitution they have become its staunchest defenders. They present themselves as being the only true guarantors of the unity of Spain, resisting statutory and constitutional reforms, while we have seen that the PSOE, in opposition, argued that precisely in order to guarantee this unity, some reforms would be needed. The PP in Catalonia continues to depend on the decisions of the Madrid leaders, though there are signs of different interests and strategies, however rarely reflected in the programmes.

A new view about the Constitution began in 1982, when AP tried to reach agreements with centre-right parties and persons. Finally, AP changed its name and leadership. Conservative victories in some ACs during the 1980s helped to convince the party about the advantages of the State of Autonomies. As far as programmes are concerned, 1989 is the year of the turn. The State of the Autonomies was now praised. 'Unity and autonomy' became a slogan. In the 1993 general elections, the idea was to 'improve the State of the Autonomies', but continuing 'the process of homogenising competencies' and 'excluding all issues that constitute the basic nucleus of the political unity of Spain' above all 'the classic competencies that are inherent to the concept of sovereignty.'[32] To cite Hernández Mancha in the Catalan campaign of 1987: 'For us, the only nation is Spain, no matter how angry this makes them. ... Catalonia is a wonderful region of Spain, make no mistake about it.'[33]

With the arrival of Vidal-Quadras to the leadership of the PP of Catalonia, the local party finally decided that the main enemy was not the PSC, but Catalan nationalism. He went further into the theoretical debate on the state and the nation. Following some theorists on nationalism since Kohn, Vidal-Quadras constructed a dichotomy between two antagonic types of nations, claiming:

> [T]he ethical superiority of what we have called Nation-project over what is known as Nation-essence (...) The Nation-project ... deals with the conception of the Nation as a spiritual principle that is encouraged by the State, ... a State that aspires for its existence and conduct to an ethical justification as a guarantor and instigator of liberty, dignity and the material and cultural progress of each of the individuals-citizens that comprise it ... the ... Nation-project, articulated around a constitutional pact that introduces a rationality that overcomes the state of nature, does not fully renounce emotional cohesion based on historical, religious, linguistic or ethnic factors and concretised in the deployment of nationalising symbols and liturgies, but without giving into the temptation of unrestrained appeal to instinctive tribal identity.[34]

He concluded:

> For the Basque and Catalan citizens, it is far better to continue being politically, constitutionally and emotionally Spaniards than self-determining themselves at the hands of those who subject to refined psychological torture those children who speak Spanish.[35]

Interestingly, at the same time, the manifesto of the Partido Popular de Catalunya of September 1995, titled 'a renewed Catalanism', evoked 'a reasonable (*centrado*) Catalanism, characterised by moderation, good sense and dialogue, tolerant and conciliatory in style.'[36] But it did not relinquish claiming some essences 'of the Catalans' work, inspiration and spontaneous creativity', with 'a collective personality, of which we are proud and that no one can usurp'. In consequence, 'the Catalanism that the Partido Popular de Catalunya considers more spiritually enriching and more genuinely Catalan,'[37] also invoked supposed essences of the Catalan character, and competed with the nationalists on how 'true' Catalanism should be.

In 1996, the statewide PP completed its 'autonomist turn'. Even constitutional reforms were mentioned, though not federalisation. The PP won the following elections, but needed the votes of CiU to govern. In a clear example of the interrelationship between levels (but also of the supremacy of the state level), Vidal-Quadras, the successful agitator, was withdrawn since his strategy of confrontation was no longer timely and was disconcerting. But when Aznar had won an absolute majority, a new process of reflection on the state began. The Congress held by the party in 2002 introduced the term 'constitutional patriotism'. Removed from its original philosophical background, the term refers to seeing the Spanish Constitution as the one and only legitimate tool to solve the problems of state. The Constitution is now seen as a success without precedent in Spanish history, even as its final coronation. To change it, seems sacrilegious.

Curiously, the Spanish nation as a pre-constitutional, pre-existing unit, is also defended, though Spanish nationalism is no longer spoken of. The term 'nationalism' is relegated to accusing the 'others', the 'ethnic' nationalists, opposed to and essentially different from the liberal, open Spanish 'patriotism'. This discourse achieved hegemony within the PP.[38] Alternative conservative discourses insisting on historical rights (e.g. the 'neo-foralists') were abandoned or even outlawed. 'Healthy' regionalisms in combination with folklore and the defence of the principle of subsidiarity and decentralisation are seen as compatible with the new line.

The programme for the Catalan elections of 2003 only devoted 6 of its 230 pages to questions of self-government. The claim for 'More self-government for Catalunya' appears on page 219 – and the name of the country now is written in Catalan. But, in short, the PP stands for

> concentrating the political development of Catalonia on the improvement in the quality of self-government, abandoning sovereignist approaches or asymmetrical federalisms that merely bring about uncertainty, and ruptures in constitutional consensus.[39]

The PP, however, lost the general elections of 2004. Since then, and especially during the debate on the new Catalan statute, a strategy of confrontation with the socialist government was pursued, in the name of the cohesion of the Spanish territory and the unity of the nation, and against the alleged privileges for some AC. In the opinion of the PP, important reforms, such as those of the Statutes, should only be carried out through pacts between the major state parties. It is true that the Catalan PP took part in the debates on the statute in Catalonia, but it did so in a lukewarm way and finally voted against. In the end, the Catalan section participated, although somewhat half-heartedly, in the mass anti-statute campaign led by the statewide PP.[40] The main argument was that it was the Spanish nation that has created the AC. If governments are elected there, this does not mean that there is any sovereignty of the regional *demoi*. They are elected by the Spaniards of the region, to whom the Spanish sovereign nation has delegated this task. The PP continues to abominate 'federalist fantasies', especially asymmetrical ones, and the idea of a plurinational Spain.

Convergència i Unió

Convergència Democràtica de Catalunya has still not really clarified its final goal. More because of its practice than its programmes, however, after so many years, we are now able to distil some principles. First of all, the party strives for gaining Spanish acceptance of the plurinational nature of the state and recognition of Catalonia as a nation. While the ideal form of the state is not defined, it is assumed that the Spanish state, as a state held in common, in some way or another, will subsist. Catalonia would therefore remain a nation without its own state. There is a basic idea of Spain being formed by four nations or nationalities (not 7 or 17). Trias Fargas had already spoken of Spain as a 'nation of nations.'[41] The Spanish Constitution is valued as 'a unique platform of coexistence in the political experience of the state as a whole,'[42] but criticised for lacking specifications on the role of the nationalities and the powers of the autonomies, as well as their financation. However, Convergència has shown itself reluctant to push constitutional change, preferring to exploit possibilities of interpretation and new readings.

At least before 1996, mentioning self-determination had a merely symbolic function in Convergència's discourse. It was not a real strategic goal. The party, somehow, begs its leave not to insist further, hinting at the fact that self-determination lacks a social majority in Catalonia. If it is mentioned at all, this calms the sovereignist current within CDC, and can be used as an element of pressure.[43] Instead of advocating statehood, CDC insisted on the decline of the nation state in Europe. In this context, independence appears as somewhat out of time. Although the party's Euro-optimism has now cooled down, it is still important, and CiU has always given almost unconditional support for European integration. In 1996, Pujol reasoned the practical exclusion of the independentist alternative in the following way:

> Catalonia is not going to separate from Spain for several and powerful reasons. Let me give you two. First, it does not aim to. And second, if it aimed to, it could not, and not just because of Spanish opposition. Therefore, the fear of secessionism is not rational.[44]

At least from the Pujolist point of view, the nation is more important than to have a state of one's own. Worse than a Catalan nation without a state is a Catalan state that is nationally de-catalanised.[45]

The CDC has never devoted much effort to formulating the alternatives of statehood or new frontiers. The notion of the Catalan Countries has never played a major role in the programmes or practices of CiU. Convergent interventionism aimed gradually to increase competencies. Autonomy was always 'insufficient', and it would be necessary to go 'further'. There is a limit: calculations are always made so as not to traumatise the rest of the state. In this way, the so often prophetised 'exhaustion of its ideology'[46] did not take place.

As long as CiU was in the Catalan government, 'piece of cake' policies were plausible. Quite differently from the discourse and the practice of many nationalist movements, Pujol always rejected the strategy of the worse for the state, the better for the stateless nation. The opposite position was taken: 'it is good for Catalanism if Spain does well.'[47] The history of CDC is full of declarations to be Spanish. Before his party's national council, on 13 December 1992, Pujol argued: 'Catalan nationalism as we understand it – and in agreement with much of Catalan tradition – is reformist. It is so in Catalonia, and it is so ... in the rest of the State.'[48] Along these lines of a nationalism that foresees continuing in a common state, Pujol was always interested in maintaining a good relation with the crown, a possible guarantor of a future plurinational state.

During the 1980s and 1990s, the party shifted from left-of-centre to right-of-centre. It lost some of its initial drive, partially becoming a voting machine, at the service of the leader. It appeared satisfied, after having incorporated the centre parties and some split-offs from the ERC. After many years in government in Catalonia, it arguably did more administrating than successful nation building. In such a situation and facing growing competition from the ERC, what can in part be called a sovereigntist turn took place.

At the X Congress, held in November 1996, and after having lost ten seats in the elections of 1995, the party, formally, began a new stage. There was a generational change, and some 'sovereigntist' young politicians joined the leadership. In a speech delivered on 8 October, Pujol himself hinted at the combination of continuity and conditioned change on the question of statehood:

> We have always insisted on trying to raise the autonomic ceiling without altering either the Statute or the Constitution. We believe that political decisions can be made within these frameworks that so permit. We are sure of this. But it might so happen that things occur or resistance arises that is supported by interpretations of the constitution that may force us to change our opinion. In this case, we ought to consider reforming the Statute and the Constitution.[49]

The Congress document itself did not propose a new statute, and neither did it insist on constitutional reform. But the basic idea now is self-determination, even if the end is left open:

> [R]ight from the start, we do not, due to coherence with our legitimate right to self-determination, renounce any qualification: asymmetrical federalism, confederation, a state of our own … or the State of the autonomies, because if only conceptually and as a denomination, this enunciation has much potential to make the above mentioned articulation (of Catalonia inside Spain, KJN) become a reality.[50]

The Declaration of Barcelona of 1998, drafted in conjunction with the Basque PNV and the Galician BNG, seemed to confirm the sovereigntist turn that the media were speaking of. Despite this, at the moment of truth, the declaration had no effect whatsoever on the good running of the agreement with the PP for the governability of Spain. Rather it was a necessary complement for internal use, as many members and some leaders abominated any agreement with the PP.

While the electoral programmes of 1999 and of 2000 insisted once again on the possibilities offered by strengthening the State of the Autonomies, deploying the Spanish Constitution and performing new transfers, inside CDC, the XI Congress, held in 2000, used some rhetoric of self-determination, and strengthened the notion that the party now would go for far-reaching reforms. Asymmetrical mechanisms like veto rights and bilateralism were now mentioned.

The slowly changing party was finally challenged by the tripartite coalition treaty in 2003 which previewed the reform of the Statute of

Autonomy that CiU, during so many years in government, had never seriously considered. In consequence, the CiU platform for the 2004 general elections finally broke with this: 'from Catalonia, we seek to start a new bilateral relationship with the State through a new Statute of Autonomy', a 'new national Statute of Catalonia ... that does not water down Catalan self-government in the framework of a uniform, homogeneous model', in addition to the classic *caveat* that it should be 'based on respect for the Constitution, but defending an interpretation thereof that enables a higher degree of self-government.'[51] But in the complicated Catalan and Spanish multiparty system, strategies mattered more than platforms: in the Catalan debate, CiU tried to put the PSC against the ropes, radicalising as much as possible the text of the *Parlament* in order to endanger the relation between Catalan and Spanish socialists – while reaching afterwards, in Madrid, an agreement with the Spanish socialists on a far more moderate Statute – and trying to leave the PSC out of the picture.

Unió Democràtica de Catalunya, occasionally, still refers to the confederal discourse of its foundation. But contemporary speeches of party leader Duran i Lleida usually go in a more cooperative direction:

> We do not want to identify our demands with the creation of a State. Unió Democràtica never did so. We sustain the concept of interdependence as positive compared to independence. Moreover, we know perfectly that in the European community there is no room for attempts at separatism.[52]

In 1995, Duran proposed a mixed horizon, 'confederal in things that set us apart and federal in what we might have in common.'[53] European integration 'involves the progressive debilitation of the concept of state and the disappearance of frontiers.'[54] This did not take place, and a more realistic tone was adapted: 'Our main challenge is to reach an agreement with the institutions of the State for the political representation of Catalonia in the EU.'[55]

In spite of defending a communitarian definition of the nation ('the nation is an original community, prior to the state, and is as natural and necessary for man as the institution of the family itself'[56]), Duran now sees 'the need to extend national conscience, rather than radicalise it,'[57] and he considers that for many Catalans, it is not Catalonia but Spain that is their national referent, and that this deserves respect. With more clarity than CDC, Unió salutes direct participation in the Spanish government, should the opportunity arise. According to Duran, 'political Catalanism must govern in Spain.'[58]

Esquerra Republicana de Catalunya

Of all the parties analysed, the ERC stands out, as it has undergone the most relevant changes to its programme. Currently, the party stands for independence. During the 1980s, some disorientation had reigned. The ERC had formed part of Jordi Pujol's governments, even when CiU had an absolute majority (1984). In theory, Heribert Barrera stuck to old confederal positions, without excluding independence as a last resort, but this was mere rhetoric. Barrera took it for granted that for his people, the nation of reference would be the Catalan Countries, but he implicitly had to admit that the very same elements of defining a nation that he enumerated, above all national conscience and common will, could not be found everywhere in the Catalan Countries.[59] During these years, Esquerra continued to criticise the State of the Autonomies, but the increasingly numerous proposals were not aimed at its abolition, but at its reform, above all, statute reform.

Under the liberal leader Hortalà, the ERC seemed to become a satellite to CiU. This process was opposed by some newly joined militants. Angel Colom, Josep Lluís Carod-Rovira, and others came either from 'la Crida', a civic, direct action movement in support of the language and against the LOAPA, or from left-wing nationalist parties that had remained outside the *Parlament*. This process of assembling independentists continued until 1995, when militants of the armed group Terra Lliure stopped laying their primitive bombs and joined ERC.[60]

The new, young militants led Esquerra's slow change towards a party that stood for independence in the first place. The programme for the 1987 municipal elections said just this: 'Now, municipal councils for independence.'[61] Independence increasingly prevailed over republicanism or leftism, and the party became more pan-Catalanist. The programme for the 1988 Catalan elections presented a road map for independence, albeit starting with the reform of the Statute. It was clearly admitted that not all of Catalonia's national problems depended on Madrid. Catalan society lacked national cohesion, while globalisation, with an increasing probability of the disappearance of the language, required achieving its own state. In 1989, a crucial year for the party, the new programme realistically asserted that the only path to the national vertebration of Catalonia would be to win the social majority. And that only a non-essentialist project could catch all elements of the people:

> It should be cosmopolitan and universalist and respect and encourage diversity. It should conceive culture as a changing dynamic, of multiple realities in permanent transition. It should assume that all

grafts and mixed cultural forms are the heritage of the civil, plural and contradictory community.

This went against traditional leaders like Barrera who had warned against 'cultural crossbreeding'. It also meant a new interpretation of the role of the Catalan language, which still would be a basic element of integration, but mainly an *instrument* to constitute the political community, which is the main goal.

Esquerra, therefore, started to separate language and nationalist political conscience: 'for large sectors of the population, feeling Catalan or not is not strictly correlative with the use of the language, and neither does it translate linearly into a feeling of belonging to a common community, the nation'. In the same year, 1989, at the December Congress, the independentists finally won and took over the leadership of the party. In the *Parlament*, ERC forced a motion in favour of the right to self-determination which passed with the votes of CiU and others, also thanks to the abstention of the PSC. The international context, following the fall of the Berlin wall, was also favourable to the independentists. The 1992 electoral programme showed the new orientation plainly in its title: 'Towards independence'.

Under Colom's populist leadership, Esquerra was seeking a young, radical electorate, even in the linguistically castilianised regions. Independentism replaced the previous, nominally federal/confederal posture. This new orientation, this new style led to considerable electoral growth. By 1992, ERC was the third force in the *Parlament*; in 1993, it recovered its representation in *las Cortes*; in the 1995 Catalan elections, almost ten per cent of votes went to ERC – and CiU lost its absolute majority.

Officially, the party's ideological declarations were presented as continuist, as mere updates of the 1931 programme.[62] But they increasingly highlighted the right to self-determination. There was always a door left open for federal solutions, the 'creation of a state or any other own legal-political structure', but in the long run, 'obtaining the independence of the Catalan Nation within a United Europe constitutes an irremediable goal', a formula copied from the Scottish Nationalists. Independence, in the context of globalisation and European integration, was not superfluous (as those that believed in the end of the nation state thought), but necessary for the Catalan nation. In spite of this, much of the programme for the general elections in 1996 was devoted to improve the situation of the 'Catalan nation as a territory within the Spanish State.'[63] Thus, Angel Colom, in a booklet widely distributed inside and outside the party, spoke at length of a new, 'national' statute of autonomy (with really exclusive competencies), and of the confederal restructuring of the state,[64] which, deep down, might be preferable.

When the CiU supported first the PSOE, then even the PP Spanish governments, this favoured the ERC. But Colom's personalist leadership, his somewhat erratic strategy, which some considered was directed too much at stealing CiU votes, ended in party crisis which led to a split-off headed by Colom himself. Under Carod-Rovira, the ERC performed a left turn as was made plain by the XXII Party Congress of 1998, when the party identified primarily as the Esquerra Nacional or National Left. Progress towards independence could only be made 'getting closer to it day to day', 'based on the modest degrees of autonomy of which we dispose,'[65] and denouncing the inconsistency of a Spanish state, which presents itself as being democratic but denies the right to self-determination. Against a reinvigorated Spanish state, the party gave greater importance to more realistic goals. Thus, the XXIII Congress of 2001 speaks, above all, of statutory and constitutional reforms, presenting long lists of proposals heading increasingly towards federalism, now more clearly conceived as asymmetrical, claiming representation of the nations in the Senate, with the right of veto on matters that affected their existence.[66]

The programme for the 2003 Catalan elections no longer features independentism in the forefront, rather it insists on the presence of Catalonia in Europe and in the world. Somehow, the balance between state/independence and nation/identity was readjusted again: the latter regains greater coverage.[67] The XXIV Congress of 2004, right in the middle of discussions on the statute, insists on what has come to be called social independentism:

> ERC's actions must be understood ... as necessary steps towards the shaping of a majority social bloc for the future exertion of the right to self-determination, if possible to the extent that ERC becomes the prime force of the left and of Catalanism. With this goal, and transitorily, Esquerra is committed to collaborating with the political forces that wish to do so in transforming the State into a federal, plurinational republic.[68]

This can clearly be related to the party's arrival in government in 2003. Significantly, the programme for the 2004 general elections now concentrates especially on 'achieving a plurinational, pluricultural, and plurilinguistic State'[69] (meaning a Spanish one). The accent lies on reforming the state and participating more in it, not becoming separate from it.

This return to federalism, with asymmetrical or confederal touches, left more populistic independentism behind, but insisted on the statehood that any federal or confederal system also involves. In his way, Carod-Rovira could claim to be more federalist than the Spaniards ('Are there any federals in Spain?', *Avui*, 4 January 2006), who would be lacking the political culture of 'pactisme' (pacting). 'Catalan federalism ... has always demanded its own State and, often, has opened the doors to an Iberian understanding, including Portugal, with no hegemonies or paternalism.' Just changing names and nominally converting the AC into federal entities would not do. 'Perhaps we could, at this stage, federate with the Spain of the autonomies and they, within, could organise themselves as they deem most fitting.'

In concluding

Catalanism has always been a challenge for the Spanish would-be nation state. In Catalonia, the transition witnessed a broad range of programmatic proposals as to how to organise the Spanish state. Today, the political game at its different levels has established its rules. The parties interact more; programmes are drafted taking into account the positions of adversaries and (possible) allies. Electoral practice at different levels (local authorities, AC, state, Europe) provides the possibility of presenting *à la carte* programmes. The incentives to play the game according to rules are manifold.

Now, the more radical positions that existed during the transition have been abandoned. The PSOE is no longer self-deterministic, the successors of AP not only accept the Spanish Constitution, including Article 2, but even consecrate it, and so on. Despite the narrowing of the range of party positions, in Catalonia, a rich diversity of programmatic positions still exists, between programmes that declare that there is enough autonomy now, that powers should be increased, that there is a need to reinterpret the Statute and/or the Spanish Constitution, that developing the state in the direction of symmetrical or asymmetrical federalism would be desirable, that a confederation would satisfy national rights, that a (eventually conditional) right of self-determination should be recognised. Independence is only defended by a minority, and often conditional on continuous lack of recognition of the nation by the state.

Notes

1. See Ismael E. Pitarch, Joan Botella, Jordi Capo and Joan Marcet, *Partits i parlamentaris a la Catalunya d'avui: Període de la Generalitat provisional (1977–1979)*, Edicions 62, Barcelona, 1980.

2. See Gabriel Colomé, 'The "Partit dels Socialistes de Catalunya"' in José M. Maravall, Gabriel Colomé, Antonio Missiroli, Patrick Seyd, Einar Berntzen, Lieven de Winter, Michalis Spourdalakis and Wolfgang Merkel, *Socialist parties in Europe*, Barcelona: Institut de Ciències Polítiques i Socials, 1991, pp. 35–61; Gabriel Colomé, *El Partit dels Socialistes de Catalunya: estructura, funcionament, i electorat (1978–1989)*, Barcelona, 1989. Eugeni Giral Quintana, *Partit dels Socialistes de Catalunya (PSC-PSOE). Cronologia (1978–1999)*, Institut de Ciències Polítiques i Socials, Barcelona, 2002.

3. Jordi Font, 'El catalanisme del PSC' in Josep Termes and Jordi Casassas (eds), *El nacionalisme com a ideologia*, Barcelona, 1995, pp. 107–23.

4. Socialist Manifesto, 'Míting de la Llibertat', 22 June 1976.

5. Partit Socialista de Catalunya. Documents aprovats en el seu Congrés Constituent, celebrat l'1 de novembre de 1976, Barcelona, 1976.

6. Arcadi Calzada and Carles Llorens, *Reconstrucció nacional. On es troba Catalunya, a vint anys del franquisme i quinze de les primeres eleccions al Parlament?*, Barcelona, 1995, p. 159s.

7. Rafael Ribó, *Sobre el fet nacional: Catalunya, Països Catalans, Estat espanyol*, Barcelona, 1977, p. 31.

8. Ibid., pp. 41, 43.

9. Ibid., p. 123.

10. *Nous Horitzons: Nuestra utopía*. PSUC. Cincuenta años de historia de Cataluña, Barcelona, 1986.

11. *La Vanguardia*, 19 October 1993, in Faulí 1995 (see below), p. 135.

12. See Josep Faulí, 'El PP de Catalunya prefereix la catalanitat al catalanisme' in Josep Termes and Jordi Casassas (eds), *El nacionalisme com a ideologia*, Materials de treball i estudi, Barcelona, 1995, pp. 135–42.

13. See Juan Marcet, *Convergencia Democrática de Cataluña: El partido y el movimiento político*, Madrid, 1987; Juan Marcet, 'The Parties of Non-State Ambit: The Case of Catalonia', in Lieven de Winter (ed.) *Non-State Wide Parties in Europe*, Barcelona, 1994, pp. 163–78; and Juan Marcet and Jorid Argelaguet, 'Nationalist parties in Catalonia. Convergència Democràtica de Catalunya and Esquerra Republicana' in Lieven de Winter and Huri Türsan (eds), *Regionalist Parties in Western Europe*, London and New York: Routledge, 1998, pp. 70–86.

14. Convergència Democràtica de Catalunya: Programa econòmic i social, Gener, 1977.

15. Montserrat Baras and Jordi Matas Dalmases, 'Els partits polítics i el sistema de partits' in Miquel Caminal Badia and Jordi Matas Dalmases (eds), *El sistema polític de Catalunya*, Madrid, 1998, p. 163.

16. Ibid., p. 167.

17. Francesc-Marc Álvaro, 'CDC i Jordi Pujol, catalanisme sostingut. Una aproximació periodística a l'evolució recent del nacionalisme moderat hegemònic' in Termes and Casassas 1995, p. 131.

18. Convergència i Unió, *Un programa de govern per a la ciutadania dels 80*, 1980.

19. Joan B. Culla i Clarà, 'Unió Democràtica de Catalunya: Le parti démocrate-chrétien catalan (1931–1989)' in Mario Caciagli, Lieven de Winter, Albrecht Mintzel, Joan B. Culla and Alain de Brouwer, *Christian Democracy in Europe*, Institut de Ciències Polítiques i Socials, Barcelona, 1992, pp. 83–110.

20. Baras and Matas, 1998, p. 167.

21. Esquerra Republicana de Catalunya, *Principis Bàsics*. Aprovats per l'Assemblea de constitució del Partit d'Esquerra Republicana de Catalunya, Barcelona, juny de 1931.
22. See Carles Santacana, 'El pensament nacionalista d'ERC (1975–1992)' in Termes and Casassas, 1995, p. 146.
23. Esquerra Republicana de Catalunya: Declaració de principis bàsics, Barcelona, 18 de novembre de 1978.
24. Santacana, p. 148s.
25. Eduard Company, 'Socialisme català i nacionalisme espanyol' in Termes and Casassas, 1995, p. 197.
26. Partit dels Socialistes de Catalunya (PSC-PSOE) (ed.): PSC 25 anys: 1978–2003, Madrid, 2003.
27. Calzada and Llorens, 1995, p. 168.
28. PSC, *Ciutadans pel canvi: Noves oportunitats per a Catalunya*, 1999.
29. Fernando Peregrín Gutiérrez, 'El nacionalismo heterodoxo de Pasqual Maragall', *Claves de Razón Práctica*, No. 147, 2004, pp. 58–66.
30. Rafeal Ribó and Massimo D'Alema, *La Reforma de l'Estat/Riforma dello Stato*, Roma, 1997, p. 24.
31. Miquel Caminal, *El federalismo pluralista: Del federalismo nacional al federalismo plurinacional*, Barcelona, 2002.
32. Josep Faulí, 'El PP de Catalunya prefereix la catalanitat al catalanisme' in Termes and Casassas, 1995, pp. 135–42.
33. Ibid., p. 137.
34. Aleix Vidal-Quadras, *Identidad y libertad* (Una ojeada en escorzo a las contraindicaciones éticas de los nacionalismos secesionistas), Revista de la Facultad de Derecho de la Universidad Complutense, monográfico 21, Madrid, 1997, p. 212s.
35. Ibid.
36. Partido Popular de Cataluña, *Un catalanismo renovado*. Manifiesto del Partido Popular de Cataluña al cumplirse los quince años de autogobierno. Septiembre, 1995, p. 5.
37. Ibid., pp. 7, 8, 10.
38. See Xosé-Manoel Núñez Seixas, 'From National-Catholic Nostalgia to Constitutional Patriotism: Conservative Spanish Nationalism Since the Early 1990s' in Sebastian Balfour (ed.), *The Politics of Contemporary Spain*, London and New York: Routledge, 2005, pp. 121–45.
39. Partido Popular de Catalunya, *Compartimos un proyecto por Catalunya*, Programa Elecciones Autonómicas, 2003, p. 219.
40. Klaus-Jürgen Nagel, 'Verfassungs- und Statutsreformen in Spanien: ein föderalistischer Frühling?', *Jahrbuch des Föderalismus 2005*, pp. 458–74 and Klaus-Jürgen Nagel, 'Autonomiestatute und/oder/statt Föderalismus? Zum Stand der Reform des spanischen, Staates der Autonomien', *Jahrbuch des Föderalismus 2006*, pp. 395–408.
41. See Cesáreo R. Aguilera de Prat, *Partidos y estrategias nacionalistas en Cataluña, Escocia y Flandes*, València, 2002, p. 138.
42. J. Rigol, UDC, 1997, cited by Aguilera, 2002, p. 261.
43. Aguilera, 2002, p. 192s.
44. Ibid., p. 135.

45. Calzada and Llorens, 1995, p. 200.
46. David Walker, 'Convergència Democràtica de Catalunya: Its successes and its Problems', *Regional Politics & Policy*, Vol. 1, No. 3, 1991, p. 284.
47. Calzada and Llorens, 1995, p. 202.
48. Alvaro, 1995, p. 131.
49. Ibid., p. 152.
50. Convergència Democràtica de Catalunya, *Convergència, la força decisiva per a Catalunya*. X Congrés L'Hospitalet – 8, 9 i 10 de novembre de 1996, 1997, p. 27. However, (asymmetrical) federalism was clearly preferred to independence.
51. Convergència i Unió, *Duran per Catalunya*, Programa Eleccions Generals, 2004, p. 21.
52. Josep Antoni Duran i Lleida, *Catalunya i l'Espanya plurinacional*, Barcelona, 1995, p. 114s.
53. Ibid., p. 154s.
54. Josep Antoni Duran i Lleida, 'Guanyar el nostre futur', *La segona nacionalització de Catalunya. IV Escola d'Estiu d'UJDCC L'Ampolla*, dijous 25 de juliol de 1996.
55. Josep Antoni Duran i Lleida, 'Europa federal, Europa plural. De la utopia a la realitat', ESADE, 19 de juny de 2001.
56. Duran, 1996.
57. Josep Antoni Duran i Lleida, 'Unió al servei de les persones: un compromís per compartir plegats', Conferència al Teatre Nacional de Catalunya, Barcelona, 3 d'abril de 2006.
58. Ibid.
59. Santacana, 1995, p. 150.
60. David Bassa, Carles Benítez, Carles Castellanos and Raimon Soler, *L'independentisme català (1979–1994)*, Barcelona, 1995.
61. Santacana, 1995, p. 151.
62. Esquerra Republicana de Catalunya, *Declaració ideològica*. 19è Congrés Nacional, Barcelona, 1993.
63. Esquerra Republicana de Catalunya, *La teva veu, Cap a la independència*. Eleccions a les Corts espanyoles, 1996.
64. Angel Colom, *Esquerra, República, Catalunya*, Barcelona, 1995, p. 51.
65. Esquerra Republicana de Catalunya, 22è Congrés Nacional, Girona, 4 i 5 juliol 1998. Ponència Política, 1998.
66. Esquerra Republicana de Catalunya, 23è Congrés Nacional. Tarragona, 17–18 març 2001. Ponència Política, 2001.
67. Esquerra Republicana de Catalunya, Una nació europea, democràtica i solidària. Eleccions catalanes, 2003.
68. Esquerra Republicana de Catalunya, 24è Congrés Nacional. Ponència d'Estratègia Política, 2004.
69. Esquerra Republicana de Catalunya, *Eleccions a Corts Generals de l'Estat espanyol 2004. Programa electoral*, 2004.

Part II Irish Perspectives

8
Equality as Steady State or Equality as Threshold? Northern Ireland after the Good Friday (Belfast) Agreement, 1998

Jennifer Todd

Introduction: Equality and ethnic conflict regulation

It is possible to identify two starkly opposed positions on the regulation of ethnic conflict.[1] On the one hand, there is the view that such conflict is in important part driven by a popular perception of unequal treatment on the basis of ethnic category, such that the equal recognition of opposed ethnic identities, equal institutional opportunities and provisions for cultural expression, equality for opposed national aspirations, and an equalisation of group economic condition allows a diminution of conflict and a moderation of ethnic demands. On the other hand, there is the view that ethnic conflict is primarily elite-driven with elites framing popular grievances in ethnic terms, so that the institutionalisation of ethnic equality and more generally the appeasement of ethnic demands rewards intransigence among leaders and congeals social divisions. Debates on the relative priorities of defeating terrorism or of remedying the grievances of subjected populations refer to precisely these principles, as do debates on the role of egalitarian measures (from affirmative action policies to consociational institutions) in ethnic conflict prevention and regulation.[2]

That the two positions sketched above are partial and overly schematic is not in doubt. Ethnic conflict is multiply determined, both popular perceptions and elite interests are involved, and each is affected by the wider geopolitical context: constitutions, state-borders, kin-states, external guarantors and international norms.[3] Even when we focus on endogenous factors, ethnic conflict is also about identity and dignity and the sense of place in the world: perceived insult here can open whole populations to ethnic mobilisation. *When* particular inequalities become ethnic grievances, or *when* particular changes are seen as opportunities for power-accretion is a product of popular perceptions and political mobilisation.[4] *When* popular attitudes and identifications define political options, and *when* elite negotiations and reformulations allow shifts in popular views and renegotiations of popular identities, and of what form and to what extent, are important and tricky questions on which there is still surprisingly little empirical research. Even accepting the need for reform of inequality, the hard questions have to do with the amount and form of equality and the commensurability of the units between which equality is sought.[5]

The positions sketched above remain a useful starting point for analysis because they open up an agenda for empirical research on the effects that equality policies – and more generally institutional part-satisfaction of ethnic demands – have on ethnic demands and ethnic identities.[6] Current debates between liberal nationalists and consociationalists on the one hand, and state-centred integrationists and transformationalists, on the other hand, too often presuppose the effect of equality policies on ethnic identities. Liberal nationalists and consociationalists presuppose that ethno-national identities are persistent and that recognising them does not change them; transformationalists assume that institutional certification of identities will make change more difficult.[7] This chapter gives qualified support to the view that ethno-national conflict can best be regulated by promoting equality between ethno-national groups, but for quite different reasons than those put forward by liberal nationalists. I argue that in at least some cases equalisation strategies work *because* they provoke change in the identities and attitudes and solidarities of groups. As this occurs, the equality provisions become less useful, precisely because they are ensuring equality between inappropriate units. Equality must therefore be seen as a threshold rather than a steady state, one that is necessary to pass in order to proceed to more participatory and indeed transformative forms of politics.

I take Northern Ireland as a case study, appropriately because a strong equalisation policy since the late 1980s, and in particular since the Good Friday (Belfast) Agreement of 1998, has been correlated with a moderation of conflict and because there is considerable scholarly attention paid to the degree of communal inequality over time and the effects of the reform programme and equality legislation. In this chapter I work from the premise that substantive communal inequality was an important grievance for Catholics and for nationalists up to the 1990s.[8] However there is a distinction between remedying inequality and constituting a new equal ethnic balance: Irish government officials in witness seminar and interview were clear that their strategy was the former not the latter.[9] If inequality has to be eliminated, equality is unstable. In Northern Ireland it can be seen as a threshold – more precisely a series of thresholds – rather than a steady state. A threshold is a step that is difficult to cross, but once crossed it allows change to proceed swiftly.[10] The process of crossing those thresholds gives rise to new ways of conceiving of identity and understanding interests, not least among Protestants and unionists, which problematises previous formulations of equality. In this sense, there is (a form of) conflict transformation triggered by (a qualified) egalitarianism. Rather than equality freezing identities, then, it is best justified as a way of provoking change in them.

Reframing the debates over the Good Friday Agreement, 1998

The Good Friday Agreement (GFA) sets out provisions for a new political and constitutional configuration in Northern Ireland, on the island of Ireland and between Ireland and Britain. It was later amended, but not radically changed, in the St Andrews Agreement of 2006. The document is detailed: an outline of its provisions and commentary on them is provided in other texts.[11] In this section, after a brief overview of the provisions, I focus on the debates about their effects. I argue that the definition of the endogenous aspects of the Agreement as 'consociational' is too narrowly institutional and that a focus on the wider egalitarian provisions and impact of the Agreement allows us to better assess its significance and understand its effects. After a brief introductory section which sets out its aspirations for a 'new beginning' in Northern Ireland, the GFA deals in turn with constitutional issues, representation and governance within Northern Ireland (strand one), North–South institutions (strand two), British–Irish institutions (strand three), issues of equality and rights, issues of decommissioning, security, criminal justice and prisons. Each issue was contested between the parties, and each marks a compromise with different winners and losers on each set of issues.[12]

The Agreement affirms the fact of British sovereignty, while a majority in Northern Ireland so wish, but the ground of that sovereignty is now the will of a majority of people in Northern Ireland. At the same time, the right of national self-determination of the Irish people, to be exercised by agreement between the two parts of the island is at once affirmed and qualified (the only choices are British or Irish sovereignty). In parallel, articles 2 and 3 of the Irish constitution are to be changed to express an aspiration to Irish unity rather than a territorial claim to the whole island.[13] The fact that it is the people of Ireland who are seen as the bearer of the right of national self-determination (in the event of a united Ireland), while the people of Northern Ireland have the right of choice of jurisdiction, suggests a complex categorisation of the relative status of these peoples which, while it remains implicit in the Agreement, is open to innovative elaboration.[14] Yet these innovations, which on a nationalist understanding put Northern Ireland into a different constitutional position than any other part of the UK, were not incorporated into British law, permitting unionists to argue that the GFA, like the Northern Ireland (1998) Act which followed, is a confirmation of British sovereignty and a strengthening of the unionist position.[15] Whether this constitutes the squaring of a circle, or a unionist victory remains in dispute.

On strand one, the Agreement takes and adapts consociational features in its design of the Assembly and Executive. There is proportionality in elections through the PR STV system, with 108 seats (the relatively large number potentially gives space for small parties). Membership of the executive is assigned broadly proportionally to party strength in the assembly by the d'Hondt mechanism: this system is more inclusive and open to variation in popular will than is voluntary coalition and no party with sufficient strength in the assembly can be excluded. There are (egalitarian) safeguards for the communal blocs in assembly voting procedures: members are designated as nationalist, unionist or other, and voting is by parallel consent and/or weighted majority in contentious situations. In essence, this is proportionality with communally egalitarian safeguards, conceived as emergency brakes rather than as barriers to all change.

Strand two outlines a North–South Ministerial Council (with a standing joint secretariat), accountable to the Northern Ireland Assembly and the Irish Dáil (Parliament), whose existence is mutually interdependent with that of the Assembly, and whose duties include the setting up of North–South implementation bodies with clear operational remits.[16] A parallel British–Irish Council, without mandatory implementation bodies, is instituted in Strand Three. British–Irish coordination and cooperation as institutionalised in the Anglo-Irish Agreement of 1985 is continued, despite some changes in the form of the Intergovernmental Conference, through the British–Irish Intergovernmental Conference and Secretariat.

Beyond these changes in the political institutions, there are far-reaching innovations in 'mainstreaming' equality policy, in human rights and in reform of the security forces and justice system to create an even playing field in civil society for nationalists and unionists.[17] In addition, provisions for decommissioning, demilitarisation and prisoner releases have slowly ended not just the 'war' but the war culture of Northern Ireland.

As is well known, the implementation of the Agreement has been very uneven. For two-thirds of the time since 1998, the executive has been unable to form and for much of the period the Assembly has been suspended. The crises continued after the reinstitution of the Assembly and executive in 2007. Nonetheless much has been achieved: decommissioning, demilitarisation, prisoner releases, thorough reform of policing, strong equality legislation and more integrated work places than before, functioning North–South institutions which serve as examples of what is possible on a wider scale in the future, substantive moderation of the policies of the 'extreme' parties, the Democratic Unionist Party (DUP) and Sinn Féin,[18] and considerable evidence of rethinking in sections of the population.[19]

Equally well known, the numbers of peace walls separating Protestant and Catholic neighbourhoods has increased and communal segregation appears to be increasing, low-level communal violence (intimidation, harassment, pipe-bombs, intermittent sectarian attacks) is endemic, and some see the new DUP/Sinn Féin executive as functioning simply by dividing the spoils of office between their constituents.[20] If individuals rethink in private, they have failed to make the leap into public change.[21] If the balance sheet is one of success, movement is certainly slower and less far-reaching than anticipated in 1998.

Much of the scholarly debate on the merits of the GFA has focused on its consociational characteristics such as proportionality in elections and in executive formation, grand coalition, bloc vetoes and segmental autonomy.[22] This has been justified by liberal nationalists on egalitarian grounds. It is often seen as the realisation of the vision of the New Ireland Forum of 1983–4, which brought together the nationalist parties in the Irish state and the SDLP and argued, on liberal nationalist principles, that new structures should accommodate both the right of nationalists 'to effective political, symbolic and administrative expression of their identity' and the right of unionists to 'effective political, symbolic and administrative expression of their identity, their ethos and their way of life'.[23]

The consociational features of the GFA have also faced trenchant criticism on the grounds that they tend to 'freeze' communal identities and preclude 'conflict transformation'. The most radical critics see it as misconceived, a vehicle for entrenching communal identities and communal opposition. Others argue that the form of consociationism is at fault: Horowitz argues that the voting system and the mode of executive formation does not give incentives to voters to vote for moderate parties, or to parties to form alliances and look for cross-community support.[24] Defenders of the consociational elements of the Agreement, in contrast, argue that the GFA is in essence a fair, pragmatic and realistic way to regulate conflict in a situation where voters will continue to vote, and to think of themselves as, nationalists and unionists, Irish and British, for the foreseeable future: ethno-national identities are long-lasting and difficult to shift, and equality between them is the fairest form of settlement.[25]

Consider, however, that the consociational form of representative institutions, and, in particular, the form of designation as unionist, nationalist or other in the Assembly, may have less causal effect than either set of protagonists suppose. Three reasons lead to this view, one to do with the nature of identities, one to do with the nature of institutions and one to do with the overall frame of the Agreement.

- Consociational political institutions do not freeze identities, because identities are at once more deeply embedded in everyday activities and social relations which outlast political change, and also more open to shift, than this view allows.[26] Much more important in highlighting identities and distinctions at everyday level than the procedures for designation in the Assembly were a range of provisions dating before 1998, on monitoring in employment, housing lists, equality legislation in employment, together with the 'mainstreaming' of equality legislation in the 1998 (Northern Ireland) Act, the emphasis on 'parity of esteem' and the new procedures for recruitment to the security services.[27]

- The consociational form of the institutions is of less direct relevance than critics and defenders argue, because how institutions function is more dependent on informal coordination practices and expectations than on formal rules. Thelen has shown how institutional change can take place from the bottom, in series of layers, shifts, conversions which have to do with collective practices and expectations rather than with top-down design.[28] We have seen this through most of the history of Northern Ireland where formally universalistic and democratic institutions were for long 'converted' to communal purposes, or simply – as in 1974 – failed to function. The consociational representative institutions in Northern Ireland in 1998 were embedded in radically changing provisions for security, employment equality and rights, and in a strengthened British-Irish understanding. This meant that the institutions stood to function quite differently than did superficially similar consociational institutions in 1974: in particular, nationalists had significantly greater opportunities for making a policy difference. The real question about the institutions of the GFA was whether they would be converted into a new arena for an older communal conflict, or instead channel and partially change the coordination practices of the parties and expectations of the leaders, and perhaps also of the public. They most certainly did moderate the policies and practices of the political elites in government.[29] However, there was much less translation between elite rethinking and public attitudes than might have been expected.[30]

- The consociational form of representative institutions was only one part of the Agreement, and the part which has, arguably, had least effect. The representative institutions were functioning for no more than a third of the period between June 1998 and June 2008, while the equality legislation, security reform and North–South and British–Irish provisions were ongoing for most of the same period. These latter provisions resolved long-standing inequalities, and put in place new opportunities. Unionists, nationalists and republicans saw a radical change in the balance of power and status within Northern Ireland.

All of this is to suggest that the consociational architecture was a sufficient condition neither of the failures nor of the successes of the Agreement. If it was one necessary condition of success, its role here was strongly conditioned by wider public and political expectations that in turn had more to do with the equalisation policies and wider geopolitical changes than with the specific political arrangements.[31] Nor was it a major factor provoking the failures of the agreement. In the initial years, it was the impact of the equality and security provisions of the Agreement – prisoner releases, restraints on marches, republican advance, 'parity of esteem' in policing, a sense of falling behind economically, of being marginalised – that most worried unionists.[32]

More important than consociationalism as an endogenous condition of both the successes and the failures of the GFA was the egalitarian thrust of the Agreement, and indeed of previous legislation from the 1989 Fair Employment (Northern Ireland) Act. This increasingly strong legislation was correlated with increasing equalisation of communal condition.[33] In 1971, Catholics (with over a third of the economically active population) made up 14 per cent of professionals, 16 per cent of male managers and 8.2 per cent of those in the top 250 civil service jobs. In 2001 (with over 40 per cent of the economically active population) they had 43 per cent of professional employment and (among men) 39 per cent of managerial, and almost a third of the top 250 civil service jobs. By 2005 a policing system was functioning with equal recruitment of Catholics and Protestants. Entrenched inequalities in educational funding were remedied in the 1990s.[34]

A level of parity of esteem, including Irish language provisions and street signs, was institutionalised. Catholics remained twice as likely to be unemployed as Protestants and were disproportionately present in the remaining pockets of deprivation and poverty.[35] However this was no longer at the centre of public attention, or a major public grievance: in 1968, 74 per cent of Catholics believed that Catholics were discriminated against; in the 2000s, only 20 per cent did.[36] Nor were the remaining inequalities treated as political priorities by Sinn Féin. The 'equality agenda' was one of three Sinn Féin priorities in the 1997–8 negotiations but by the 2000s, it was junior Sinn Féin spokespersons who pointed out the remaining problems. Debates continued over public symbolism,[37] but the centre of political attention, and the focus of Irish government efforts, had to do with institutional changes (in criminal justice, in the devolution of policing) the effects of which would not be immediate. It appears that nationalists and republicans are content with the substantive change in inequality, and are not prioritising the demand of full equality of communal condition.

Hayward and Mitchell show how unionists have tended to take equality legislation as meaning 'equality for nationalists' and loss for unionists.[38] Unionists responded in at least two different ways. From 1985 onwards, mainstream unionists were quick to point to the asymmetries of the legislation which permitted the Irish government to represent nationalists while the British government took responsibility for the entire population, and the inherent injustice of treating unionist loyalty to the state as equivalent to nationalist identification with the Irish nation.[39] If unionist identity was inherently state-centred, as many liberal unionists believed, changing the character of the state did not treat unionists and nationalists equally but instead undermined the entire presuppositions of unionist identity. Deep disappointment and privatisation were common among those unionists who identified with the British state, and ultimately the 'structural unionist' programme of the UUP was rejected by the electorate.[40] But these unionists, once it became clear that there remained opportunities for them, came to accept the inevitable. In Aughey's words, they 'swallowed the toad' of the Agreement and reprioritised the elements of their identity accordingly.[41] Studies show a significant 'thinning' of the content of British identity, a tendency among some to open to Irish linkages (while retaining a British self-categorisation) and an increasing number who accept an Irish element to their identity.[42] To offer to these groups equality for their 'British identity', when they are in the process of enforced and difficult change in their understanding of this identity, is at once insulting and counterproductive.

Another group of unionists applied equality norms strictly, if inappropriately, generating some of the worst problems of the implementation period. The Glenbryn protest against small Catholic schoolgirls walking to school, or the Harryville protest against Catholic church attendance were legitimated for protestors by the sense that if Protestants were not permitted to march in Catholic neighbourhoods, neither should Catholics be allowed to walk where they wished. The argument that Protestant identity was being 'taken away', that nationalist advance was at Protestant expense, and that Protestants were not able to be effective in arguments with republicans and should be left to develop their own strong identity before cross-community involvement was demanded all rested on a notion of equal and opposite ethnic groups and ethnic identities.[43] Treating equality as something which required unionists to become a mirror image of republicans would indeed lead to segregation and continuing conflict rather than cooperation.

Taking the broad view beyond representative institutions to popular perspectives, we can see the successes of the GFA as including a change in the tenure of politics, a depoliticisation of the issue of inequality, and an acceptance of gradualist politics: surveys show that the majority of both unionists and nationalists 'could live with' a constitutional settlement other than their choice.[44] Indeed it has promoted a level of identity change. The 2007 Life and Times survey shows only a minority of the population who see themselves as 'Irish only' or as 'British only': this is a significant change from 1999, the only time a comparable question was asked, and the respondents themselves see it as quite different from their parents' attitudes.[45] A cultural threshold is being crossed. It is no longer possible to read ethnic self-conceptions, national identifications and political perspectives from political 'bloc' voting, nor is that voting in any simple sense expressive of 'identity-politics'.

The crossing of that threshold has been, and remains, difficult, particularly for some unionists and it appears to many that divisions are unchanging, even increasing. In part, this is a function of the delay in translating the political architecture of the GFA into on-the-ground effects (in demilitarisation and decommissioning, in policing changes, in cross-border opportunities, in safety). In part it is the undoubted difficulty of identity shift in a deeply divided society: interviews show widespread shifts in assumptions and values, but they also show that interactional obstacles and entrenched understandings made change crisis-ridden, reversible.

One major political failure lay in the failure to communicate and translate change from elite and institutional level to everyday social relations and institutions which crucially affect public attitudes and identity. Very limited choices were presented to the mass public – those in the process of rethinking their views had few ways of testing the collective water on small public choices. The communication channels between public attitudes and political choices which had begun to be explored, for example, by Colin Irwin's surveys, were now substituted by government-commissioned research.[46] The Civic Forum was wound down.[47] This was less a product of the consociational architecture of the Agreement than of the elite-centred implementation process.

Equality as threshold: Loosening the ethnic from the nation state

The Northern Ireland case study exemplifies many features common to 'internal' or 'ethnic' conflicts. The communities in conflict constitute themselves and their political loyalties in radically asymmetrical and often oppositional ways. The quest for an egalitarian settlement is therefore unstable and crisis-prone, for the following reasons:

- Not all interests and identities, in particular oppositional identities, *deserve* to be treated equally.
- Not all interests and identities *can* be treated equally within the same institutions. Equal institutional recognition of oppositional identities and cultures requires segmental, and perhaps eventually territorial, autonomy. This in turn is likely to reproduce and intensify the oppositional character of the identities.
- Institutional equality does not mean the same to each community or benefit both equally. Equality in relation to the symbols and cultural substance of the state may be worth significantly less to those (like unionists) who constitute their identity in terms of the state, than it is to those whose identity is constituted outside of state institutions. For the latter, parity of esteem gives a level of certification, increasing confidence and solidarity. For the former, parity of esteem decertifies their identity, requires that they change either its content or its mode of relation to the state, and decreases solidarity and confidence.

- The resultant process of change in identities, cultural interests and political preferences means that equality itself becomes a 'moving target'.

Short of leaving in existence an inequality which has had major effects in intensifying grievances and allowing radical politicisation, there are two possible ways out. The first path – enforcing equality as a steady state – is to insist on full equality, to the point of shared sovereignty, enforced by outside actors (in the Northern Ireland case by the British and Irish governments).[48] The second path – equality as threshold – is to justify the equality provisions of the GFA as a means through which all citizens are equally to be enabled to participate in politics, culture and economy.[49]

In Northern Ireland, the governments have not chosen to enforce equality as a steady state. They have not moved towards joint authority, they have not insisted on enforcing absolute equality in display of flags, emblems or in numbers of marches; they have not introduced quotas into general employment legislation. In interviews, government officials and negotiators were clear that they were attempting to address legitimate grievances, rather than attempting to create a fully equal bi-national order.[50] Nor have the main political parties argued that they do so. The principle that each national culture and allegiance (British and Irish) should be equally recognised and institutionalised and that each group (nationalist and unionist, Protestant and Catholic) should have equal conditions and status was once the minimal demand of moderate nationalists. Now even the more extreme nationalist party recognises it as inappropriate, in large part because the groups themselves are in the process of change.

The second path, equality as threshold, focuses on the idea of the GFA as a 'new beginning' to politics on the island. It requires that the past, well-documented inequalities in relation to Irish national culture, Catholic access to employment and nationalist political influence be removed. National equality or 'parity of esteem' is a situationally justified transitional norm, necessary to arrive at a situation where no one is substantively disadvantaged or advantaged because of their ethnic or religious background, national loyalty or cultural identity. Once this threshold is reached (and one good test is when the participants recognise that it is reached), further change can be opened to deliberative politics that is not reducible to community-based standards of equality. Rather than giving Protestants incentives to develop forms of community and identity equal (and opposite) to nationalists, this approach gives incentives to remove communal inequality in order to build a plural and participatory polity.

Treating equality as a threshold (or more precisely as a way to cross a series of thresholds) means that governments act as doctors rather than as scientists or lawyers, aware that the necessary medicines are also poisons, and ready to change treatment as soon as processes of regeneration (identity shift, communal plumping for new options) begin. It means that the egalitarian norms are means to overcome entrenched patterns, rather than organising principles of new patterns. That does not mean that the emerging society is norm-less, but it is to prioritise individual over communal ends, at the same time as recognising that communal injustice may effectively rule out individual fulfilment. As in medicine, judgement on when to insist on the full dose of medicine and when to reduce it, is governed by rule of thumb and pragmatism, when it is sensed that recovery is underway. The task for social scientists is not to find institutional formulae which will *in general* promote conflict resolution, but rather to identify the mechanisms which preclude and those which encourage change away from division and towards participation. In the case of Northern Ireland, those mechanisms include the remedying of gross communal inequality, but not the enforcement of strict communal equality.

What would recovery look like in Northern Ireland? There would certainly be more varied combinations of ethnic identity, national loyalty and political choice. Today some unionists, like Sir Kenneth Bloomfield, may see more dignity in a united Ireland; some nationalists may see no point – merely economic disadvantage – in a united Ireland.[51] Should these arguments become more frequent there would not be a move beyond the nation state but a move beyond the ethnic basis of the nation state. The need to eliminate gross ethnic and national inequalities would remain. But liberal nationalist concepts of equality would have to change to allow for multiple intersecting combinations of ethnic, national and political perspectives.

Notes

The chapter draws as background on as yet unattributable interviews conducted in an IRCHSS-funded research project at University College Dublin, 'Breaking Patterns of Conflict' and on a wider set of interviews (the John Whyte Archive) of which this is a part. An earlier version of the chapter was given to the pre-conference IPSA workshop 'Beyond the Nation State', Queens University Belfast, September 2007. The arguments are drawn from a much longer text co-authored with Joseph Ruane now in its final stages of completion, and has benefitted from the comments of John Baker and Iseult Honohan.

1. For the purposes of this chapter I use the term 'ethnic conflict' in the broad sense referring to group conflict where the groups are at least partially defined in decent terms.
2. For examples of the latter, see J. McGarry and B. O'Leary, *The Northern Ireland Conflict: Consociational Engagements*, Oxford University Press, Oxford, 2004; F. Stewart (ed.), *Horizontal Inequalities and Conflict: Understanding Group Violence in Multi-ethnic Societies*, Basingstoke: Palgrave Macmillan, 2008; R. Taylor (ed.), *Consociational Theory: McGarry and O'Leary and the Northern Ireland Conflict*, London: Routledge, 2009.
3. See for example D. A. Lake and D. Rothchild (eds), *The International Spread of Ethnic Conflict: Fear, Diffusion and Escalation*, Princeton University Press, Princeton, 1998; A. Guelke, *Northern Ireland: The International Perspective*, Dublin: Gill and Macmillan, 1988.
4. Doug McAdam, Sidney Tarrow and Charles Tilly, *Dynamics of Contention: Cambridge Studies in Contentious Politics*, Cambridge: Cambridge University Press, 2001, pp. 124–59.
5. W. N. Espeland and M. L. Stevens, 'Commensuration as a Social Process', *Annual Review of Sociology*, Vol. 24, 1998, pp. 313–43; J. Baker, K. Lynch, S. Cantillon and J. Walsh, *Equality: From Theory to Action*, Basingstoke: Palgrave Macmillan, 2004.
6. For positive assessments of the effects of part-meeting ethno-national demands for self-determination, see M. Guibernau, 'National Identity, Devolution and Secession in Canada, Britain and Spain', *Nations and Nationalism*, Vol. 12, No. 1, 2006, pp. 51–76; M. Keating, *Plurinational Democracy: Stateless Nations in a Post-Sovereignty Era*, Oxford University Press, Oxford, 2001.
7. See, respectively, J. McGarry and B. O'Leary, 'Consociational Theory, Northern Ireland's Conflict and its Agreement. Part 1: What Consociationists Can Learn From Northern Ireland', *Government and Opposition*, Vol. 41, No. 1, 2006a, pp. 43–63; J. McGarry and B. O'Leary, 'Consociational Theory, Northern Ireland's Conflict and its Agreement. Part 2: What Critics of Consociation Can Learn From Northern Ireland', *Government and Opposition*, Vol. 41, No. 2, 2006b, pp. 249–77; and R. Taylor, 'The Belfast Agreement and the Politics of Consociationism: A Critique', *The Political Quarterly*, Vol. 77, No. 2, 2006, pp. 217–26.
8. For evidence and analysis, see J. Ruane and J. Todd, *Dynamics of Conflict in Northern Ireland*, Cambridge University Press, Cambridge, 1996, pp. 116–203; J. Whyte, *Interpreting Northern Ireland*, Clarendon, Oxford, 1991, pp. 65–6.
9. See acknowledgements above.
10. See the extended discussion in Ian Lustick, *Unsettled States, Disputed Lands*, Ithaca: Cornell University Press, 1993, pp. 26–56.
11. R. Wilford, *Aspects of the Belfast Agreement*, Oxford University Press, Oxford, 2001; McGarry and O'Leary 2004, pp. 1–61.
12. J. Ruane and J. Todd, 'The Belfast Agreement: Context, Content, Consequences', pp. 1–29 in J. Ruane and J. Todd (eds), *After the Good Friday Agreement: Analysing Political Change in Northern Ireland*, Dublin: University College Dublin Press, 1999.
13. This was overwhelmingly passed in a constitutional referendum held in May 1998.

14. This would be parallel with Spain, see J.-M. Comas, 'Spain: The 1978 constitution and centre–periphery tensions', pp. 38–61 in J. Ruane, J. Todd and A. Mandeville (eds), *Europe's Old States in the New World Order: The Politics of Transition in Britain, France and Spain*, University College Dublin Press, Dublin, 2003.

15. B. Hadfield, 'The Belfast Agreement, Sovereignty and the State of the Union', *Public Law*, Winter, 1998, pp. 599–616. See also D. Godson, *Himself Alone: David Trimble and the Ordeal of Unionism*, London: Harper Collins, 2004, pp. 617–8.

16. J. Coakley, B. Laffan and J. Todd (eds), *Renovation or Revolution: New Territorial Politics in Ireland and the United Kingdom*, Dublin: University College Dublin Press, 2003.

17. B. Osborne and I. Shuttleworth (eds), *Fair Employment in Northern Ireland: A Generation On*, Blackstaff, Belfast, 2004; Colin J. Harvey (ed.), *Human Rights, Equality and Democratic Renewal in Northern Ireland*, Oxford: Hart Publishing, 2001; M. Cox, A. Guelke, F. Stephens (eds) *A Farewell to Arms: Beyond the Belfast Agreement* (2nd edition), Manchester: Manchester University Press, 2006.

18. P. Mitchell, P. G. Evans and B. O'Leary, 'Extremist Outbidding in Ethnic Party Systems Is Not Inevitable: Tribune Parties in Northern Ireland', *Political Studies*, Vol. 57, No. 2, 2009, pp. 397–421.

19. G. Ganiel, *Evangelicalism and Conflict in Northern Ireland*, New York: Palgrave Macmillan, 2008, pp. 104–5, pp. 141–8.

20. P. Shirlow and B. Murtagh, *Belfast: Segregation, Violence and the City*, London: Pluto, 2006; Neil Jarman, 'No Longer a Problem? Sectarian Violence in Northern Ireland', Belfast: Institute for Conflict Research, 2005; R. Wilson and R. Wilford, *The Trouble with Northern Ireland: The Belfast Agreement and Democratic Governance*, Dublin: Tasc at New Island, 2006.

21. J. Todd, 'Identity Shift in Settlement Processes: The Northern Ireland Case' in G. Ben-Porat (ed.), *The Failure of the Middle East Peace Process? A Comparative Analysis of Peace Implementation in Israel/Palestine, Northern Ireland and South Africa*, Palgrave Macmillan, New York, 2008.

22. J. McGarry (ed.), *Northern Ireland and the Divided World*, Oxford University Press, Oxford, 2001, pp. 36–89; P. Dixon, 'Why the Good Friday Agreement is not consociational', *The Political Quarterly*, Vol. 76, No. 3, 2005, pp. 357–67; McGarry and O'Leary, 2004; 2006a; 2006b; Taylor, 2006; 2009.

23. New Ireland Forum, *Report*, Stationery Office, Dublin, 1984, para. 4.15.

24. D. L. Horowitz, 'The Northern Ireland Agreement: Clear, Consociational and Risky', pp. 109–36 in McGarry (ed.) 2001.

25. McGarry and O'Leary, 2004, pp. 19–22.

26. J. Todd, 'Social Transformations, Collective Categories and Identity Change', *Theory and Society*, Vol. 34, No. 4, 2005, pp. 429–63. For examples, see J. Todd, T. O'Keefe, N. Rougier and L. Cañás Bottos, 'Fluid or Frozen? Choice and Change in Ethno-National Identification in Contemporary Northern Ireland', *Nationalism and Ethnic Politics*, Vol. 12, No. 3–4, 2006, pp. 323–46; J. Todd, N. Rougier, T. O'Keefe, L. Cañás Bottos, 'Does Being Protestant Matter? Protestants, Minorities and the Re-Making of Ethno-Religious Identity after the Good Friday Agreement', *National Identities*, Vol. 11, No. 1, 2009, pp. 87–99.

27. On mainstreaming, see C. McCrudden, 'Equality and the Good Friday Agreement', pp. 96–121 in Ruane and Todd (eds) 1999.

28. W. Streek and K. Thelen (eds), *Beyond Continuity: Institutional Change in Advanced Political Economies*, Oxford University Press, Oxford, 2005; K. Thelen, 'How Institutions Evolve: Insights from Comparative Historical Analysis' pp. 206–40 in J. Mahoney and D. Rueshemeyer (eds) *Comparative Historical Analysis in the Social Sciences*, Cambridge: Cambridge University Press, 2003.

29. C. Gormley-Heenan and R. MacGinty, 'Ethnic Outbidding and Party Modernization: Understanding the Democratic Unionist Party's Electoral Success in the Post-Agreement Period', *Ethnopolitics*, Vol. 7, No. 1, 2008, pp. 43–61; Mitchell et al., 2008.

30. On the effects on unionism, see H. Patterson and E. Kaufmann, *Unionism and Orangeism in Northern Ireland since 1945: The Decline of the Loyal Family*, Manchester: Manchester University Press, 2007, pp. 218–59.

31. J. Ruane and J. Todd, 'Path Dependence in Settlement Processes: Explaining Settlement in Northern Ireland', *Political Studies*, Vol. 55, No. 2, 2007, pp. 442–58.

32. Godson, 2004, pp. 474–84; C. Farrington, *Ulster Unionism and the Peace Process in Northern Ireland*, Basingstoke: Palgrave Macmillan, 2006, pp. 152–62; Patterson and Kaufmann, 2007, pp. 224–5.

33. Osborne and Shuttleworth, 2004, pp. 1–23.

34. R. D. Osborne, 'Education and the Labour Market', pp. 65–87 in Osborne and Shuttleworth, 2004.

35. P. Hillyard, D. Patsios and F. Semillon, 'A Daughter to ELSI–NILSI: A Northern Ireland Standard of Living Index or Problematising Wealth in the Analysis of Inequality and Material Well-Being', *Social Policy and Society*, Vol. 6, No. 1, 2007, pp. 81–98.

36. J. Hughes, 'Attitudes towards Equality in Northern Ireland: Evidence of Progress?', pp. 166–83 in Osborne and Shuttleworth, 2004.

37. C. McCall, 'From "long war" to "war of the lilies": "Post-conflict" Territorial Compromise and the Return of Cultural Politics', pp. 302–17 in Cox, Guelke and Stephens, 2006.

38. K. Hayward and C. Mitchell, 'Discourses of Equality in Post-Agreement Northern Ireland', *Contemporary Politics*, Vol. 9, No. 3, 2003, pp. 293–312.

39. A. Aughey, *Under Siege: Ulster Unionism and the Anglo-Irish Agreement*, Belfast: Blackstaff, 1989.

40. For analysis, see Patterson and Kaufmann, 2007, pp. 218–59.

41. A. Aughey, ' Learning from *The Leopard*', pp. 184–201 in R. Wilford (ed.) *Aspects of the Belfast Agreement*, Oxford University Press, Oxford, 2001, p. 193.

42. C. Mitchell and J. Todd, 'Between the Devil and the Deep Blue Sea. Nationality, power and symbolic trade-offs among evangelical Protestants in Northern Ireland', *Nations and Nationalism*, Vol. 13, No. 4, 2007, pp. 637–55. In the Life and Times 'identity' module, 2007, where the 'Moreno' question was asked for the first time, only 35 per cent of Protestants said they were 'British not Irish', considerably fewer than the 51 per cent in 1999 who (to a different set of options) said they did not feel Irish at all (http://www.ark .ac.uk/nilt/2007/Identity/IRBRIT.html).

43. G. Spencer, *The State of Loyalism in Northern Ireland*, Basingstoke: Palgrave Macmillan, 2008, pp. 186–7, pp. 241–2; Rural Community Network, *You'd Feel You Had No Say: Rural Protestants and Community Development*, Cookstown: Rural Community Network, 2002; Todd et al., 2009.
44. See http://www.ark.ac.uk/nilt/2007/Political_Attitudes/FUTURE1.html.
45. Life and Times, 'identity' module, http://www.ark.ac.uk/nilt/2007/Identity/IRBRIT.html (accessed January 2009). It is interesting and deserves separate analysis that young Catholics are more likely to say 'Irish only' than their elders.
46. C. Irwin, *The People's Peace Process in Northern Ireland*, Basingstoke: Palgrave Macmillan, 2002.
47. L. S. Palshaugen, 'The Northern Ireland Civic Forum and a Politics of Recognition', *Irish Political Studies*, Vol. 20, No. 2, 2005, pp. 147–69.
48. S. O'Neill, 'Mutual Recognition and the Accommodation of National Diversity: Constitutional Justice in Northern Ireland' in A.-G. Gagnon and J. Tully (eds), *Multinational Democracies*, Cambridge: Cambridge University Press, 2001.
49. M. S. Williams, *Voice, Trust, and Memory: Marginalized Groups and the Failings of Liberal Representation*, Princeton: Princeton University Press, 1998.
50. See acknowledgements above. Analysis is not yet complete, but it is clear that this was the perspective of many significant actors in the process, both Irish and British.
51. Kenneth Bloomfield, *A Tragedy of Errors: The Government and Misgovernment of Northern Ireland*, Liverpool University Press, Liverpool, 2007, p. 258.

9
Nation and Neighbourhood: Nationalist Mobilisation and Local Solidarities in the North of Ireland

Niall Ó Dochartaigh

Introduction: Nationalising the local

A central ambition and achievement of modern nationalism is to extend collective identifications beyond the local spaces of everyday life. Nationalists assert the primacy of the national as a scale of solidarity and identification which subsumes and transcends solidarity and identity at regional and local level. Nationalism achieves this despite the fact that the national scale usually extends far beyond the more intimate and densely connected spaces of everyday life. As Agnew puts it, 'the spatial practices of everyday life have always maintained a local place specificity that defies sweeping up into national territorial containers.'[1] Crucial to this achievement is the embedding of the national scale in the spaces of everyday life.

The intense infrastructural penetration of the modern state[2] embeds the national scale and outer boundaries[3] of sovereign states in the spaces of everyday life through state institutions such as schools and hospitals, through legal and regulatory frameworks that fit a huge variety of local elements into a national framework, and through the creation of circuits of movement for education and employment that are strongly shaped by state frameworks, even if they are not limited by them. The presence of the state in everyday life reinforces, reifies and naturalises the outer boundaries of the state in the most subtle and powerful way through the taken-for-granted institutions of everyday life, utterly embedded in a particular national territorial framework. It is not that the national displaces the local as a scale of consciousness and solidarity. As Agnew notes, the local remains the primary scale of political socialisation and 'the densest informal and spontaneous network ties are intensely localized even today.'[4]

Rather, the national scale gains power from its embedding in the spaces of everyday life. The national operates through the local and 'The national story is seen through local eyes.'[5] The naturalisation of the national as the primary scale of solidarity and identification can be seen as a central aim and achievement of the modern state, an achievement that is maintained and reproduced in interaction in the local spaces of everyday life. In the absence of a nation state, however, asserting the primacy of the national scale is a much more difficult project.

The national and the local in counter-state nationalism

Much of the literature on nationalism is aimed at explaining the strength of nationalism and the power of nationalist ideologies to mobilise and to create solidarities, particularly when contrasted with the comparative failure of class-based mobilisation.[6] But an important distinction needs to be made here. Critiquing the 'manichean' distinction between ethnic and civic nationalism, Brubaker argues, a more useful and less ambiguous distinction can be drawn between 'state-framed' and 'counter-state' nationalism.

> In the former, 'nation' is conceived as congruent with the state, and as institutionally and territorially framed by it. In the latter, 'nation' is imagined as distinct from, and often in opposition to, the territorial and institutional frame of an existing state or states.[7]

State-framed nationalism gains much of its strength from the material resources at its disposal, the administrative and coercive power of the state. But it also draws strength from the naturalisation of state territory as 'national' territory, through the embedding of the territorial framework of the state in the spaces of everyday life. The difficulty in embedding and naturalising an alternative national territorial framework in everyday life without the apparatus of the state is central to understanding the comparative weakness of counter-state nationalism.

For the purposes of this chapter, counter-state nationalism is defined as a nationalism that proposes an alternative territorial framework for national identity and sovereignty to that offered by an existing sovereign state, emphasising the territorial dimension to Brubaker's definition. It covers both separatist and irredentist nationalism but not oppositional nationalisms that simply seek to take control of an existing state territory, nor state nationalist irredentism, on the basis that the former does not challenge the territorial framework while the latter deploys the resources of a state.

In the absence of the powerful and naturalising territorial framework provided by state boundaries, counter-state nationalists are much more dependent for legitimation and mobilisation on strongly naturalised local solidarities and identities that are in tension with state-framed identities. Local identities and solidarities can act as powerful legitimating forces and provide a strong base for counter-state nationalist mobilisation, but their very strength undermines the nationalist project to assert the primacy of the national scale over the local. This hinders efforts to build national scale solidarities and identities on which to mobilise. As a consequence, the tension between national and local scales of identification and solidarity presents a central ongoing challenge for counter-state nationalists. The contrast in relationships between the national scale and the local scale is a central and defining distinction between state-framed and counter-state nationalism.

This is not to say that counter-state nationalists do not also have powerful resources for naturalising their preferred national territorial frameworks. Existing administrative frameworks at regional and local level, political organisations, cultural associations and territorial concentrations of ethnic populations can all act as naturalising resources for counter-state nationalists, embedding an alternative territorial framework in everyday life and presenting a serious challenge to a state's nationalisation of parts of the national territory. Nonetheless counter-state nationalists rarely have the resources for asserting the primacy of the national scale comparable to those available to state-framed nationalists. This chapter argues that the difficulty of asserting the primacy of the national scale in the absence of state structures is central to explaining the relative weakness of counter-state nationalism.

Counter-state nationalism in Ireland

The argument of this chapter is illustrated by reference to the most recent period of mobilisation of militant Irish nationalism, between the late 1960s and the mid-1990s. The chapter argues that specifically regional and local identities and solidarities were central to this mobilisation, that militant nationalists found it difficult to maintain a fit between the national movement and these sub-national scales, and that this partly explains the unevenness and relative weakness of this mobilisation. While violence in Northern Ireland during this period was on a scale unmatched elsewhere in Western Europe since the end of the Second World War, the numbers of those taking part in political violence were comparatively small and militant nationalist mobilisation was extraordinarily uneven. Militant mobilisation was intensely and almost exclusively concentrated North of the Irish border, in predominantly Catholic urban working-class districts and in predominantly Catholic rural areas although not equally concentrated in all such areas.[8]

There were much weaker clusters of militant mobilisation South of the border, notably in rural areas close to the border, in Dublin and in parts of Munster where the IRA had been strong in the early 1920s. The vast majority of those who were mobilised in militant republican organisations came from districts directly affected by the conflict at local level. That is, immediate personal experience in the local environ-ment was the key element in this militant mobilisation. This uneven-ness was not simply an effect of the border. During the Irish war of Independence from 1919 to 1921, mobilisation was similarly uneven, with violence concentrated in Dublin and the southern province of Munster.[9] The minimal mobilisation that took place throughout most of Ireland suggests strongly that neither the bonds of nationalist solidar-ity nor the dreams and poems of nationalist intellectuals that figure so prominently in some explanations of the power of nationalism[10] were crucial explanatory factors in this militant mobilisation.

Nationalist movement, local mobilisation

Civil rights

When mass mobilisation began in Northern Ireland on civil rights issues in late 1968, the Irish national framework was only weakly embedded in the structures and processes of mobilisation. Although all-Ireland organisa-tional structures were a distinguishing and determined feature of militant Irish republican organisations, mobilisation for the civil rights campaign was organised primarily at sub-national scales. Organisations such as the Northern Ireland Civil Rights Association (NICRA) operated at the regional scale (from the Irish nationalist perspective) covering Northern Ireland as a unit while some of the most important civil rights organisations, including the Campaign for Social Justice and the Derry Citizens Action Committee, were locally concentrated and sometimes determinedly locally focused.

The fact that the movement focused on issues that were effectively bounded by the Northern Ireland state ensured that this initial mobilisa-tion, while enjoying varying degrees of support throughout Ireland, was very much a Northern mobilisation, addressing specific regional issues, despite republican efforts to nest it within an all-Ireland context. The civil rights mobilisation strengthened the context of Northern Ireland as a territorial framework for mobilisation creating, from the nationalist point of view, a dramatic regional imbalance in mobilisation. One consequence of this was that the solidarities, the networks, the collective identities and the resources generated by the civil rights campaign were intensely concentrated within the boundaries of the Northern state.

The regional framework was not the only sub-national scale deeply embedded in the civil rights mobilisation. Many of the civil rights grievances related to the behaviour of local authorities and significant forces within the movement invoked local scales in the mobilisation, legitimating themselves and mobilising support as local alliances and local movements. Thus the unique situation in Derry, where the Unionist party could take 60 per cent of seats on the local council with only a third of the vote, was repeatedly framed by moderate civil rights leaders in the city as a local civic issue. The campaign in the city was run by a local organisation that was not only quite separate from the NICRA but was also strongly resistant to cooperation with NICRA. When this local group announced its first public protest, it declared that the theme of the meeting would be 'What is wrong with our city?' and 'What can be done about it?' and that the meeting would be 'concerned solely with a campaign to root out the causes of discontent and disharmony in the Derry area'. Together, these statements amount to a determined refusal to nest the local problems within a wider Northern Irish or Irish context.[11]

Street violence and no-go areas

From the first major confrontation at a civil rights march in Derry in October 1968, the escalating violence took on an uneven territorial character. Urban violence was focused on the interface between predominantly Catholic areas and urban commercial centres and increasingly, as time wore on, on the interfaces between predominantly Catholic and Protestant working-class districts. Urban working-class Catholic districts near urban centres and sectarian interfaces became the prime focus of violence, and although those involved in the violence at these battlegrounds often came from further afield, they tended to come from working-class districts to the rear of the 'frontlines'. The result was that the initial violence was very intensively concentrated in a small number of urban working-class districts, all of them north of the Irish border.

Militant opposition to the state first took direct territorial form with the establishment of a short-lived no-go area in January 1969 in

Derry's Bogside from which the police force was excluded for several days. Subsequently no-go areas were established in Derry again in April 1969, and most dramatically in August 1969 when 'Free Derry' was administered for several weeks behind barricades by the Derry Citizens Defence Association (DCDA), a local coalition of leftists, moderates and republicans. Similar developments took place in Belfast in August 1969. Militant mobilisation in direct confrontation with the state thus took direct territorial form at local level, inevitably strengthening the importance of the local as a scale of organisation and mobilisation. Opposition to the state was strengthened through the fit that now existed between rejection of the state and the spaces of everyday life in these districts. While this was a source of strength for oppositional forces, identifying militant opposition as a component of local identity, it also localised this opposition and rejection of the state became identified with a scattered archipelago of local spaces.

The initial shift to the use of physical force in the form of vigilante groups and local defence committees was legitimised on the basis of local concerns for neighbourhood defence, was organised locally and, for the most part, was focused on specifically local aims. As a consequence, the initial mobilisation of militant Irish nationalism was very strongly localised. In Derry the first organised involvement of Irish republicans in the use of physical force took the form of local vigilante patrols by the 'St. Columb's Wells Protection Association' established in January 1969, for example.[12] In the summer of 1969 a variety of local defence associations were established in working-class Catholic areas of Belfast and Derry. Not only were these committees concerned primarily with the local environment, they were also strongly local in their organisational structures and had very little contact with one another, despite the prominent involvement of republican militants. 'It emerged at one point that no one on the Derry Defence Committee knew who the officers on the Belfast Defence Committee were.'[13] When republicans and left-wingers within these committees sought to broaden out from the local context they faced difficulties in asserting the primacy of other scales of solidarity over those of the local.

Nationalism and neighbourhood in the IRA

Mobilisation

The Provisional and Official IRA campaigns that began in 1970 emerged primarily from local experiences of confrontation and this new militant mobilisation was intensely locally concentrated. This contrasts starkly with mobilisation for the previous IRA campaign, in the 1950s, when IRA volunteers from all over Ireland were brought together to launch a border campaign in accordance with a centrally planned strategy.[14] The very thinly scattered national character of the mobilisation of the 1950s was arguably central to the weakness of that campaign. The far more densely localised mobilisation of 1969 and 1970 provided a critical mass of militant activists concentrated in certain locations that was central to the strength of the new IRA campaigns. At the same time, it created a radically unbalanced and uneven mobilisation and a situation in which the balance between the national and the local was heavily tilted towards the local.

When organised violent attacks began in the spring of 1970, they came from a bewildering variety of sources. In addition to the Provisional and Official IRA and the small splinter group, Saor Éire, a number of freelance groups also began to carry out small-scale attacks. The groups now carrying out attacks consisted, to a great extent, of small groups of teenagers and young adults bound by intensely local ties of kinship and friendship. Many of those who would later be prominent IRA activists moved between the Provisional and the Official IRA in 1970 and 1971, looking for a home for their hostility to the state and state security forces.[15] In some cases local IRA units maintained a distance from both the Official and Provisional IRA national leaderships for several months after the split, as was the case with the Ballymurphy IRA unit in which Gerry Adams was prominent at the time.[16]

The fact that local units could continue to operate without deciding on their allegiance to either national leadership, that some young militants were moving between both organisations in search of a home for their militancy and that others were setting up their own independent units, emphasises that militant mobilisation was driven not by the centralised strategies of national organisations but by small, tightly knit local networks.

Veteran republicans involved in the campaigns of the 1940s and 1950s recognised the novelty and distinctiveness of this new mobilisation. One former Official republican recalls how an older IRA veteran referred to many of the new recruits of 1969 and 1970 as 'the streets men', men who had joined the IRA to fight for their streets in the context of intense localised violence from late 1969 onwards (in conversation with former Official republican activist, 2007). It was recognised that these recruits were not motivated by the same ideological nationalist concerns with sovereignty and national self-determination that loomed large for the small group that had kept the IRA going over the previous decades.

The evidence of many former members of the IRA on the factors lead-ing to their mobilisation in the late 1960s and early 1970s is striking for the weak presence of nationalist rhetoric and ideology in their explana-tions. Only rarely do the interviewees who spoke to Rogelio Alonso, for example, mention the kind of factors that some scholars of nationalism imagine makes the blood boil and nationalist fervour rise. Many of these new recruits recognised that they fitted uneasily and awkwardly into the category of Irish nationalist, accepting that the term added little to their explanation of their actions. 'I never considered myself a great nationalist', as one of Alonso's interviewees put it.[17]

Instead, many former IRA members cite local events and the desire for local 'defence' as the prime factor motivating their involvement. Some recruits also emphasised scales well beyond the national, arguing that their involvement was driven by identification with anti-imperialist and revolutionary struggles worldwide. Irish nationalism in its classic, traditional form, is mentioned by some interviewees, notably the sig-nificance of historical narratives of British repression and a historical Irish struggle for freedom from British rule, but the overriding impres-sion is of a mobilisation in which the local context loomed much larger than the national.[18] Whether they cited local defence, Irish history or international solidarity, the great majority of those who mobilised were united by the radicalising experience of direct and collective violent confrontation with the state at local level.

And if the immediate local environment, rather than the imagined national community, was crucial in motivating militant mobilisation, it was also crucial to the mechanics of mobilisation as locally con-centrated networks of friendship and kinship provided the base for the new mobilisation. As demonstrated comprehensively in the social movement literature, mobilisation takes place overwhelmingly through pre-existing ties. 'Social networks at the base of society have emerged as the most common sources of recruitment into social movements', as Tarrow puts it.[19] One former IRA member from Creggan estate in Derry explained his initial involvement with the Fianna, the Republican scouting movement through which many recruits moved into the IRA: 'A bunch of us were in a football team – we were all buddies and all brought up in Creggan so it seemed the right thing to do at the time.'[20] In this account, a friendship network focused around an existing local organisational structure (the football team) and united by a strong sense of local identity is cited to explain involvement in a militant national-ist mobilisation. The national scale is notable for its absence from this explanation.

This is not to say that nationalism was absent, simply to say that the balance between national-scale identifications and those at the scale of the regional and local were heavily tilted towards the regional and the local. The creation of an archipelago of resistance, of distinctive local territories in which militant nationalism was dominant, strongly localised that nationalism. At one level the Irish flags fluttering from lamp posts in Creggan and the Bogside and Ardoyne and the Lower Falls served as symbols of Ireland, of an Irish national framework that transcended the boundary between North and South and between component parts of the national territory. In the local urban context of Derry or Belfast, however, they also served as powerful symbols of local identity, distinguishing these small working-class communities sharply from other parts of the cities, even from other districts where nationalist voters were the overwhelming majority.

The IRA at one level mapped onto Irish national identity and the Irish national scale, but on the ground it mapped onto particular working-class neighbourhoods, and particular rural areas. Militant Irish nationalism thus became heavily localised and its symbols provided a way to identify with the local neighbourhood, in opposition to the state, but in a way that did not strongly embed the Irish national framework in everyday life. In giving concrete territorial expression to a national framework competing with the state, these neighbourhoods were a source of strength for militant nationalists, to the extent that they denaturalised state territorial sovereignty, but they simultaneously defined and characterised the nation as a series of separated local spaces, localising the national, and cutting across the nationalist aim of uniting and evening out space, and of asserting the primacy of the national scale.

Legitimation

Just as civil rights activists and local defence committees had done in 1968 and 1969, militant nationalists in the early 1970s regularly invoked the local scale as a prime source of legitimation, claiming a popular mandate for the IRA campaigns from the 'people of Ballymurphy' or the 'people of the Bogside'. A 1976 *Republican News* article on the Provisional IRA bombing campaign, for example, implicitly rested the IRA's mandate on local networks and neighbourhoods, arguing that 'behind those bombers, is a massive structure based on streets and districts, whose existence is dependent upon the active support and mandate of the people.'[21]

When asked in 1972 whether IRA bombing might stop in response to 'public demand', Martin McGuinness, then in charge of the Derry

Provisional IRA, similarly rested the IRA's mandate on local support when he told a reporter that 'Well, we will always take into consideration the feelings of the people of Derry. Those feelings will be passed on to our GHQ in Dublin, you know.'[22] In this formulation the 'people of Derry', rather than 'the people of Ireland' was clearly the 'public' that McGuinness felt the Derry IRA was answerable to. Implicitly, the IRA in the city was resting its mandate not on national support but on local levels of support.

Given the centrality of the local to the legitimation strategies of the IRA, militant nationalists had to be extremely careful that the national scale they represented did not conflict too directly with the local scale. If the IRA claimed legitimacy at the local scale, it also opened it up to challenges at that scale, challenges that invoked the primacy of the local in opposition to, rather than in support of, the Irish national scale. One incident in 1972 illustrates the way in which local solidarities could be marshalled in opposition to militant nationalism. In May 1972, members of the Official IRA in Derry abducted and killed William Best, a teenager from Creggan who was home on leave from the British army. Best was a local youth and, like other local youths, he had been involved in rioting against the British army during his period of leave, emphasising the extent to which he was still bound up with local networks.

As McCann put it, 'his killing outraged that very feeling of communal solidarity which the last three years had created and which was absolutely essential to the maintenance of Free Derry.'[23] The killing of Ranger Best led to vigorous protests in Derry led by local women demanding that the Official IRA end its campaign. Local critics characterised the Official IRA as an external force, alien to the city and to the traditions of the city, partly because of its Marxist ideology. 'You are not wanted, you are an alien influence' as one local priest said to an Official IRA commander who sought to address a 'peace meeting' in the wake of the killing.[24] An analysis asserting the primacy of the national scale might characterise the actions of the Official IRA in this case as the killing of a British soldier by a militant Irish nationalist movement, an attack on the outside from the inside. But it could also be characterised as the killing of a local Derry boy by an external force, an Irish national organisation headquartered in Dublin, further externalised by its Marxist ideology. Militant Irish nationalists could be externalised at local level by asserting the primacy of the local over the national. The need to avoid an opposition between solidarities at the local and national scales acted as a powerful and ongoing source of constraint on the activities of militant nationalists.

The need to respond to local priorities also strongly constrained the capacity of the IRA to secure territorial bases from which the state was excluded. When barricades were built around a new Free Derry area in July 1971, for example, it not only kept the security forces out of the area but also disrupted state services such as public transport and street lighting. The immediate local need for state services was in tension with the militant nationalist project to erode state sovereignty. When the local tenants' associations negotiated for the removal of barricades in order to allow the return of public bus services to the no-go area in October 1971, they did so with the support of 'all organisations' in the area, code for the support of both the Provisional and Official IRA.[25]

Militant nationalists were under intense local pressure to minimise the rupture with the state because of the disruptive effects this rupture produced at local level. The nationalist aim of ending British state sovereignty in Ireland could not be successfully invoked in opposition to this local pressure to maintain state services in the area, given that the local scale was so central to the legitimation of militant nationalism. If the IRA claimed to be acting primarily for the people of the Creggan and the Bogside, then it was difficult to invoke Ireland's 'struggle for freedom' in opposition to concrete local needs that necessitated compromise with the state.

Organisation

The relative strength of the local scale in relation to the national is reflected too in the organisational structures of both the Official and Provisional IRAs during the early years of the conflict. In both movements national leaderships had very problematic relationships with powerful local units. IRA units throughout the North were dominated by new members who had come into the movement through local networks, had been mobilised by local events and who appear to have been quite weakly integrated into the national movement. Nell McCafferty, a Derry Labour Party and civil rights activist who was living in Dublin in the early 1970s, recalls a surprise visit from the head of the Official IRA.

> Sometime in the autumn of 1971, I opened the front door of Patsy Murphy's house in Hatch Place to find Cathal Goulding, the chief of staff of the Official IRA, standing there. He asked could he come in and talk ... I ushered him in. He wanted to know about the men in the Derry branch of his army. Their numbers had grown considerably, and he had no idea who the new men were or what they were like.[26]

At least partly because of the weakness of central control, local units had a high degree of autonomy, reflected in the wide latitude they enjoyed in making operational decisions. This situation gradually changed as central approval of individual operations became the norm in the late 1980s. The extent of this local autonomy, and the strength of local units in relation to the national leadership, is illuminated by one early confrontation between the central leadership and the IRA in Belfast. When senior national leadership figure Ruairí Ó Brádaigh made a rare and mild public criticism of an IRA action in Belfast in the early stages of the conflict it drew a furious response from the IRA in Belfast who demanded that the central leadership refrain from such criticism.[27] In circumstances where local units had wide latitude to decide on operations, this was effectively an insistence that local units, rather than the national leadership, should be allowed to drive the campaign and decide its direction.

To a great extent the character and pace of both Official and Provisional IRA campaigns were being dictated by specific local circumstances, rather than by a centrally directed and controlled strategy at national level. The fact that IRA units were organised geographically, and that IRA members generally operated in, or close to, their local areas, strengthened the IRA's local credentials and its claim to local legitimacy but also eroded the national as a scale of action and identification. It presents a direct contrast with the way in which state forces are circulated through national territories in such a way that regional and local connections are weakened in favour of the national. This is not to say that the IRA might easily have done otherwise. It is simply to reinforce the point that counter-state nationalists face a much greater struggle than state nationalists to assert the primacy of the national scale.

As the Provisional IRA reorganised and prepared for a 'long war' from 1976 onwards, the organisation moved away from the local brigade structure to the use of smaller Active Service Units (ASUs) in order to make it more difficult for the security forces to map the structures of the organisation or to link particular attacks to particular local units.[28] Nonetheless IRA members continued, to a great extent, to operate within their home areas. Thus when eight IRA members were killed during an attack on Loughgall RUC station in 1987, all of them came from nearby villages or towns in East Tyrone and North Monaghan. And, according to Moloney, the South Armagh Brigade, based in the largest and most populous rural district in which Catholics were an overwhelming majority, insisted on retaining its localised brigade structure in the face of this national reorganisation.[29]

Ultimately the Provisional IRA did enjoy considerable success in asserting the primacy of the national scale over the local, of absorbing this locally based mobilisation into a national movement and of nationalising local networks and mobilisations, although that process took several years. This was not by any means a natural and inevitable process. The struggle to assert the primacy of the national over the local was an extremely difficult one, and the tension between the national scale and other scales of identification and solidarity remained a central difficulty and a constant and significant source of constraint on the actions of militant Irish nationalists.

Regional imbalances in mobilisation

As with the civil rights campaign, the very fact that the key issues mobilising militants were directly related to conditions within the boundaries of the Northern Ireland state, strengthened the regional context of Northern Ireland as a territorial framework for mobilisation and created a striking regional unevenness in militant Irish nationalist mobilisation. Both the Official and Provisional republican leaderships, from quite different perspectives, viewed this regional imbalance in mobilisation as a central challenge, and a central impediment to national mobilisation.

In 1975, for example, the veteran Official IRA figure Sean Garland, concerned with the extreme weakness of the movement south of the Irish border and the movement's failure to generate the 'involvement of the mass of the people' throughout Ireland, argued that 'The imbalance that the six County [Northern Ireland] situation creates in the entire country has been one of the greatest difficulties we have had to face and fight.'[30] From a quite different perspective, the difficulties with this imbalance were also acknowledged in a 1976 column by 'Brownie', generally regarded as a pen name for Gerry Adams: 'We need to expand our struggle onto a Thirty-Two County basis. We are fighting for National Freedom but one major drawback appears to be that we are restricting ourselves a great deal to the North.'[31]

The aim of correcting that imbalance, and of mobilising nationalist opinion throughout Ireland, was central to a key speech by senior Provisional republican Jimmy Drumm in 1977 that marked a major shift in direction by the Provisionals:

> [A] successful war of liberation cannot be fought exclusively on the backs of the oppressed in the six counties ... [but requires] the mobilization of the working-class in the 26 counties. We need a positive tie in with the mass of the Irish people.[32]

For militant nationalists concerned with asserting Ireland as a whole as a framework for political mobilisation and solidarity, the intensely regionally and locally concentrated mobilisation in the north, creating a stark unevenness in nationalist mobilisation, was seen as a central challenge, and a central weakness of militant Irish nationalism.

Conclusion: National and local scales in counter-state nationalism

In the absence of a naturalising state framework that embeds the national scale unobtrusively in everyday life and that contributes to building a sense of national identity and national solidarity, counter-state nationalists necessarily draw heavily on localised solidarities and identities as a base for mobilisation. Local identities resonate in the spaces of everyday life and provide a firm base for collective action and mobilisation in the absence of a powerfully naturalised national identity. Because of this heavy dependence on the local scale, counter-state nationalists face a continuous and ongoing struggle to assert the primacy of the national scale against the local. They are severely constrained by the need to maintain an alignment between national frameworks and the local solidarities on which they are dependent. This tension between the national scale and the spaces of everyday life is a central challenge for counter-state nationalists and is an important factor in explaining the relative weakness of counter-state nationalism.

Nationalism, as a set of abstract ideas about identity, ancestry, common commitment and shared destiny, seems to have been a relatively marginal component of militant mobilisation in the North of Ireland while solidarities based on more restricted and localised face-to-face communities seem to have been much more influential. Uneven militant mobilisation reflects the importance of specific local experiences of violent confrontation and the associated development of local oppositional networks and repertoires of contention that involve confrontation with authority. The balance between national and local scales of identification and solidarity was heavily tilted towards the local in this mobilisation, contributing to the sharp geographical unevenness in militant mobilisation.

Nationalist movements may be able to harness local identities and solidarities to a broader nationalist project, but the tension between the two scales remains a central problem for counter-state nationalists. Counter-state nationalism, heavily dependent as it is on local scales of identity and solidarity, faces a constant challenge to assert the primacy of the national over the local. The balance between the national and the local is quite different to the balance in state nationalism, and the primacy of the national scale is much less securely established in counter-state nationalism.

Notes

1. J. A. Agnew, *Place and Politics in Modern Italy*, Chicago: University of Chicago Press, 2002 p. 18.
2. M. Mann, *The Autonomous Power of the State: Its Origins, Mechanisms and Results* in J. Hall (ed.) *States in History*, Oxford: Oxford University Press, 1986.
3. A. Paasi, *Territories, Boundaries, and Consciousness : The Changing Geographies of the Finnish-Russian Border*, Chichester and New York: J. Wiley & Sons, 1996.
4. Agnew, 2002, p. 32.
5. Ibid., p. 25.
6. B. R. Anderson, *Imagined Communities: Reflections on the Origin and Spread of Nationalism* (revised 2nd edition), London: Verso, 1991; E. Gellner, *Nations and Nationalism*, Malden, MA: Blackwell, 2005; W. Connor, *Ethnonationalism: The Quest for Understanding*, Princeton: Princeton University Press, 1994.
7. R. Brubaker, 'The Manichean Myth: Rethinking the Distinction between "Civic" and "Ethnic" Nationalism' in H. Kriesi, K. Armingeon, H. Siegrist and A. Wimmer (eds), *Nation and National Identity: The European Experience in Perspective*, Zürich: Verlag Rüegger, 1999, p. 67.
8. R. Murray, 'Political Violence in Northern Ireland 1969–1977' in F. W. Boal, J. N. H. Douglas and J. A. E. Orr (eds), *Integration and Division: Geographical Perspectives on the Northern Ireland Problem*, London and New York: Academic Press, 1982, pp. 309–32; M. T. Fay, M. Morrissey, M. Smyth, Cost of the Troubles Study (Organisation), INCORE. *Mapping Troubles-Related Deaths in Northern Ireland, 1969–1994*, Derry: INCORE, 1997.
9. P. Hart, 'The Geography of Revolution in Ireland 1917–1923', *Past & Present*, Vol. 155, No. 1, 1997, pp. 142–76.
10. Connor, 1994.
11. N. Ó Dochartaigh, *From Civil Rights to Armalites: Derry and the Birth of the Irish Troubles*, Cork: Cork University Press, 1997, pp. 24–5.
12. Ibid., p. 41.
13. E. McCann, *War and an Irish Town*, Harmondsworth: Penguin, 1974, p. 71.
14. T. P. Coogan, *The IRA* (6th impression edition), London: Fontana, 1980, pp. 380–5; J. B. Bell, *The Secret Army: The IRA, 1916–1979*, Dublin: Poolbeg, Swords, Co., 1989.
15. P. Bishop and E. Mallie, *The Provisional IRA*, London: Corgi, 1988, pp. 155–6.
16. Interview with Gerry Adams. See E. Moloney, *A Secret History of the IRA*, London: Penguin, 2002, p. 73 and H. Patterson, *Ireland since 1939*, London: Penguin, 2006, p. 164.
17. R. Alonso, *The IRA and Armed Struggle*, London and New York: Routledge, 2007, p. 38.

18. R. Alonso, *The IRA and Armed Struggle*, London and New York: Routledge, 2007; A. Feldman, *Formations of Violence: The Narrative of the Body and Political Terror in Northern Ireland*, Chicago and London: University of Chicago Press, 1991; R. English, *Armed Struggle: The History of the IRA*, London: Pan, 2004.

19. S. G. Tarrow, *Power in Movement: Social Movements and Contentious Politics* (2nd edition), Cambridge and New York: Cambridge University Press, 1998, p. 124.

20. L. Clarke, K. Johnston, *Martin McGuinness: From Guns to Government*, London and Edinburgh: Mainstream, 2001, p. 29.

21. Peter Arnlis, 'The Nature of Strategy, Politics, Revolution and British Withdrawal', *Republican News*, 27 March 1976, cited in H. Patterson, *Ireland since 1939*, London: Penguin, 2006, p. 165.

22. News clip from the early 1970s shown in P. Taylor, *Provos*. BBC, UK, 1997.

23. E. McCann, *War and an Irish Town*, Harmondsworth: Penguin, 1974, p. 107.

24. Ibid., p. 108.

25. N. Ó Dochartaigh, *From Civil Rights to Armalites: Derry and the Birth of the Irish Troubles*, Cork: Cork University Press, 1997, p. 278.

26. R. W. White, *Ruairí Ó Brádaigh: The Life and Politics of an Irish Revolutionary*, Bloomington: Indiana University Press, 2006, pp. 250–2.

27. Ibid., pp. 180–1.

28. E. Moloney, *A Secret History of the IRA*, London: Penguin, 2002, pp. 156, 160.

29. Ibid., p. 220.

30. H. Patterson, *Ireland since 1939*, London: Penguin, 2006, p. 131.

31. Brownie, 'Agitate Educate Liberate', *Republican* News, 22 May 1976, quoted in H. Patterson, *Ireland since 1939*, London: Penguin, 2006, p. 166.

32. H. Patterson, *Ireland since 1939*, London: Penguin, 2006, p. 160.

10
Modern Irish Nationalism – Ideology, Policymaking, and Path-Dependent Change

Cillian McGrattan

Introduction

This chapter examines the role that Irish nationalism played in the 30 years of inter-communal violence that have been euphemistically named the 'Northern Ireland troubles' (1968–98) and, since the Good Friday Agreement of April 1998, in the decade-long attempt to find common political ground in the North. The chapter eschews a simplistic causal depiction of the 'Northern Ireland problem' as being one of antagonistic ideologies and modes of belonging (British versus Irish; unionists versus nationalists; Protestants versus Catholics).[1] Instead, it borrows from recent theoretical insights into the importance of political actors and key decisions in constructing ethnic contention,[2] and claims that the failure to reach a compromise was not solely due to unionist obduracy but that modern Irish nationalism pursued a consistently maximal policy agenda that effectively ruled out accommodation with moderate unionist tendencies.

This is not to deny the obstructionist tactics and anti-Catholic rhetoric of extreme Unionists such as Ian Paisley, nor should it be taken as an ideological criticism of what was a rational and defensive policy trajectory. Rather, the chapter examines one case of how constitutional policy goals can mobilise opinion and carry through across time and thereby (inadvertently) contribute to long-term inter-communal polarisation.

The Horowitzean model would suggest that inter-communal polarisation is not all that remarkable – in fact it may even be inevitable.[3] Thus, in the Northern Irish case, moderate, constitutional nationalists in the form of the Social Democratic and Labour Party (SDLP) were threatened by the more extreme agenda of Sinn Féin and the Irish Republican Army (IRA), which favoured immediate British army and government withdrawal rather than incremental reform and gradual moves towards reunification.[4] However, the archival material suggests that, as regards Irish nationalism specifically, the Horowitzean model is misleading and profoundly inadequate: potential IRA outbidding, while a factor in SDLP decision-making, was not the primary concern in the mobilisation of the North's Catholics. Rather, the SDLP and successive Dublin governments pursued a consistent policy agenda that prioritised Southern involvement in Northern Ireland, even at the expense of possible power-sharing settlements with Ulster unionist actors.

Importantly, this was not simply a reaction to unionist distrust and suspicion of change – demonstrated in the May 1974 Ulster Workers' Council strike, which elicited widespread support across all sections of the Protestant population and contributed decisively to the collapse of the 'Sunningdale' power-sharing experiment. Instead, a stringent nationalist policy agenda had been fixed as early as 1971 and carried through across time in an essentially rational, coherent process in which the SDLP sought to 'bank' perceived concessions and move towards the end goal of gradual and inevitable reunification.[5] From that date, an alternative and more moderate policy based on power-sharing within the North was eschewed in favour of mobilising opinion around a reunification project. This effectively sidelined Ulster unionism and institutionalised an incremental policy trajectory.

While challenging the conventional wisdom as regards modern Irish nationalism, this chapter also points towards an alternative perspective on the study of nationalist politics in general. A temporally sensitive approach moves the focus from ideological and strategic disputes and overt decision-making to the 'hidden' or subterranean level of cross-time constraints and historical processes. Thus this chapter charts the emergence and persistence of a specific policy agenda across four decades of Irish nationalism. While a certain evolution of thought has occurred as nationalists adapted to changing circumstances, the general framework of the original policy agenda – namely, an increasing role for Dublin in the affairs of the Northern state – has remained constant. In effect, this touchstone has been institutionalised in nationalist policy direction and has carried across time in a self-reinforcing, path-dependent fashion.[6] The chapter maps this historical sequence and describes how the early choices of the SDLP and Dublin administrations effectively set the framework for future nationalist policymaking.

Key decisions: The radicalisation of Irish Nationalism, 1970–3

A historically informed perspective moves beyond the idea that ideology or ethnicity act as primary determinative forces; instead, it prioritises agential choices, policy interventions, and identifiable political processes as being instrumental to the emergence and persistence of nationalist identification and contention. The resilience of Irish nationalist policy direction suggests why this may in fact be the case. It demonstrates

(a) how historical decisions create incentives to mobilise;
(b) how policy interventions confer structural advantages and legitimate grievances; and
(c) how, by ruling out once-plausible alternative goals and strategies, nationalist mobilisation can create self-perpetuating or self-reinforcing processes that account for long-term continuities and gradual changes in political outcomes.

In other words, despite the fact that policies are (theoretically) more liable to sudden change than formal institutions,[7] in the case of Irish nationalism key decisions taken in the early years of the conflict carried through across time to constrain later options.

Formed in August 1970, the SDLP was initially an uneasy umbrella group that encompassed several of the leaders of the Northern Ireland civil rights movement. While it harboured a desire to win over the Protestant population to the cause of socialism and moderate nationalism, it is unclear how this could ever have been accomplished given the fact that many unionists believed that key members such as Gerry Fitt, John Hume, and Austin Currie were responsible for the Northern crisis.[8] The party accepted the principle that Northern Ireland's constitutional position could not change without the consent of a majority of its people and called for periodic referenda to reduce the importance of the national question.[9] Initially, the SDLP participated in the unionist-dominated devolved government at Stormont and sought to use its position to bring about reforms to alleviate the position of Catholics in the North.[10] Despite a certain unease with its participatory attitude, the party refused to go as far as the IRA in calling for the abolition of Stormont and sought to contrast its socialist principles with the 'sectarianism' of both republicans and the Unionist Party.[11] Indeed, in June 1971, the SDLP reacted favourably to the offer by the Northern Ireland Premier,

Brian Faulkner, for seats on governmental policy committees. However, this initial reformist agenda was irrevocably overturned the following month when, after the shooting of two unarmed Catholics in Derry by the British army, the party walked out of the Stormont parliament.

Importantly, the SDLP's abstentionism and disillusionment with the Stormont system had occurred *before* the introduction of internment without trial in August 1971. Internment was directed almost completely against Catholics and precipitated a massive escalation of violence and the total alienation of nationalists from the state.[12] Yet, despite this, the SDLP sought a return to the political sphere. A September 1971 position paper, for instance, envisages a new devolved institution based on power-sharing and with an 'Irish dimension'.[13] Participation in a majoritarian system was now off the table, instead, the document argued any '"solution" that ignored the inter-dependence of the two parts of Ireland would be meaningless'. It held that 'a 100-member Commission broadly representative of the entire Northern Ireland community' should replace Stormont. The 'second draft' of the paper argued that the 'Westminster model of government' should be abandoned and replaced by a proportional system.[14] It also envisaged the end of Stormont and argued that a 'Council of State' could administer Northern Ireland on an interim basis. Crucially, it called for cross-border institutions to provide for economic and social cooperation, and to 'provide the machinery for ... policing of the border'.

The SDLP's policy formation in the period following internment was cumulative and fundamental rather than pragmatic. The party sought to channel Catholic opinion around its own agenda and did not simply strike out for the first available option in response to the radicalisation of 'street politics' or the IRA campaign. This process began in the summer of 1971 but continued through the key events of Bloody Sunday (30 January 1972) and the imposition of direct rule from London (March 1972). Indeed, the party recognised its crucial role in Anglo-Irish politics:

> If [we] refuse absolutely to enter in negotiations at any time ... it is very likely that the Westminster government will decide on complete integration [of Northern Ireland with the UK] as the only possible solution. It should, therefore, be borne in mind throughout that our decision on the question of negotiating may well influence the nature of that eventual solution.[15]

Until the summer of 1972, however, the party felt constrained by its abstentionist position of not talking while internment continued.

However, a series of political miscalculations by republicans offered the party a chance to move beyond any outbidding threat. These included the killing of an off-duty Catholic soldier in Derry in May and the breakdown of an IRA ceasefire on Bloody Friday (21 July) when over 20 bombs exploded in Belfast city centre, killing nine people and injuring over 130 others. The party openly attacked republicans for 'selling out' the internees by continuing with the violence and attacked the 'lunatic fringe' of extremists who, it said, had created an 'inflexible' political climate.[16] In addition, it challenged its supporters to repudiate the IRA which had, it said, proved itself to be politically incompetent. The party claimed that such 'opposition to the men of violence' would also entail supporting its decision to enter talks.[17]

The overt rhetoric was mirrored in a tougher, more nationalistic stance in its private documents, which elaborated an institutional system based on either joint sovereignty for Northern Ireland or a three-way division of power between Dublin, Belfast, and London. These papers were premised on the idea that unionists should no longer have a veto over change in the North, but that Irish nationalists should also have a say in the design of any future proposals. The internal discussions, therefore, called for the party to 'stop talking in mealy-mouthed terms of the anti-Unionist population or the minority but [to] play the card of Irish nationality as hard as the Unionists play the British national card'.[18] The resulting document, *Towards a New Ireland*, was published in September 1972.[19] In it, the SDLP called for the creation of an 'interim system of government' for the North in which an 84-member assembly would be elected by PR. It also called for a 'national senate' to harmonise laws and institutions, to 'plan the integration of the whole island', and to draw up a new constitution.

Whereas Irish government policy had been split between ad hoc conciliation and overt irredentism,[20] the SDLP's assertive nationalism and opposition to physical force republicanism resonated with its general thinking and offered it an ally and a foothold in Northern politics. Civil servants advised the government that the SDLP's September 1972 paper, *Towards a New Ireland*, 'gives considerable support to the idea that the Irish government has a *right* to be consulted by Britain.'[21] By the winter of 1972, Dublin officials had drafted a series of proposals premised on the idea that a 'meaningful North–South link' would form part of an 'interim solution', which would be 'sufficiently dynamic and evolutionary to create a climate which ultimately might lead to Irish unity.'[22] Following the publication of the White Paper of March 1973 in which the British government acceded the need for an 'Irish dimension' and a 'cross-community' government the SDLP and Dublin began to draw ever closer. While the logic of this rapprochement can be traced back to 1971, it informed the general approach of the two sides towards the political talks of October–December 1973, which culminated in a power-sharing executive being set up and a Council of Ireland being agreed upon.

The available evidence suggests that the latter took priority to the point where the SDLP were willing to sacrifice their erstwhile unionist executive partner, Brian Faulkner, to secure a strong Irish dimension. As John Hume told the Irish government liaison, Sean Donlon, in September 1973:

> Now that Faulkner was at his weakest … it [was] more important than ever that he should be inextricably tied to a fully worked out and agreed Council before the [power sharing] executive was formally established.[23]

The SDLP's decision to walk out of the Stormont system in July 1971 overturned an original reformism and instituted a new agenda of banking concessions and downplaying losses in the pursuit of further gains. This was based on the perception of opening opportunities and created a self-reinforcing framework that encompassed later policy options. Accommodation and moderation were effectively ruled out and the key idea was to create a situation where, through increased Dublin involvement and 'harmonisation' between North and South, reunification would become practically inevitable.

Successive Dublin governments also bought into this agenda, and, despite having ostensibly wider responsibilities than the Northern party, Dublin also seemingly believed that Ulster unionists could be outmanoeuvred by constitutional mechanisms. The principle of consent remained, but in this strategic vision it was rendered virtually meaningless as unionists would eventually be presented with a *fait accompli*. Prior to the crucial talks on the future of Northern Ireland with the British government, which were held at Sunningdale in December 1973, Irish government ministers were advised to cooperate with any new political institutions, but that, in so doing, they should go no further than accommodating 'the minimal requirements of responsible Northern Protestant opinion.'[24]

Nationalist policy entrenchment

The radicalisation of Catholic politics continued to constrain the SDLP's leadership during the latter half of the 1970s and shaped Hume's attempts to outmanoeuvre Ulster unionism through the introduction of concepts borrowed from the European Community. For Hume, the EC demonstrated that political institutions could accommodate communal rights and facilitate the expression of cultural identities. His application of this insight to Northern Ireland, however, sought to undercut traditional unionist suspicion of constitutional and institutional change by portraying it as a veto on progress. Instead, he claimed that unless Britain became a 'persuader' for Irish unity and removed the constitutional guarantee, unionists would never negotiate with Irish nationalists to reach what he termed an 'agreed Ireland.'[25]

This apparent re-casting of the Northern Ireland problem was influential in the proceedings of the New Ireland Forum, which was convened in 1983–4 by the then Taoiseach, Garret FitzGerald, to enable Irish political parties to reach a consensus on possible ways forward. It was also designed to provide a mechanism to bolster the SDLP against a resurgent republican movement in the wake of the hunger strikes of the early 1980s. The Forum's conclusions chimed with the traditional nationalist understanding that any solution must occur in an all-Ireland framework and all but ignored unionist unease with affording Dublin a central role in the running of the North.

In part, the closer relationship between London and Dublin set the context for the intergovernmental Anglo-Irish Agreement (1985), which offered the Irish Republic an institutionalised and consultative role in the North in return for increased security cooperation. Although that role could be tempered by the devolution of a power-sharing administration in Belfast, there is evidence to suggest that it is doubtful whether London believed that this was actually possible given unionist apprehensions on this issue.[26] Indeed, as an exercise in 'coercive consociationalism,'[27] the Agreement was self-defeating. In fact, its logical implications favoured a pan-nationalist convergence around Dublin's involvement and the idea of 'joint authority' rather than an internal power-sharing arrangement. In practice, it contributed to an increased pan-nationalist approach and militated against inter-communal compromise. Despite failing to deliver tangible constitutional change, for nationalists the Agreement marked another gain in the reunification project. In short, the pro-Dublin and anti-power-sharing logic of the Agreement meant that Northern nationalist policymaking would lead towards pan-nationalist (namely, Dublin, Northern republicans, and Irish America) alignment rather than the cultivation of cross-communal alliances.

Following the Anglo-Irish Agreement, the changed political context lent credibility to Sinn Féin leader Gerry Adams's idea that constitutional politics rather than simply physical force would more effectively lead to the achievement of the IRA's objective of the withdrawal of British state forces. While the Agreement facilitated the emergence of a Sinn Féin peace strategy, it did not inexorably lead to the April 1998 or May 2007 accords. Simply stated, for republicans, it afforded substance to the possibility of opening up another front in the 'armed struggle'.

The groundwork for that second front was prepared ironically through John Hume's attempt to wean republicans away from violence by talking with Gerry Adams in 1988. The stated objective of the Hume–Adams dialogue was to find a 'common strategy on bringing about Irish unity, and also on the issues affecting nationalists in Northern Ireland.'[28] While the parties disagreed over the nature of British state involvement – the SDLP seeing Westminster as a neutral presence and Sinn Féin arguing that it exerted an imperialist influence over Ireland – both agreed that Britain should act as a persuader for Irish unity. In other words, unionist consent should take a backseat to the reunification project and the (unsupported) belief that Britain should redirect its resources to facilitating the end of partition. Thus, while a formal convergence remained off the agenda, the thrust of SDLP and Sinn Féin policy direction continued along a maximal path. Moderate power-sharing proposals, as advocated by the Ulster Unionist Party in the late 1980s, were ignored and Northern nationalism targeted the more radical proposal of joint governmental authority.

The Sinn Féin peace strategy certainly marked an overhaul of the Provisional IRA's raison d'être; yet, importantly, this overhaul occurred within the parameters of a layered, anti-partitionist trajectory. The landmark speech by Secretary of State Peter Brooke in November 1990 precipitated a gradual rethinking of the republican position. In particular, Brooke's conclusion that 'The British government has no selfish strategic or economic interest in Northern Ireland, our role is to help, enable, and encourage' challenged the republican depiction of the British state presence in Ireland as a neocolonial power – a fact that the subsequent Soviet and Cold War collapse further underlined. However, neither the backchannel discussions with the British government nor the joint Dublin–London, Downing Street Declaration of December 1993 offered the possibility that Westminster would finally assume the role of 'persuading' unionism to accede to a united Ireland. Despite this, the growing US influence following the Clinton election in 1992 provided a 'compensatory mechanism,'[29] while the end of the Thatcher premiership provided a renewed impetus for republicans to engage with constitutional politics.

The shifting political opportunities of the early 1990s encouraged republican moves towards constitutionalism, and it was in this changed context that the August 1994 ceasefire definitively ushered in a new alternative to the physical force campaign: TUAS (a 'Totally Unarmed Strategy', or, to more sceptical observers, the 'Tactical Use of the Armed Struggle').[30] The underlying objective was that if Sinn Féin 'could get agreement with the Dublin government, the SDLP, and the Irish-American lobby on basic republican principles ... [then that would] create the dynamic that would considerably advance the struggle'. No longer would British army withdrawal be an immediate prospect and the inevitable result of the armed campaign; instead, the leadership explained, 'Another front has opened up and we should have the confidence and put in the effort to succeed on that front.'[31]

This was a shift in strategy rather than a complete revision of policy direction. The overriding objective remained the reunification project – regardless of the polarising effect that project would create within the unionist constituency – which almost seamlessly continued under the Sinn Féin peace strategy. On the one hand, for example, a party policy strategist, Mitchel McLaughlin, argued at the party's 1994 Ard Fheis (conference), 'The unity of the Irish people will be achieved by a process of national reconciliation, never by force.'[32] On the other hand, Adams claimed at the same conference that

> [t]he unionists must be told plainly that, contrary to their illogical belief, the Six-County area does not belong to them. It belongs to all our people equally, irrespective of falsely created majorities and minorities.[33]

In short, 'reconciliation' was not to be confused with 'consent'. This disjuncture characterises the political development of Northern nationalism in the decade since the signing of the Good Friday Agreement in which there is an apparent contradiction between pursuing long-term reunification and reaching a compromise with Ulster unionism. Instead, Catholic mobilisation is maintained through a strategy of incrementally banking perceived 'concessions' and the pursuit of gradual unification.[34]

Conclusions

By focusing on overt changes in rhetoric and discourse on the one hand, or on strategic initiatives on the other, scholars of modern Irish nationalism have tended to overlook the layered and cumulative nature of the Irish nationalist project, and hence underestimate not only its mobilising potency but its very real meaning for Catholic politics in the North. The tendency to view Irish nationalism solely as a discourse or an ideology misses underlying policy continuities and fails to account for why nationalism apparently shifted so far without reaching an accommodation with Ulster unionism. Scholars working within this area typically explain the nationalist–unionist disjuncture in terms of Irish nationalism's 'irreconcilable irredentism' or of it being an 'incoherent ideology' and a 'nuanced discourse.'[35] Certainly, personal and ideological preferences may condition individual choices. However, as this chapter has pointed out, political outcomes are also the result of the cumulative effect of cross-time decision-making: the SDLP's July 1971 decision to leave Stormont set in place a policy trajectory that carried through across time to affect later choices – Dublin involvement was prioritised and an internal, power-sharing settlement was consistently de-valued.

Arguably, the discourse or ideological approach to Irish nationalist political development is based on a functionalist outlook. In other words, strategic shifts in nationalist discourse are assumed to have emerged from the immediate needs and correspond to the perceived benefits of contemporary political elites – the benefits explain the changes. That functionalism may result from what is ostensibly a reasonable starting point, but one that reveals certain teleological assumptions. In contrast, a temporally sensitive perspective explains outcomes by their causes, not their consequences.

As this chapter has demonstrated, the archival material raises serious questions for backwards-reading approaches that parachute in ethno-nationalist theory with little regard for the historical facts,[36] when in fact the empirical material suggests a great deal of policy continuity across time. In part, this almost wilful disregard of chronology is implicit in the logic of outbidding in which a deterministic downward spiral of ethnic contention negates the need to specify why historical decisions were made or even if they were possible in the first place. The result is that conflict and division are explained away from the outset. Again, it suggests that leaders were not simply deploying nationalist rhetoric in order to make 'off-camera' deals. Unsurprisingly, political elites and rank-and-file supporters tended to share a similar vision, which was coloured by previous actions and experiences.

More pertinently, the historical record reveals two main lacunae in the dominant theoretical approaches to the Northern Ireland conflict. Firstly, while the SDLP were conscious of the threat of IRA outbidding, this was not a primary concern. Indeed, from the summer of 1972 onwards, the party actively sought to make the most of the changed opportunities British state intervention and unionist division had created. In this regard, the Horowitzean-inspired idea of a dual party system[37] is too simplistic for the Northern Ireland case: on the one hand, both nationalists and unionists competed for concessions from Westminster, and on the other, the 'greening' of the SDLP was the result not simply of a fear of outbidding but rather from the rational strategy of maximising its gains. The evidence from the SDLP's party papers and the Dublin archives reveals that from the early 1970s key Irish nationalist actors were engaged in a self-reinforcing process of banking gains and targeting further concessions with an end goal of gradual reunification. Certainly, until 1974 the idea of a Council of Ireland provided the mechanism in which this would occur.

While both the SDLP and Dublin subscribed to the principle of consent this was in effect no more than paying lip service to a political ideal that would be bypassed through increased cross-border harmonisation. The then Minister for Foreign Affairs, Garret FitzGerald hinted at this dual purpose in October 1973:

> The Council of Ireland would hold out to the majority of the Irish people a prospect of progress towards the unity that is their aspiration. At the same time the power given to a majority in Northern Ireland to determine the pace of this evolution would provide them with the guarantees they seek against being forced unwillingly into a united Ireland.[38]

Indeed, the response of the unionist *Newsletter* points towards deep-seated and entrenched suspicions of the nationalist project that accounts for the Ulster Workers' Council strike of 1974: 'It is a case of "Heads I win, Tails you lose."'[39]

The second lacuna the case study highlights is related to an overly simplistic causal linking between ethno-nationalism and political conflict. Just as the outbidding thesis fails to reflect accurately the historical record, the idea that the troubles happened because of antagonistic nationalisms is profoundly inadequate in the face of available archival evidence.[40] This may be because the underlying assumptions of the 'ethnic conflict' approach to Northern Ireland are rarely questioned. Certainly, pre-existing ethnic groups were present at the start of the conflict, but it was political decisions and omissions that created and maintained the conflict. The failure to look beyond the basic assumption that the presence of antagonistic ethnic groups engendered the troubles conflates cause and effect. In Northern Ireland, elections, political rhetoric, or historical understandings may have had ethnic characteristics but there is nothing intrinsically ethnic about those events and narratives – they become 'ethnicised' when they are used in a particular way and for a particular purpose.[41] To ignore the actions and choices through which this process occurs is to recycle dominant understandings without really explaining very much. Arguably, this is possible only when ethnic conflict theories are read back into the historical record with little concern for context or nuance.

Instead, the chapter stressed the importance of examining choices and decisions and their enduring effects. It claimed that even small and apparently insignificant decisions may have large and long-term consequences. Thus the SDLP's walkout from Stormont in July 1971 created the circumstances where the once-viable option of committee participation was removed from the negotiating table and more fundamental reforms were prioritised. The chapter mapped how these carried through in a path-dependent fashion in which concessions were banked and the end goal of gradual reunification maintained despite widespread evidence of unionist disquiet. Voices who spoke up and argued for the more moderate goal of power-sharing, such as the party's first leader, Gerry Fitt, or founding member, Paddy Devlin, were marginalised.[42]

While the case study highlighted certain problems with the dominant theoretical approaches to Northern Ireland, it also pointed to three possible areas for developing claims about the emergence and persistence of ethnic contention. Firstly, it demonstrated the utility of examining how policy interventions constrain options downstream. Secondly, it described how this process worked in that critical historical choices can carry through in a self-reinforcing, path-dependent fashion – once-viable alternatives are left behind, moderate voices are marginalised, and support is mobilised around a specific agenda. Finally, it suggested that only by paying attention to the context in which nationalism becomes causally determinative instead of relying on importing hazy theoretical constructs can we hope to gain an insight into how nationalist politics remain such a potent force in the modern world.

Notes

This chapter is based on doctoral research that was sponsored by the Department for Employment and Learning, Northern Ireland. I would like to thank Dr Aaron Edwards and Professor Henry Patterson who commented on earlier versions of this chapter.

1. Brendan O'Leary and John McGarry, *The Politics of Antagonism: Understanding Northern Ireland*, London: Athlone Press, 1997, pp. 3–4.
2. For example, Rogers Brubaker, *Ethnicity without Groups*, London: Harvard University Press, 2004; Kanchan Chandra, 'What is Ethnic Identity and Does it Matter?' *Annual Review of Political Science*, Vol. 9, 2006, pp. 397–424; Joseph Ruane and Jennifer Todd, 'The Roots of Intense Ethnic Conflict May Not in Fact be Ethnic: Categories, Communities, and Path Dependence', *Archives européenes de sociologie*, Vol. 45, No. 2, 2004, pp. 20932.
3. Donald L. Horowitz, *Ethnic Groups in Conflict*, London: University of California Press, 2000.
4. Gerard Murray and Jonathan Tonge, *Sinn Féin and the SDLP: From Alienation to Participation*, Dublin: O'Brien Press, 2005; Peter McLoughlin, 'John Hume and the Revision of Irish Nationalism', unpublished PhD thesis, Queen's University, Belfast, 2005.
5. Alvin Jackson, *Home Rule: An Irish History, 1800–2000*, London: Weidenfeld and Nicolson, 2003, pp. 293–4.
6. Douglass North has defined path-dependency as 'the constraints on the choice set in the present that are derived from historical experiences in the past'; *Understanding the Process of Economic Change*, Oxford: Oxford University Press, 2005, p. 52. See also Paul Pierson, *Politics in Time: History, Institutions, and Social Analysis*, Oxford: Princeton University Press, 2004.
7. See Paul Pierson, 'Public Policies as Institutions' in Ian Shapiro, Stephen Skowronek, and Daniel Galvin (eds), *Rethinking Political Institutions: The Art of the State*, London: New York University Press, 2006.
8. See Cillian McGrattan, 'Dublin, the SDLP, and the Sunningdale Agreement: Maximalist Nationalism and Path-Dependency', *Contemporary British History*, Vol. 23, No. 1, 2009, pp. 61–78.
9. McLoughlin 2005.
10. Fitt pointed out at its first press conference that 'We support the maintenance of Stormont at the present time as it is the only institution which can bring about the reforms we desire', *Irish News*, 22 August 1970.
11. One of its leaders, Ivan Cooper, repeatedly attacked the IRA and called on the party to 'step out of our entrenched position' and tackle sectarian divisions; *Irish News*, 1 May 1971.
12. Niall Ó Dochartaigh, *From Civil Rights to Armalites: Derry and the Birth of the Irish Troubles*, Basingstoke: Palgrave Macmillan, 2004.
13. 'Draft working document, September 1971', Public Record Office of Northern Ireland (hereafter PRONI), D/3072/1/30/1.
14. 'Draft working document, Second Draft, 17 September 1971', in ibid.
15. 'Some notes on future SDLP policy, March 1972', PRONI D/3072/1/33/2.
16. *Irish Independent*, 25 May 1972; *Irish Times*, 23 May 1972.
17. *Irish Times*, 27 July 1972.
18. 'Northern Ireland – a Condominium? August 1972', PRONI D/3072/1/30/1.
19. *Towards a New Ireland*, SDLP, Belfast 1972.
20. Ronan Fanning, 'Playing it Cool: The Response of The British and Irish Governments to the Crisis in Northern Ireland, 1968–9', *Irish Studies in International Affairs*, Vol. 12, 2001, pp. 57–85.
21. 'SDLP proposals, 21 September 1972', National Archives of Ireland (hereafter NAI) DFA/2004/7/2698.

22. 'Council of Ireland Paper 1 [December] 1972', NAI DT/2003/16/430.
23. 'Report of a meeting, 20 September 1973', NAI DT/2004/21/670.
24. 'Status of Northern Ireland, December 1973' NAI DT/2004/21/627.
25. John Hume, 'The Irish Question: A British Problem', *Foreign Affairs*, Vol. 58, No. 2, 1979–80, pp. 303–4.
26. Eamonn O'Kane, *Britain, Ireland, and Northern Ireland since 1980: The Totality of Relationships*, Abingdon: Routledge, 2007.
27. O'Leary and McGarry 1997, pp. 220–41.
28. Murray and Tonge 2005, p. 166.
29. Henry Patterson, *Ireland Since 1939: The Persistence of Conflict*, Oxford: Oxford University Press, 2006, p. 324.
30. The TUAS document is reprinted in Eamonn Mallie and David McKittrick, *The Fight for Peace: The Inside Story of the Irish Peace Process*, London: Mandarin, 1997.
31. Ibid., pp. 422–3.
32. Linenhall Library, Northern Ireland Political Collection, P5685.
33. Gerry Adams, 'Presidential Address to Sinn Féin Ard Fheis, 1994', www.sinnfein.ie/pdf/Speech_ArdFheis94.pdf, accessed 20 November 2008.
34. Cillian McGrattan, 'Northern Nationalism and the Belfast Agreement', in Brian Barton and Patrick Roche (eds), *The Northern Ireland Question: The Peace Process and the Belfast Agreement*, Basingstoke: Palgrave Macmillan, 2009.
35. Christopher Farrington, 'Reconciliation or Irredentism? The Irish Government and the Sunningdale Communiqué of 1973', *Contemporary European History*, Vol. 16, No. 1, 2007, pp. 89–107; Katy Hayward, 'The Politics of Nuance: Irish Official Discourse on Northern Ireland', *Irish Political Studies*, Vol. 19, No. 1, pp. 18–38, 2004.
36. McLoughlin 2005.
37. Paul Mitchell, 'Party Competition in an Ethnic Dual Party System', *Ethnic and Racial Studies*, Vol. 18, No. 4, 1995, pp. 773–93.
38. *Newsletter*, 3 October 1973.
39. Ibid.
40. O'Leary and McGarry 1997; see also McLoughlin 2005, p. x.
41. Brubaker 2004; Chandra 2006.
42. See Paddy Devlin, *Straight Left – An Autobiography*, Blackstaff, Belfast 1993.

Part III Comparative Analysis

11
The Effectiveness of Federal Responses to Ethnic Conflict

John Coakley

Introduction

There was a time when the ideal of the multinational state seemed to many to be a valuable end in itself. As Lord Acton put it in a celebrated essay, 'the coexistence of several nations under the same state is ... one of the chief instruments of civilisation'. It represented, he argued, 'a state of greater advancement than the national unity which is the ideal of modern liberalism.'[1]

This conception of harmony between nations or ethnic groups within the boundaries of the same state has been subjected to demanding tests. In practice, it was advanced more vigorously by the political left than by the right. For the so-called Austro-Marxists in the Habsburg monarchy and the Bolsheviks further to the East, peaceful coexistence between national groups within a multinational state was an achievable end, even if the blueprints advocated in the respective cases clashed. But imperial collapse immediately after the First World War and the turmoil of the decades that followed, together with the later fragmentation of European-led empires, punched a deep hole in the notion that a stable multinational state could be sustained. The ideal survived, of course; but, with every subsequent disintegration of a multinational entity, its attractiveness as a long-term solution was further eroded. Switzerland and India persisted as examples of what is possible at best, when the model works; but the dying days of the Soviet Union and of Yugoslavia illustrated an alternative and much less appealing scenario – what may happen at worst, when the model fails.

Public policy considerations reinforce intrinsic academic interest in seeking to identify the circumstances in which such multi-ethnic states are stable in the long term. Rather than pursuing the whole gamut of potentially relevant conditions, though, this chapter explores the strategies used by constitutional architects anxious to design a durable federal system which accommodates a set of territorially concentrated ethnic groups. The pathology of 'failed cases' may be a useful starting point. If we ask what the former Soviet Union, Czechoslovakia and Yugoslavia had in common which sets them apart from other multinational or multilingual federations such as Switzerland, Canada and Belgium, the most obvious point is that the collapse of the federal structure coincided with the fall of a powerful centralising institution, the Communist Party.

It may indeed be the case that some exceptional centralising force is needed to hold ethnic federations together. The two words in the phrase 'ethnic federation' draw attention to two major dimensions which may be used to examine the survival prospects of such entities. The first is the character of the federation itself: the extent to which its component parts are truly independent of the centre, or alternatively are substantially constrained by political forces there. The second is the extent to which the component parts are indeed 'ethnic' (or linguistic, or defined by reference to some other cultural characteristic): their cohesiveness and completeness in this respect. These two dimensions (the character of the relationship between the centre and the regions, and the match between regional boundaries and underlying ethnic or other cultural divisions) form the basis for the two main sections of this essay. A short concluding section speculates on the implications for political stability.

The federal option

The federal approach is just one of a broad range of strategies open to the multi-ethnic state in managing its relationship with its minority populations.[2] It may be distinguished conceptually from other territorial approaches, but its distinctiveness is not always clear-cut, a point developed in the first subsection of this section.[3] Furthermore, even when some kind of territorial management is the instrument of choice, the relationship between centre and regions need not be symmetrical. We therefore need to consider further those cases where the territorial structure of the state provides for two or more types of relationship between centre and region. This issue is considered in the last part of this section.

The federal model

Discussion of the concept of federation often proceeds as if the term refers to a clearly defined, categorical political structure. The implication is that a state either falls into this category, or it does not – an understanding that runs through the large literature in this area.[4] There is surprisingly little disagreement among authors as to which states are federal and which are not. The dominant (indeed, near universal) view is that most countries in the world are unitary, or at least non-federal, and that 24 are federal, authors disagreeing on only a small number of borderline cases. A range of countries, 14 in all, have had a long-established status as federations: Argentina, Australia, Austria, Brazil, Canada, Germany, India, Malaysia, Mexico, Nigeria, Pakistan, Switzerland, the USA and Venezuela. Two others replaced larger ethnic federations that disappeared with the collapse of communism (Bosnia and Herzegovina in the former Yugoslavia and Russia in the former Soviet Union; the third comparable former federation, Czechoslovakia, was replaced by two unitary states). A further three are micro-states which have become independent recently, made up of archipelagos in the Caribbean (St Kitts and Nevis, independent from the UK, 1983), the Indian Ocean (Comoros, independent of France, 1975) and the Western Pacific (Micronesia, independent of the USA, 1982).[5] Another, the United Arab Emirates, also appeared in 1971 as part of the process of decolonisation. Two more, Belgium and Ethiopia, became federal states as a consequence of internal restructuring. The two remaining cases, Spain and South Africa, resemble these, in that their federal status emerged as a consequence of domestic reform, though observers are not in full agreement regarding their status.[6]

The near-unanimity on the content of this list is surprising, since efforts to define federalism or federation have by no means achieved general agreement.[7] Indeed, it has for long been recognised that, to the extent that a federation is characterised by a division of power between centre and regions, the applicability of this term to a particular entity is not always entirely clear: the pattern of power distribution between the two levels is critical. Thus, for example, Ivo Duchacek devised a well-known 11-point scale describing the relationship between centre and regions.[8] This ranges from the extreme where the central government exercises most (indeed, all) power, totalitarian centralism, to that where there are no central authorities, temporary associations of states. In between, at the mid-point, we find the federal position. Stretching out to this from the totalitarian pole we find four other categories: authoritarian centralism, pluralistic but centralised unitary states, moderately decentralised unitary states and highly decentralised unitary states. Stretching from the mid-point (the federalist one) to the other pole we find confederation, permanent regional organisations or common markets, inter-governmental organisations such as the United Nations and its specialised agencies and permanent leagues of states.

More systematic efforts have been made to quantify the centralisation – regional autonomy continuum. Broadly speaking, they fall into two categories. First, and most obviously, efforts have been made to measure the distribution of *political resources* between the centre and component units in an effort to assess the relative institutional power of sub-national government. Thus, for example, Lane and Ersson devised an 'institutional autonomy index' – a scale running potentially from 0 to 10. This was based on four criteria: degree of federalism and degree of local government discretion (three points each) and existence of provisions for special territorial autonomy and for functional autonomy (two points each). When applied to the states of Western Europe, country scores ranged from Switzerland (the country with the most generous provisions for autonomy, with seven points) to Greece, Ireland, Luxembourg, Portugal and the UK (one point each).[9]

More recently, Marks, Hooghe and Schakel have devised a more comprehensive 'regional authority index', a scale running potentially from 0 to 24 for any one sub-national tier. Three-fifths of the weight of the scale (15 points) are accounted for by indicators of the degree of self-rule, using four measures: extent of regional autonomy, policy scope of regional governments, degree of fiscal autonomy of regions and existence of independent regional representative institutions (four points each, except for the first criterion, which is weighted at three points). The remaining two-fifths are accounted for by four measures of shared rule: level of recognition of regions in the national legislature, role of regional governments in co-determining national policy, influence of regional representatives on distribution of national tax revenues and influence of regions over the process of constitutional change (two points each, except for the last, which is weighted at three points).[10]

This index is a significant advance on other indices in two respects. First, its broad scope enables it to capture with some subtlety a wide range of characteristics of regional authority; it thus reveals meaningful variation not only in space (its authors have applied it to 42 democracies – 29 OECD countries, a further seven EU member states and six other European states), but also in time (they computed measures for each year from 1950 to 2006).[11] Second, the index tackles effectively the difficult problem of multiple tiers and asymmetrical territorial structure: scores are computed separately for each tier and for any territories for which special provision is made, and these are weighted by population in generating the overall country index. For the year 2006, the index ranged from 0.0 (eight small countries) to 30.5 (Bosnia and Herzegovina; in such cases as this, where there is more than one sub-national territorial tier, the score may exceed the theoretical maximum for any one tier, 24).

The second broad approach is to measure the distribution of *fiscal resources* between the centre and component units in an effort to assess the relative power of sub-national government. This is more easily quantifiable but, because of variations in standards of reporting such data cross-nationally, more difficult to interpret. Lijphart, for example, used the proportion of all tax receipts attributed to the central government as an approximate measure of centralisation in 15 unitary and six federal states.[12] Looking at the matter from the opposite perspective, Lane and Ersson used the proportion of all public expenditure accounted for by local and regional government as an indicator of autonomy in 18 European states.[13] Its easier availability and more 'objective' status mean that this kind of index has been very widely used, from policy-oriented bodies such as the World Bank to academic researchers.[14] One important initiative in this direction, based on public finance data but seeking to advance a broader understanding of decentralisation, distinguishes three dimensions: fiscal (sub-national revenue and expenditure as a proportion of all), administrative (sub-national taxation and transfers as a proportion of all sub-national grants and revenues) and political (the existence of municipal and regional elections). Using confirmatory factor analysis, it was possible to derive factor scores for each country on each of these dimensions based on 1996 data, scores which could be used as a plausible indicator of decentralisation.[15]

The existence of two important measures of autonomy below the level of the central state invites us to compare the two and, in particular, to explore the implications of each for conventional definitions of federal systems. Given their different starting points and methods of scoring cases, there is a surprising level of convergence between measures of this kind in general; that between the 'regional authority index' of Marks et al. and a decentralisation index based on Schneider's work is illustrated in Figure 11.1. Here, the horizontal axis refers to the score of each country on the regional authority index and the vertical axis to a composite decentralisation index, based on the mean of Schneider's three dimensions, fiscal, administrative and political decentralisation (the equal weighting of these three measures is of course arbitrary, as is normal in additive indices of this kind). The relatively strong association between the two indices is reflected in the clustering of countries reasonably close to the regression line, from bottom left to top right. The decentralisation index displays some capacity to distinguish federal

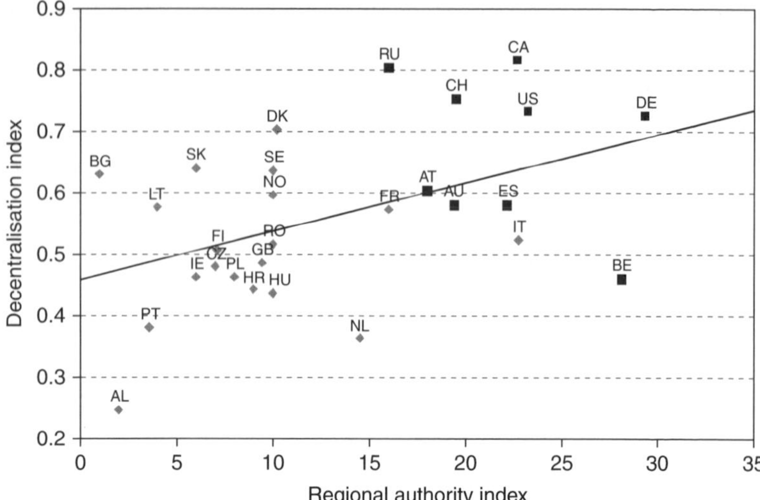

Figure 11.1   Decentralisation index (1996) and regional authority index (2006), selected states

Note: The decentralisation index is the mean of three factor scores (for fiscal, administrative and political autonomy). Diamonds refer to unitary states and squares to federal states ($r = 0.46$, $p < 0.05$, $n = 28$).

Source: Derived from Schneider (2003), and Liesbet Hooghe, Arjan H Schakel and Gary Marks (2008) 'Appendix B: Country and Regional Scores', *Regional and Federal Studies*, Vol. 18, No. 2–3, pp. 259–74.

states (shown as black squares) from unitary ones (grey diamonds): five of the nine federal states are higher on this axis than the highest-ranked unitary state, Denmark. But the regional authority index is more impressive in this respect: all nine federal states score more highly on this (i.e. they are located further to the right) than the cluster of unitary states, excluding Italy, which has a high score on this measure.

However, one would not expect the regional authority index to offer a clear differentiation between federal and unitary states: it does not purport to measure the strength of a particular regional tier, but rather that of all significant sub-national tiers. If we focus only on the primary regional tier in a federal system, ignoring the relative power of other tiers, we get closer to the federal model. Figure 11.2 re-computes the regional authority index, this time focusing on a single sub-state level, that of the highest regional tier.[16] This shows unitary states (grey bars) ranging from Bulgaria (1.0) to the Netherlands (14.5) and federal states (black bars) ranging from Russia (15.0) to Bosnia and Herzegovina

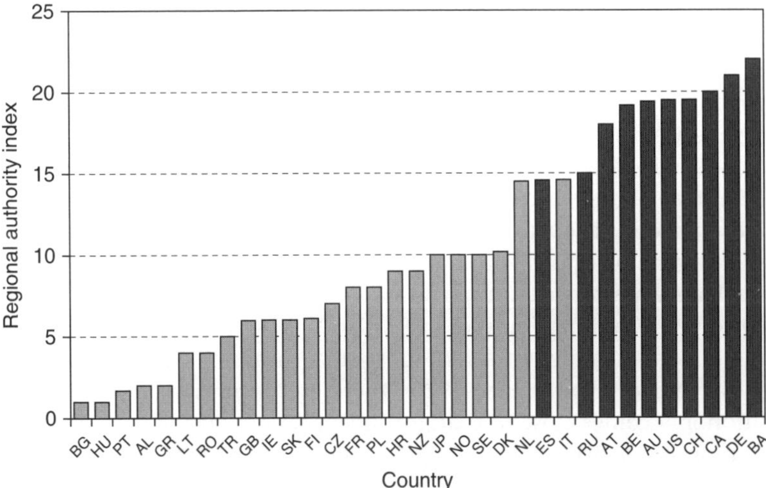

Figure 11.2   Regional authority index for tier one regions, selected states, 2006
Note: Grey bars refer to unitary states and black bars to federal states.
Source: Derived from Hooghe, Schakel and Marks (2008), and from data available at www.
unc.edu/~hooghe/data_ra.php.

(22.0). In between these, two countries tie on 14.6, but with Spain (commonly classed as federal) fractionally below Italy (not so classified). This, however, illustrates the perils of using the 'federal' label rather than implying any inadequacy in the index.

The asymmetrical variant

In federal states, the great bulk of the population typically lives in a set of regions which, however great the disparities in their demographic, economic and other resources, bear the same formal relationship to the central government. But there are circumstances where a portion of the population has fewer powers than typical federal units or, more rarely, where certain areas enjoy more autonomy than such units.

The most characteristic examples of the former are capital territories (such as Washington, DC, and Canberra, the Australian Capital Territory) – entities considered to be of such national importance as hosts of central government institutions that the central authorities have a particular interest in their management. The other set of examples is rather different: territories remote from the capital and suffering from structural disadvantage (whether deriving from peripheral geographical or ethno-cultural status, or socio-economic marginalisation) such that direct administration from the centre is considered appropriate. The territories of northern Canada and the tribal areas of Pakistan are examples. By contrast, there are circumstances where certain component units of federations may enjoy more power than others: the Basque Country, Catalonia and Galicia in Spain, for instance, or the republics in the Russian Federation which enjoy more powers than other federal units because of their status as ethnic homelands.

Even states which are otherwise unitary may make arrangements to endow certain regions with a high level of autonomy. Thus, for example, France has conceded a special status to Corsica, the UK has devolved power to subordinate entities in Scotland, Wales and Northern Ireland and Finland has allowed a very substantial measure of self-government to the Åland Islands since 1920. There are circumstances where this autonomy comes close to outright independence, as in the case of the relationship between the Isle of Man, Jersey and Guernsey and the UK, or a range of other microstates whose foreign relations and defence are managed by an adjacent power.

The ethnic dimension

The central question in this chapter is not the shape of federal arrangements as such, but the manner in which they respond to ethnic divisions. The first part of this section looks at precisely this question: the general relationship between federal structure and ethnic realities. The second part looks at certain options open to states in responding to the pattern of ethnic distribution on the ground, by exploring the general issue of boundary definition, one which arises not just in federal states but also in unitary ones.

The phenomenon of ethnic federalism

As we have seen, federal arrangements vary not just in the degree of power held by the units in the primary sub-national territorial tier but also in the extent to which power is symmetrically distributed among these units. Arrangements of this kind may have few implications for ethnic minority demands and expectations, or such implications may be profound. The capacity of federal structure to respond to ethnic conditions will depend, of course, on the geographical distribution of ethnic groups. If these are widely dispersed, it is unlikely that any territorial arrangements will be able to offer them the prospects of a homeland; but if they are territorially concentrated this prospect indeed arises. In the rest of this section, the focus will be on the latter type of ethnic group: one which is sufficiently territorially concentrated to facilitate the delineation of its boundaries on an administrative map.

Of 24 contemporary federal states, relatively few seek to reflect ethnic divisions in their first tier regions. To begin with, in six cases a settler society of European origin has structured itself along federal lines in response to issues of size and scale: the USA, Mexico, Brazil, Venezuela, Argentina and Australia. This is not to deny the salience of ethnic issues in these countries; but political cleavages substantially cut across or otherwise ignore ethnic fault lines, and territorial structure was not designed to accommodate such differences. The same could be said of the United Arab Emirates, Austria and Germany, and the three microstates (St Kitts and Nevis, Comoros and Micronesia). In the case of Austria and Germany, contemporary federal arrangements are a recognition of long-standing geopolitical divisions, and in pre-1918 Austria these had a strong ethnic (or 'national') component. We might add to this category another two where federal structure cuts across ethnic divisions, even though these are powerfully articulated in contemporary politics: Malaysia and South Africa.

The South African and especially Malaysian cases illustrate the central dilemma in federal solutions to problems of ethnic conflict, the dilemma that has just been discussed: the territorial division lines implicit in ethnically based federation can realistically be drawn only in circumstances where the relevant ethnic groups are sufficiently geographically differentiated. This condition is not present in peninsular Malaysia; even though there are areas where Chinese and Indians are spatially concentrated the overall pattern is one of intermingling with the largest group, the Malays. Even if the boundaries of South Africa's provinces were to seek to follow those of the country's main linguistic or ethnic groups, similarly, they would be able to do so only imperfectly. But there are countries (such as Spain and Russia) where the boundaries of the component units in the system have been devised precisely to facilitate ethnic autonomy, or where long-established internal boundaries have been endowed with fresh significance with a view to protecting the interests of certain minority groups (as in Canada and Switzerland). In each of these cases the numerically dominant groups (speakers of Castilian Spanish, ethnic Russians, Anglophone Canadians and German Swiss) are themselves internally partitioned under the federal system: between 14 of Spain's 17 autonomous communities, between at least 57 of the 83 federal subjects of Russia, between nine of Canada's ten provinces, and between 19 of Switzerland's 26 cantons.[17] In Spain, the three remaining autonomous communities, Catalonia, the Basque Country and Galicia, have a status of special autonomy in view of their historical and cultural distinctiveness, as do 21 republics, four autonomous districts and one autonomous province in Russia. In Canada, the province of Quebec constitutes a focal point of francophone loyalty, while in Switzerland the francophone population is distributed over six cantons and the Italian-speaking population is concentrated in one.

In the cases just described, federal arrangements make certain concessions to ethnic realities by endowing spatially concentrated minorities with a measure of autonomy in their own regions, though perhaps dividing them between several such units (as in the case of French-speaking Switzerland) or making provision for a form of ethnic autonomy that is largely nominal (as in the case of the Russian republics, in only a few of which the titular nationality is numerically dominant). In all of these cases, the most numerous group does not have an autonomous territory of its own but is divided among several federal components (which in the case of Spain and Russia enjoy a constitutional status that is at least symbolically inferior to that of the special minority regions). In a small number of cases, straightforward ethnic federation (the creation of a federal structure that matches ethnic divisions, group by group, as closely as possible) has been attempted. But, as has been mentioned already, the three most clear-cut examples of this, the Soviet Union, Yugoslavia and Czechoslovakia, have already disappeared.[18]

The best surviving examples, Belgium and Bosnia-Herzegovina, are also outstanding cases where the integrity of the state is threatened. In Belgium, the status of Brussels (overwhelmingly francophone, but located in central Flanders) has acted as an obstacle to disintegration; the city has been given separate status as a third bilingual region alongside Dutch-speaking Flanders and French-speaking Wallonia. Bosnia-Herzegovina, a loose federation of two entities (an ethnic Muslim-Croat federation and a 'Serbian Republic'), has been sustained since the Dayton Agreement of 1995 more by international pressure than by the will of its peoples to live together. Pakistan might be added to this list. Although the main groups there are dispersed throughout the country, each of the four provinces is home to one of the country's major ethnic groups (Punjabis, Pashtuns, Sindhis and Baloch, respectively); but the country is held together by a more powerful central government than is the case with either of the two other ethnic federations just discussed.

The three remaining cases illustrate stages in the progressive institutionalisation of ethnic divisions. India's federal system was based originally on traditional territorial units – princely dominions or units of British rule – whose borders largely ignored ethnic and linguistic ones, but a reform process ensured that after 1956 a new network of states would conform much more closely to the realities of ethnic geography.[19] Overhaul of the federal system in Nigeria and the reform of the state structure in Ethiopia in 1995 that ushered in a federal system have been described as 'a means to contain a fractious plurality of languages, ethnicity and regions.'[20] In each case, they brought the political map of the country into closer conformity with the geographical expression of ethnic division.

The politics of boundary delimitation

It seems clear, then, that states may be prevented by geographical realities from moving to the model of ethnic federation: multi-ethnic states with spatially intermingled populations may of course be federations, but it is unlikely that the federal structure will reflect any kind of real ethnic geography. However, even where ethnic groups are clearly delimited geographically, boundaries of sub-state units need not recognise these. If the central authorities wish to minimise recognition of spatially defined ethnic groups, they may seek to ensure that, if territorially defined ethnic groups are present, the extent to which they may possess their 'own' territory is obscured by the way in which lines are drawn on a map. Broadly speaking, this may be done in any of these three ways: the interdependent processes of truncation and hyper-expansion and the practice of subunit multiplication. These approaches may be adopted not just in federal states but also in relation to tiers of sub-national government in unitary states, as some of the examples that follow demonstrate.

The 'truncation' approach rests on a form of partition of ethnic territory.[21] The population of the distinct unit is given a territory of its own, but this does not extend over the whole of the ethnic territory. This may obviously occur in contexts other than the federal one. When Ireland was being partitioned in 1921, for example, the line of partition did not seek to follow the crude line of the boundary between Catholic (Irish nationalist) areas and Protestant (British unionist) ones, but partitioned the former, excluding a significant, territorially concentrated Catholic population. This did not prevent Irish secession, but it reduced its attractiveness to secessionists. When the region of Brittany was reconstituted as part of the French regional reforms in 1972, similarly, the boundaries of the pre-revolutionary Duchy of Brittany were not restored; instead, the department of Nantes was excluded and transferred to a neighbouring region. It could similarly be argued that the current autonomous communities of Catalonia and particularly the

Basque Country in Spain are 'undersized', in that they fall short of the maximalist territorial definition of nationalists.

The 'hyper-expansion' approach is the opposite. An ethnic territory is enlarged by the inclusion of an 'alien' population which will have the effect of diluting the territory's ethnic distinctiveness. This was a feature – not necessarily intended in this way – of Irish partition in 1921. The Irish Free State was truncated, as already mentioned, but Northern Ireland was hyper-expanded, laying the seeds of long-term inter-communal problems: a substantial Catholic population was included within its borders. A similar approach was adopted in interwar Czechoslovakia. There, the German-speaking population inhabited a cohesive ring around most of Bohemia, and administrative boundaries could have been drawn to maximise linguistic coherence. But these areas were instead grouped with adjacent Czech-speaking districts, so that the administrative map bore little relation to the ethnic one. The German-speaking South Tyrol is a further example: instead of being given autonomy under the provisions of the Italian regionalisation programme, it was grouped with overwhelmingly Italian-speaking areas to constitute the mixed region of Trentino-Alto Adige.

The third broad strategy has been described above, for want of a better term, as subunit multiplication. There are circumstances where internal political boundaries may follow ethnic or linguistic lines closely but the unity of ethnic or linguistic territories is still disrupted. In Switzerland, for instance, almost all cantons are unilingual (though three have significant minorities).[22] Furthermore, the third largest linguistic group, the Italian one, has its 'own' canton, Ticino. But German speakers are divided between 19 cantons, and French speakers between six. Thus, to the extent that cantons may flex their autonomous political muscles, they are doing so typically in isolation from other cantons belonging to their linguistic group. The cantonal structure, in other words, disrupts the territorial integrity of the two largest linguistic groups. Of course, this should not be taken as implying an intentional fracture of the coherence of two large language communities. It is true that each possesses a measure of language-based identity (resting on the distinctive character of the Swiss-German dialects, and on the shared historical experience of the Suisse-romande area), but the powerful political position of the cantons rests on a long-standing tradition of local independence and cantonal loyalty, and is by no means a clever device concocted by the centre to perpetuate its rule.

There are many other examples of this process in operation. In Canada, the French-speaking population is overwhelmingly concentrated in a single province, Quebec, while English speakers are divided among the remaining nine provinces. The process of regional reform in Spain has produced a quasi-federation, similarly, with Basques, Catalans and Galicians each concentrated in one of the 17 'autonomous communities', but the Castilian-speaking, 'Spanish-identifying' population is dispersed among the remaining autonomous communities, several of which are also home to other culturally distinct groups.

Although, as we have seen, these approaches may be adopted in all kinds of states, unitary or federal, there are commonly particular difficulties in adjusting internal frontiers in federal states. Whether the boundaries of component units in federations match ethnic boundaries, or whether they fail dramatically to do so, this outcome has not necessarily been achieved by any kind of conscious manipulation of the relationship between the ethnic map and the political-administrative one. Since the boundaries of the units which combine to form a particular federal system are typically very old and complex historical factors lie behind their location, they may not easily be altered, and their failure to reflect lines of ethnic division constitutes a significant factor in maintaining the integrity of the state. Thus the federal system in Malaysia cuts across ethnic divisions: in peninsular Malaysia, where the borders of the nine states coincide with the domains of traditionally hereditary rulers, the large Chinese minority constitutes a majority in only one, but makes up a big minority in others. State borders could be redrawn to provide more ethnically homogeneous areas; but there are good reasons for not doing so. In the USA, similarly, it would be possible to carve out a new state in the South which would be predominantly African-American, but a conservative constitutional tradition and public policy priorities make such a course of action highly unlikely and of questionable desirability.

This is not to say that redesignation of the territorial arrangements within a federation is impossible. In some federal states internal borders have been adjusted without provoking insurmountable local opposition. The successive waves of revision of the federal structure in Nigeria, discussed above, have been facilitated by the reality of a powerful central government, while the redrawing of the map of Germany's *Länder* after 1945 was facilitated by the collapse of the older federal system and the installation of a centralised Nazi-run state in the interwar period, rubbing clean the old boundary map. Even Switzerland and its Bern canton were able to adjust to regional demands and redraw boundaries in the 1970s: Bern by allowing the secession of the Northern Jura district and Switzerland by admitting this district to the Swiss Confederation as a new canton. India, as we have seen, represents one of the few cases where the initial federal system was replaced by one in which borders were redrawn to reflect ethnic reality more closely.

Conclusion

This chapter has, then, identified several structural features of the federal system that are conducive to maintenance of stability in multi-ethnic societies. To start with, the system may be able to defend a form of federation which is tilted in the direction of the centre, limiting the options of the constituent units. But it may also have the capacity to undermine the potential for regional revolt through the manner in which boundaries are drawn. These may result in truncation of the homeland of this minority by the exclusion of certain areas to which it might reasonably lay claim. They may result in the dilution of this homeland by the incorporation of additional areas predominantly inhabited by other groups. They may result in the partition of the homeland by dividing it into several sub-federal units, which might or might not be ethnically homogeneous. But by simply endowing the majority group with several sub-federal units rather than with a single one it changes the balance of collective decision making within the federation, giving the majority many more voices than minorities.

In the discussion above, it has been implicitly assumed that the spatial pattern of distribution of different ethnic or linguistic groups is stable. In reality, though, this is not always the case. Quite apart from differential trends in population dynamics, those in control of the central state apparatus (or, more rarely, their regional opponents) may have the capacity to create or to modify 'facts on the ground': to encourage or enforce particular kinds of migration patterns that will have an impact on ethnic geography, and therefore on the potential operation of any kind of system of territorial autonomy. It should be recalled, then, that intrastate boundaries are not just a response to ethnic facts; they may also help to shape them, and thus assist in determining the future options for territorial government.

How, then, may we respond to the question posed at the beginning of this chapter about the extent to which ethnic federations may promote or impede political stability? The examples given above suggest that ethnic federations sometimes survive, and sometimes fail. This is in line with the balanced conclusions reached by many researchers in the area. One study of fiscal politics in federal states with a strong ethnic component (India, Pakistan, Nigeria and Yugoslavia) arrived at the verdict that a strategy of 'fiscal appeasement' sometimes succeeded in buying off ethnic dissent, but it also sometimes failed.[23] Another study of political decentralisation concluded that it was 'a useful mechanism in reducing both ethnic conflict and secessionism', except in circumstances where there were strong regional parties.[24] A general analysis of the federal approach pointed out that while there was recent evidence suggesting that 'federal formulas for accommodation are at best ineffectual and at worst deeply damaging', a range of country specialists had reached a near-consensus that 'federal institutions promote successful accommodation.'[25] Careful comparative historical analysis takes us a little further: notwithstanding the difficulty in generalising, it has been suggested that federal systems which recognise a core ethnic region are more likely to collapse than those which do not.[26] This takes us back to the hazards of ethnic federation, since, as understood in this chapter, it refers precisely to the accuracy with which boundaries of federal units match ethnic ones. If they do so closely, and there is a single dominant ethnic group (as in the former Soviet Union), the system faces serious threat; if they do so in circumstances where there is a wide measure of ethnic pluralism (as in India), survival of the system may be more likely. A full explanation of survival and collapse of ethnic federations is likely, however, to require case-by-case study so meticulous as to defy the prospects for large-scale comparative analysis.

Notes

This is the revised version of a paper presented at the colloquium of the Research Committee on Politics and Ethnicity of the International Political Science Association, Queen's University, Belfast, 10–12 September 2007.

1. Lord Acton [John Dalberg-Acton], 'Nationality' in *The History of Freedom and Other Essays* [essay first published 1862], Books for Libraries Press, NY: Freeport, 1907, pp. 270–300, at p. 290.
2. John Coakley, 'The Resolution of Ethnic Conflict: Towards a Typology', *International Political Science Review*, Vol. 13, No. 4, 1992, pp. 341–56; John McGarry and Brendan O'Leary, 'Introduction: The Macro-Political Regulation of Ethnic Conflict', in John McGarry and Brendan O'Leary (eds), *The Politics of Ethnic Conflict Regulation: Case Studies of Protracted Ethnic Conflicts*, London: Routledge, 1993, pp. 1–47.
3. This point is developed further in John Coakley, 'Conclusion: Towards a Solution?' in John Coakley (ed.), *The Territorial Management of Ethnic Conflict* (2nd edition), London: Frank Cass, 2003, pp. 293–316. The extent to which federalist and decentralist arrangements lie along a continuum rather than falling into discrete categories is discussed in Jonathan Rodden, 'Comparative Federalism and Decentralization: On Meaning and Measurement', *Comparative Politics*, Vol. 36, No. 4, 2004, pp. 481–500.

4. For early general but still very useful descriptions of federalism and federation, see K. C. Wheare (1963) *Federal Government* (4th edition), London: Oxford University Press, 1963 [first published 1946]; Carl J. Friedrich, *Trends of Federalism in Theory and Practice*, London: Pall Mall Press, 1968; Ivo D. Duchacek, *Comparative Federalism: The Territorial Dimension of Politics*, New York, NY: Holt, Rinehart and Winston, 1970. Later general overviews include Preston King, *Federalism and Federation*, London: Croom Helm, 1982; Murray Forsyth (ed.), *Federalism and Nationalism*, London: Leicester University Press, 1989; Michael Burgess and Alain-G. Gagnon (eds), *Comparative Federalism and Federation: Competing Traditions and Future Directions*, London: Harvester Wheatsheaf, 1993; Bertus de Villiers (ed.), *Evaluating Federal Systems*, Cape Town: Juta and Co., 1994; Wilfried Swenden, *Federalism and Regionalism in Western Europe: A Comparative and Thematic Analysis*, Basingstoke: Palgrave Macmillan, 2006; Thomas O. Hueglin and Alan Fenna, *Comparative Federalism: A Systematic Inquiry*, Peterborough, Ont.: Broadview Press, 2006; and Michael Burgess and John Pinder (eds), *Multinational Federations*, New York: Routledge, 2007.

5. The Federation of St Kitts and Nevis consists of two islands, with a population in 2005 of 43,000; the Union of the Comoros of three islands, with a population of 798,000; and the Federated States of Micronesia of four clusters of small islands, with a population of 110,000. One comparative study of federal micro-states added Palau (Belau) as a fourth instance; see Dag Anckar, 'Lilliput Federalism: Profiles and Varieties', *Regional and Federal Studies*, Vol. 13, No. 3, 2003, pp. 107–24. Palau (population of 20,000 in 2005), however, is not usually included in lists of federations.

6. This listing of federations is based on seven sources: Duchacek 1970; A.-P. Frognier, 'Federal and Partly Federal Systems, Institutions and Conflict Managements: Some Western European Examples', in Desmond Rea (ed.), *Political Co-operation in Divided Societies: A Series of Papers Relevant to the Conflict in Northern Ireland*, Dublin: Gill and Macmillan, 1982, pp. 187–228; overviews by Elazar (1995), Watt (1999) and Denis and Ian Derbyshire (1999) reported in Jan-Erik Lane and Svante Ersson, 'The Riddle of Federalism: Does Federalism Impact on Democracy?', *Democratization*, Vol. 12, No. 2, 2005, pp. 163–82; Ann L. Griffiths and Karl Nerenberg (eds), *Handbook of Federal Countries, 2002*, Montreal: McGill-Queen's University Press, 2002; and Forum of Federations: The Global Network on Federalism (2009), available www.forumfed.org. The Derbyshires did not classify either South Africa or Spain as federal.

7. King 1982, pp. 19–23, made an important distinction between *federalism* as an ideology and *federation* as an institutional arrangement. It has been argued that this has since become the mainstream position; see Michael Burgess, 'Federalism and Federation: A Reappraisal' in Burgess and Gagnon, 1993, pp. 3–14. While this may be an optimistic judgement, this is the sense in which these terms are used in this essay.

8. Ivo D. Duchacek, *The Territorial Dimension of Politics Within, Among and Across Nations*, Boulder, CO: Westview, 1986, pp. 112–18.

9. Jan-Erik Lane and Svante Ersson, *Politics and Society in Western Europe* (4th edition), London: Sage, 1999, p. 187.

10. Liesbet Hooghe, Gary Marks and Arjan H. Schakel, 'Operationalising Regional Authority: A Coding Scheme for 42 Countries, 1950–2006', *Regional and Federal Studies*, Vol. 18, No. 2–3, 2008, pp. 123–42.

11. Gary Marks, Liesbet Hooghe and Arjan H. Schakel, 'Measuring Regional Authority', *Regional and Federal Studies*, Vol. 18, No. 2–3, 2008, pp. 111–21.

12. Arend Lijphart, *Democracies: Patterns of Majoritarian and Consensus Government in Twenty-One Countries*, New Haven: Yale University Press, 1984, p. 178.

13. Lane and Ersson 1999, p. 188.

14. For an overview of such indices, see Arjan H. Schakel, 'Validation of the Regional Authority Index', *Regional and Federal Studies*, Vol. 18, No. 2–3, 2008, pp. 143–66.

15. Aaron Schneider, 'Decentralisation: Conceptualisation and Measurement', *Studies in Comparative International Development*, Vol. 38, No. 3, 2003, pp. 32–56.

16. In the case of Russia, tier two regions were used; there, the tier one regions identified by Marks, Hooghe and Schakel have a relatively light administrative function.

17. These figures oversimplify. In Spain, for instance, some would argue that Andalusia should be subtracted from this list, in view of its special identity, and the use of stricter linguistic criterion might suggest that there are only two regions, Catalonia and Galicia, in which a majority of the population speaks a language other than Castilian; in Russia this refers to 46 provinces, nine territories and two federal cities; and in Switzerland the use of the term 'minority' or 'ethnic' to refer to the French- and Italian-speaking populations would be contested.

18. The Soviet Union dissolved into its 15 ethnic ('union') republics in 1991, and Czechoslovakia into its two republics in 1993. The dissolution of Yugoslavia began with the secession of Croatia, Slovenia and Macedonia in 1991, with Bosnia-Herzegovina (not an 'ethnic' republic) following in 1992; the two remaining republics, continuing as 'Yugoslavia' to 2002, finally went their separate paths as Serbia and Montenegro in 2006.

19. See Louise Tillin, 'United in Diversity? Asymmetry in Indian Federalism', *Publius: The Journal of Federalism*, Vol. 37, No. 1, 2007, pp. 45–67.

20. Yonatan Fesha and Coel Kirkby, 'A Critical Survey of Subnational Autonomy in African States', *Publius: The Journal of Federalism*, Vol. 38, No. 2, 2008, pp. 248–71, at p. 265.

21. See Brendan O'Leary, 'Analysing Partition: Definition, Classification and Explanation', *Political Geography*, Vol. 26, No. 8, 2007, pp. 886–908.

22. These are the cantons of Graubünden, predominantly German-speaking but with a large Romansch minority, and Valais and Fribourg, predominantly French-speaking but with German-speaking minorities of 32 per cent in each case (these statistics refer to the citizen population, not to the resident population, which contains much higher proportions of speakers of minority languages); see Switzerland, *Recensement fédéral de la population 2000: Le paysage linguistique en Suisse*, Office Fédéral Statistique, Neuchâtel 2005.

23. Eduardo Alemán and Daniel Treisman, 'Fiscal Politics in "Ethnically-Mined", Developing, Federal States: Central Strategies and Secessionist Violence', in Philip Roeder and Donald Rothchild (eds), *Sustainable Peace: Power*

and Democracy after Civil Wars, Ithaca: Cornell University Press, 2005, pp. 173–216.
24. Dawn Brancati, 'Decentralization: Fueling the Fire of Dampening the Flames of Ethnic Conflict and Secessionism?' *International Organization*, Vol. 60, No. 3, 2006, pp. 651–85.
25. Nancy Bermeo, 'A New Look at Federalism: The Import of Institutions', *Journal of Democracy*, Vol. 13, No. 2, 2002, pp. 96–110, at p. 97.
26. Henry E. Hale, 'Divided We Stand: Institutional Sources of Ethnofederal State Survival and Collapse', *International Organization*, Vol. 56, No. 1, 2004, pp. 165–93.

12
Local Space and Protest in Divided Societies

Diarmuid Maguire

Introduction

This chapter examines the dynamic nature of protest mobilisation and state response within ethnic-national locales. People in these areas are sensitive to any form of de-territorialisation or re-territorialisation at the local level. Nationally, the state exercises repressive control over ethnic-national locales by seeking to avoid secessionist challenges and restricting conflict to the local level. For those inhabiting these areas, sovereignty is not an abstract idea but a lived and normal part of everyday life. The local architecture of the everyday, such as schools, shops, and parks, contests the architecture of local inclusion and exclusion. Murals and memorials stand in support of insurgents, national flags honour them, and graffiti taunts adversaries. All of these symbols demand communal solidarity. These sentiments are reinforced by the surrounding architecture of state sovereignty, such as observation towers, barracks, or armoured vehicles. Protest is highly volatile in these areas: a few stones thrown by teenagers at security forces after school can later degenerate into a shooting battle between older insurgents and state forces.

Local grievances have clear implications for both ethnic violence and conflict resolution. The case of Northern Ireland will be discussed in terms of the transformation of state–society relations at the local level from the period of widespread ethnic violence from 1967 to 1994 to the peace process beginning in 1994. The state in Northern Ireland is now attempting to disentangle ethnic boundaries from protest boundaries. Concretely, these areas are directly rewarded for participation in the peace process with locally directed reforms. By contrast, the state of Israel seeks a two-state settlement based on nationality and is not interested in negotiating with local dissidents. Both states want to win the battle for peace but their strategies differ as a result of respective geopolitical situations and the dynamics of protest. These societies have disputed borders, their military and police forces play each other's roles, their communities are divided, and disorder occurs on the issue of national identity. The central argument here is that local space matters; it exists in a world of contested borders under globalisation.

State sovereignty has three main aspects which are the protection the state offers to its citizens from fellow citizens and other states; state regulation of national economies, mainly through protection from the effects of global commerce; and finally national identity. Kalyvas defines the sovereign as 'the one who determines the constitutional form, the juridical and political identity, and the government structure of a community in its entirety.'[1] Definitions of order and disorder mean that protest has to be observed within territorial boundaries. First, this is how protesters are regarded by the state. Most legislation surrounding protesters is expressed in terms of public disorder (i.e. within an open space). State authorities use space to control society. As Sewell writes:

> Space is an object and matrix of power. All power is, ultimately, power over people. One way of exercising control over people is by controlling the spaces where people live and work. The organization of power in the modern nation-state is particularly space-based, or territorial, in character.[2]

Second, protesters take advantage of the temporary boundary of action to express their demands politically and culturally. Third, the possibility of disorder is usually part of any message that protesters want to send to the authorities. The protesters' control of space is designed to keep state authorities guessing as to the outcome of this temporary episode.

Therefore, state and society engage in political struggle over access to and interaction within contested territory. Movements are 'spatially-conscious social actors'[3] and the authorities in turn seek to utilise space in order to control their actions.[4] In this context, protest is best thought of as a verb and movement as a noun. Obviously protest action and movement organising are related, but they should not be seen as the same thing. Protesters carry signs, chant songs, and seek to attract more people into their ranks from those outside their boundaries. For example, during the occupation of Paris in May 1968, Lefebvre notes the transformation of existing spatial practices; he writes: 'The streets become political areas, political places.'[5] Protest is defined by the capacity for disorder and the state uses the police or army to contain it. The definition of protest used here is based on disruption of authority by movements for political goals.[6] Protest does not exist purely in terms of the organisation that produced it, protest only exists during the period of disruption that it creates and therefore is not a permanent boundary on the political landscape.

Police use the principle of territoriality that is 'the active use of geographic space'[7] to control this disruption of daily life. Police authorities in Britain have placed protest in its first line of issues to be 'managed'. A police document entitled *Policing Disorder*[8] discusses the role of non-institutionalised protest; it describes how 'the mobility of protesters provides a fresh challenge to the Service in that supporters from an ideological community ... only becomes geographically based for relatively short periods before moving on to the next protest site'. It calls for intelligence and geographic mapping of the locations of protesters. Warnings have been given to protesters about adopting non-institutionalised protest making and thus being 'mistaken for terrorists.'[9] Thus the main focus, using the 'world's best practise', is 'liaison' with protesters to produce 'emotive protest with minimal disorder.'[10] Della Porta[11] has also noted there is often a 'shared interest between the police and the organizers' in containing those regarded as 'outsiders.'[12]

In divided societies, however, citizens do not see the state as protecting them from fellow citizens, from other states, or regulating the national economy in their interest. They do not identify with the borders established by the state, believing that the police and army play a complementary role in repressing their community. In short, all the problems that afflict this community – protection, regulation, identity – are depicted in national terms and centre not only on state behaviour but also on state sovereignty. As a result, Fearon and Laitin ask: what is 'the relationship between ethnic identity construction and ethnic violence?'[13] Part of the answer to this question lies in the activation of new geographic change disrupting previously quiescent ghettoes.

The framework

Spatial practices are seen here as constituting four arenas for protest activity: space as resource, resistance, retreat and right. The first is space as *resource*, places where movements prepare for mobilisation. This is true for any movement seeking to challenge power within society as movements require meeting places for planning. For example, workers have used space, provided by factories or residence to organise challenges against employers. Lack of organisational space typically means no protest. The Tiananmen protest analysed by Sewell discusses how

Beijing dormitories provided possibilities for mobilisation and communicative space for challengers.[14] Space is used for *resistance* when protestors mobilise against the state or other actors using disruptive direct action. Movements engage in protest, using public or private space, legally or illegally, with different reactions by the authorities.

A legal protest in a public space usually passes peacefully while illegal protest in a public space usually attracts less repression by the authorities than illegal protest in a private space, at least within liberal-democratic regimes. To return to previous example, students gathered in Tiananmen Square taunted the regime using non-violent protest but they were crushed by state forces. Space also provides areas of *retreat*. After an episode of contention, movements re-enter spaces they feel safe in, they reflect on what has been achieved and they provide the possibility of avoiding the authorities to struggle another day. These areas may be the surroundings in which they previously came from, that is, space as a resource or, in extreme cases, new spaces may be available to a movement elsewhere, for example, sanctuaries or other countries. In a post-Tiananmen situation, those students who escaped the crackdown went underground, to Hong Kong or other countries from where they sought to reorganise resistance.

But space can be used to proclaim the *right* to sovereignty. Here, protesters reproduce or mimic sovereign institutions at the popular level. Within segregated areas this can involve the re-creation of border guards, judiciary, tax collectors, transport, and cultural institutions. This use of space as right and its role within divided societies makes these movements unique. Societies unable to settle the issue of sovereignty create places of residence as potential spaces of resources and resistance. These locales may be spaces of retreat for militants escaping from the authorities. Above all, these spaces can be used to establish the central aim of the movement, namely the right to sovereign space over all or part of a territory with a state claiming sovereignty. It is here that the example of the Tiananmen uprising no longer fits; this protest did not seek secession or the redrawing of China's boundaries.

Table 12.1 provides a framework for understanding how a divided state uses space in dynamic conflict with its challengers. Typically, military response summarises the initial stance by state authorities towards insurgents at the beginning of the struggle. This is certainly the case in both Northern Ireland and Israel. Through repeated iterations with challengers, different sections of the state employed various spatial solutions locally. Some involve segregating protest in the four spaces of protest below, for example by isolating protestors to disrupt using local areas as a resource. As dynamics change over time possible 'solutions' might emerge

Table 12.1 Spatial strategies of states

State response to protest	Resource (Preparation)	Resistance (Mobilisation)	Retreat (Underground)	Right (Mimicry)
Military Response	Disrupt preparation by monitoring and harassing individuals.	Repression. Use Army as blunt weapon.	Curfew, raids, imprisonment or attacks on former militants.	Deny right to 'pretend' sovereignty by attacking areas.
Segregation	Isolate insurgents.	Infiltrate insurgents.	Cooperate with other governments.	Use sectarianism as opposed to sovereignty.
Possible Dynamics	Denial to management of local areas.	Repression to incorporation of movements.	Capture to release of prisoners.	Defence of sovereignty to recognise new borders.
Solution	Provide resources to local communities.	Police replace Army. Or Army becomes more 'police-like'.	Release local prisoners.	Sovereignty (re)divided with recognition of local areas.

that involve compromise by both parties. The use of solution here is obviously normative and does not mean resolution of the quarrel.[15]

For example, military withdrawal played its part in Northern Ireland but different layers of government were involved; the European Union provided a different level of government, adding a layer of complexity to the situation in Northern Ireland. Kolossov notes that due to economic reasons and 'geographic location': 'in Europe, potential separatists cannot escape the common external boundaries of the EU.'[16] However, in Israel these layers of government do not exist and Palestinians must rely on both force and diplomacy.

Tilly argues that movements must display four key elements if they are to be successful: Worthiness, Unity, Numbers and Commitment (WUNC).[17] Clearly, the failure of a movement to be WUNC-like is a plus for the state but we could apply WUNC to the state in terms of its interaction with protesters. Is the state worthy in its reaction to protest, measured perhaps by international acceptance at the state and popular level? Does the state display unity by preventing fissures in the state elite? Has the state got the numbers, measured by public opinion? Will the state show commitment when times are tough?

The remainder of this chapter will look at two case studies through the framework outlined in Table 12.1.

Northern Ireland

Tilly analyses how the imposition of a new border by authorities activates new movements or reactivates old ones. The Northern Ireland state was established by the Government of Ireland Act passed in 1920 in the Westminster Parliament. This move ceded to decades of unionist protest against Home Rule for the entire island, by partitioning off its North-East corner. The internal strength of the unionist state rested on two factors: the numerical majority of Protestant to Catholic (two to one) and the solidity of the unionist alliance. Northern Ireland is a case of 'contested sovereignty' with the struggle taking place locally over whether the North's future still lies with Britain (unionist-loyalist) or a united Ireland (nationalist-republican). Divided sovereignty and discrimination within the North meant that for the Catholic nationalist minority there was no agreement on the legitimacy of the police and the military. The demands of constitutional nationalism or militant republicanism failed to move the authorities from 1920 to 1967.

The emergence of the American Civil Rights Association inspired many within the North to advance the concept of minority rights within a majority system through the tactics of non-violent direct action. On 29 January 1967 the Northern Ireland Civil Rights Association (NICRA) was formed and new weapons of social protest were forged as a result. The state was to be confronted by protesters who did not take up arms like the Irish Republican Army (IRA) but instead organised illegal rallies, sit-ins, squats, and marches outside of traditional nationalist ghettoes. The Civil Rights Movement led nationalists out of their ghettoes onto the main streets of the province. Civil rights supporters marched from one town to another. When they were blocked by the police or counter-demonstrators they sat down on the roads. In demanding equal rights, they laid equal claim to the territory of the province. The occupation of territory allowed Irish nationalists to make up for their numerical inferiority. The police were unable to restore order in Derry and the British army was called into the province on 14 and 15 August 1969.

Michael Farrell, author and activist, described the situation in Northern Ireland spatially:

> The Loyalists were frustrated and angry. They were outraged by the existence of the 'No Go' areas behind the barricades where Crown forces couldn't penetrate and the Union Jack didn't fly. Parts of the state had virtually seceded. And they sensed that the intervention of British troops had drastically curtailed the powers of Stormont.[18]

In other words, nationalists were putting forward space as a right. But there are other conclusions to be drawn in territorial terms.

1. The civil rights movement had led a minority in a province-wide struggle against discrimination. The Northern Ireland state had partially succeeded in turning this struggle about equality into a struggle about nationalism. This was assisted by attacks on nationalist ghettoes. No longer did the Royal Ulster Constabulary have to deal purely with non-violent protestors on city streets, violent protestors armed with stones and petrol bombs defended their neighbourhoods. This assisted the state in containing the violence.
2. The shift in nationalist support to localised Citizens Defence Committees away from NICRA was a function of going on the defence rather than engaging in attack. Citizens Defence Committees had to deal not only with the RUC but also with unionist protestors. Some members of the Citizens Defence Committees were later to become active in the Provisional IRA. That is, future insurgents came from local ethnic ghettoes.

3. The arrival of the British army did not result in power being handed over to nationalists nor indeed back to unionists. The British army was a blunt weapon and it saw the Northern Ireland problem in operational terms. Arms raids by the British army were conducted with increasing frequency in nationalist ghettoes and one such raid provoked a riot in West Belfast in July 1970. The British army announced a two-day curfew for the Falls Road in response.

Misunderstandings over militants' use of local space were revealed during a meeting between representatives of the British state and the Provisional IRA in June 1972. At this meeting, British representatives found that contrary to their expectations, violence in nationalist ghettoes was not always under the control of the IRA. The two IRA representatives, Daithi O'Conaill and Gerry Adams, pointed out some of the difficulties in patrolling violence within their own areas. According to the notes, O'Conaill and Adams had stated how

> [t]hey were worried about the activities of teenagers and school children. They admitted that violence against the Army frequently started by stone throwing by children and that the opportunity was then taken to escalate the violence to shooting: they offered a list of places they thought the risk was greatest and asked if the Army could avoid them at times when children tended to congregate.[19]

Also at this first meeting between the two parties, the Provisional IRA revealed the pressure they faced hiding militants and their desire to lead a normal life. In later ceasefires the IRA demanded 'incident centres' which provided rights to this organisation albeit on a temporary basis. Through this first encounter between state authority and challenger within a divided society we can read how the state's reaction to local protest as a resource, resistance, retreat and a right was discussed.

The army clearly saw the situation within Northern Ireland in terms of terrorism, strictly related to territory. The army requested further powers to restrict control of movement within the North and across the border. In a document from the Ministry of Defence in November 1973, it was proposed that the army be entrusted with new rules of engagement that allowed for soldiers to open fire

> '[w]ithout fear of legal penalty' on 'persons merely carrying firearms'; 'persons breaking a curfew', and 'persons who failed to halt when

challenged', in areas designated by the Secretary of State or, perhaps the General Officer in Command, as 'special areas', which would typically, be exceptionally 'hard' areas in which the Army needed to regain control and which might or might not correspond with areas under curfew.[20]

This may have constituted hard line parallel diplomacy conducted by the British government: that is, initiatives taken on the political front by the state which recognised the subtleties of the local situation for groups willing to negotiate but, at the same time, were designed to maintain military dominance. But there is also considerable evidence of confusion at the state level during this period over Northern Ireland's constitutional future. Files released for the period 1972–5 reveal that United Kingdom Cabinets considered a number of plans that ranged from a united Ireland, re-division of Northern Ireland, to complete integration within the UK system.[21] The uncertainty that these considerations, which were often leaked, created in the minds of nationalist and unionist elites led to a breakdown of trust at the provincial level.

As a result, local stronghold areas within Northern Ireland became increasingly ghettoised, illustrated by wall murals of paramilitary leaders, painted warnings to outsiders, and pavements coloured according to national flags. Those who lived inside these areas did so 'under the protection' of their local paramilitary. From 1972 to 1980 the pattern of violence revolved around IRA attacks on security forces, the Protestant community and commercial premises; and unionist attacks on the Catholic community and security repression through internment, torture, and shoot-to-kill attacks on the IRA. These local areas were most affected by political violence and segregation which reinforced local ties and created separate spatial areas for mobilising protest. The important thing to note about these attacks, though, is the 'controlled' level of violence that emerges, especially after 1972. Paramilitary violence was a protest tactic used to gain media coverage, maintain organisational profile and keep enemies on the defensive. At the same time, this also represented army success in containing violence to a few key areas.[22]

In examining local areas, I coded protest events from *The Times* newspaper in the period 1969–93 in order to analyse events at the local level. From this coding, republican paramilitary activity at the level of shooting mostly came from the city of Belfast (528 reported events: 48%), Derry (156: 14%), border areas (131: 12%), rest of the North (219: 20%), and other countries (68: 6%). This overwhelming concentration on the two large cities and the border areas (74%) reflects areas of republican strength; though it must be noted that the attempts to move beyond these areas, especially in mainland Britain, represented an attempt to take the war directly to the enemy. Beyond a few 'spectaculars', like the bombing of the Conservative Party Conference in Brighton, this strategy failed to make use of additional space in Britain or in mainland Europe. Evidence on those killed in Northern Ireland from 1966 to 1999 carried out by McKittrick also demonstrates the localised pattern of violence and paramilitary activity.[23] By 1999, 3636 people had died in the conflict, 1647 (45%) came from Belfast. When McKittrick examined the Belfast figures they found that the figures were geographically concentrated within the city.

> The names of the most violent areas occur again and again in the text of this work: Falls, Andersonstown, Ballymurphy, Whiterock, Woodvale, Shankill, Crumlin, Ardoyne, New Lodge, Tigers Bay, Short Strand, and the Markets and so on. These have been the heartlands of paramilitarism, producing large percentages of the victims as well as large percentages of the prison population.[24]

Poole and Doherty remind us that throughout Northern Ireland: 'the province is subject to tremendous spatial diversity', it is 'an irregular mosaic of radically different places – not just Catholic and Protestant, but with every conceivable level in between'. This level of analysis complicates the issue of simply considering Northern Ireland as a divided society living under divided or contested sovereignty: the issue of locality has a profound effect on the related experience of individual citizens. Poole and Doherty quote Whyte on this issue:

> Areas only a few miles from each other can differ enormously – in religious mix, in economic circumstances, in the level of political violence, in political attitudes. This means that the nature and intensity of the conflict can vary widely. That in turn means that the nature of a settlement likely to bring peace can vary widely too.[25]

The battle for peace

The state utilised a number of strategies to diffuse the strength of local protest, especially after 1994, and out of the dynamics of conflict the state was able to move towards the solution that would satisfy its key adversary. The peace process occurred as a result of a confluence of external factors involving economic transformation, the involvement of the EU, and the end of the Cold War.[26] Economic unity saw the rise of an all Ireland economy operating domestically and internationally. The end of the Cold War allowed the US administration to become involved as an independent actor under no real security constraint in tampering with the 'special relationship' with the UK.[27] The ceasefire by the IRA in 1994 and its final abandonment of armed struggle by October 2005 was a strategic response to this situation. The IRA believed this new situation offered political opportunities for the eventual unity of Ireland and concrete concessions from the British government in the meantime.

The state had to deal with paramilitaries in areas of local conflict. Republican and loyalist prisoners came from local ghettoes and the state assisted negotiators by releasing prisoners thus weakening challenges from potential paramilitary rivals. Local divisions would inevitably centre on the role of the peace process and it was not in the state's interest to see the rise of anti-peace factions. Previous attempts to establish ceasefires had foundered partly due to failure to recognise this factor. This strategy has been used to good effect with the republican movement after 1994 but loyalists continued to exercise sectarian violence in traditional ghettoes in Belfast and new ones in towns like Coleraine. Loyalists feared that the possible end of 'contested sovereignty' would leave them abandoned by the UK. The fact that the UK has stated they were willing to leave the North if called to do so in a referendum is seen as a sign of their minimal commitment to the province in unionist and loyalist opinion.

The state adopted a managerial approach to the problem of contested sovereignty; turning the RUC from a force into a service. It funded local community groups and adopted equality rather than efficiency as the key goal of all government agencies. This has been an uneven process but the processes are always political even when they pretend not to be. The transformation of the state can be seen by comparing political stances in the mid 1980s to the late 1990s. Douglas Hurd, Secretary of State for Northern Ireland (1984–5), instructed civil servants to vet local community groups on the basis of their alleged links to paramilitary organisations. This meant not only were these groups to be denied funding but they had also been singled out by the British government, making these groups, in the view of one community worker who was affected by this, 'legitimate targets for paramilitary attack from the other community'.[28]

But the attitudes of the state changed after the peace process was formally declared. The Good Friday Agreement was preceded by a ceasefire on the part of the IRA since 1994. That initial ceasefire was interrupted for a period of 17 months (from February 1996 to July 1997). Bringing the IRA and its political wing Sinn Féin back to the negotiating table was seen as an important goal for both the British and Irish governments, as they both regarded Sinn Féin support for the Good Friday Agreement as crucial to any long-lasting settlement. When Sinn Féin finally signed the agreement, it was rewarded in a number of ways. Some of these rewards were direct, others indirect, for example, one involved the release of paramilitary prisoners. The effect of this was to help republican political leaders demobilise their armed militants, as well as rendering any attempts to set up breakaway organisations to be largely ineffective.

An indirect reward was the opening up of new funds for community development in nationalist ghettoes. In one way, this was to have the effect of opening up civic culture in areas that lacked resources or opportunities to advance. However, these funds were always tied to the state seeking new forms of legitimation, and the best example of this process was the announcement by the British government that a new college linked to a university was to be opened up in predominantly Catholic West Belfast. This occurred precisely one week after the Good Friday Agreement. The message was that cooperation with government would result in military withdrawal, release of prisoners, and state funding offered as an incentive.

The battle for governance within Northern Ireland was a struggle between the state and the paramilitaries for control of the ghettoes.[29] This battle was fought largely around the security issue but other areas of government were affected. For example, public transport was blocked by rioting in these areas and was replaced by community-based taxis. Punishment shootings by paramilitaries acted as a form of justice for those allegedly guilty of stealing, joyriding, or selling drugs. The state clearly needed to establish links with local community organisations in these areas as these links were seen as the only path to legitimate governance.[30] This process of participatory governance at the local level began in the 1970s but came to fruition in the 1990s. As McCall and Williamson have argued:

> Non-governmental voluntary and community organisations are not component parts of governments, but they are being called upon to play a role in governance, both at the global and the local level. They are most active in developing and transitional societies where government infrastructure is poor.[31]

At the same time, this approach was undertaken in order to reproduce the qualities of uncontested sovereignty through governance, participation, and managerialism. This managerial style has been used to address the sectarian situation in Northern Ireland and a good example of this is the 2002–3 report by Hugh Orde, the Chief Constable of the Police Service of Northern Ireland. In this report, he talked of the continuing formation of an 'inclusive police service', the creation of a 'local policing', and, where local services are allowed to work, linking up 'with their local communities.'[32] The police were clearly following the strategy of 'ordered disorder', with community consultation defined not just in terms of 'the security issue' (i.e. contestation over sovereignty) but in criminal matters more broadly.

At the same time, the European Union provided a mechanism to reinforce local cultural identity but establish cross-community ties through funding and institutional mechanisms. The EU's process of transition provides a model that is being copied in Northern Ireland. The European Economic Community preceded the European Union with the goal of developing a European form of state. The EU, created in the Maastricht Treaty of 1992, united on issues other than economics. Northern Ireland is being pushed through a similar process. It is moving from being an economic community to its own form of political union. This involves provincial representation with Britain as ultimate sovereign, Southern Ireland as potential sovereign and the EU as regional entity. This multi-layered state is pushing civil society away from sectarian locales to community groups seeking rewards and identifying with Northern Ireland as a province. This is seen as the first step in producing European unionists who are content with Northern Ireland's evolving role rather than Ulster unionists or those who seek unity within Ireland.

Comparison with Israel

Loyalists are still aggrieved by the peace process and identify with victims of terrorism elsewhere. Israeli flags now fly over loyalist areas symbolically calling for an Israeli solution to IRA terrorism. Palestinian flags are hoisted alongside the Irish Tricolours in nationalist areas symbolically uniting the struggles for Palestinian and Irish unity. But IRA terrorism is over and Sinn Féin no longer demands Irish unity. Loyalist representatives sit alongside Sinn Féin in the Northern Irish government. Thus the contrast between these symbolic gestures and reality is stark.

The very term Israel/Palestine reflects the contested nature of sovereignty within this area. The state of Israel is defined as a Jewish state while the West Bank does not 'have any formal sovereign status': it is a territory 'whose jurisdiction is yet to be decided.'[33] The two-state solution to the Israeli problem has not been realised given the ambiguous stance of the Israeli state to Palestine and the position of the Palestinian Authority. Israel keeps a close eye on Palestinian cities and villages, it controls movement of people through checkpoints, punishes militants with destruction of homes, and has constructed a security wall.

The argument here is that the main obstacle to commitment of these parties to the peace process lies in ethnic-national areas subject to both the control of the Israeli and settler communities. The spatial confrontations in these areas see ethnic identity merge with protest and ethnic violence is the result. Israel seeks to remove settlers from certain areas controlled by the Palestinian Authority but at the same time reserves the right to invade this territory. In the meantime, some Palestinian militants wage a campaign of terror both within Palestine and the State of Israel, thereby encouraging Israeli hard liners. This leaves Israelis stuck between military responses to protest combined with segregation shifting back and forth along dynamics to a possible solution. The Israelis and Palestinians are also engaged in a peace process watched over by the Middle East Quartet and Palestinian movements – Hamas and the Palestine Liberation Organization (PLO). Hamas and the PLO have become political parties and are dealing with the internal dilemma of being movements organising protests in local areas, or parties administering government more broadly.

During the first Intifada (1987–91) local Palestinian residents in the Gaza Strip, West Bank, and even in the State of Israel adopted new protest tactics. They threw stones, blocked roads and took part in a general strike in Israel. In the Occupied Territories, the Israeli Defence Force responded with bullets, in Israel there was the threat of martial law.[34] In many ways, this parallels the response of the RUC to the civil rights protest in Northern Ireland, and Palestinians won international support for their cause. Israel and the PLO negotiated the Oslo Declaration of Principles in 1993 and the Oslo Interim Agreement in 1995. Infighting emerged in the Palestinian community between pro- and anti-peace process factions with attempts to disrupt any settlement by directly attacking the State of Israel, provoking inevitable military retaliation. The division of the Occupied Territories into areas of control – A (Palestinian control), B (joint Israeli/Palestinian control), and C (Israeli control) – helped exacerbate factional struggle. The isolation and containment of Palestinians living in Israel has contributed to ethnic oppression and violence.[35]

The images of mapping (The Road Map to Peace), mental mapping,[36] walls (Klein 2005),[37] fences,[38] and barriers[39] are second nature to academics and commentators on this case. Therefore, there are a number of studies in the literature of the ethno-spatial pattern within Israel and Palestine. For example, Haim Yacobi undertook a study of Lod and makes this important theoretical point:

> I propose that the spatial organization of the city is not an organic or natural process reflecting economic issues. Rather it is integrated into unequal urban niches that spatially express power relations. These segregated battlefields are the locations in which struggles for 'the right to the city' (Lefebvre 1996) take place. Hence understanding the patterns of segregation in housing, social attitudes and everyday life is tightly linked with the analysis of minority–majority power relations.[40]

Lod along with Jaffa, Acre, Shefar'am, and Tel Aviv was one of the areas that saw Israeli Arab rioting during the first Intifada.[41] Again, using spatial imagery, this form of protest activity is referred to as representing the voice of the Arab 'Street'. As Bayet puts it, 'In the Arab World, the street is the physical place where collective dissent is expressed.'[42] We also see the role of the 'Arab Street' in the Occupied Territories resembling that of Northern Ireland's ethnic localities. These areas mimic state activity through public funerals of martyrs; they are protected by various militia and they are surrounded by symbolic walls of national and religious identity.

Jerusalem has been studied closely by Israeli political scientists and geographers. When Alfasi and Fenster compare Jerusalem with Tel Aviv they find that

> Jerusalem's municipality offers a national, homogenous and hegemonic type of citizenship with a high level of exclusion to those who do not belong to this hegemony. Tel Aviv, on the other hand, embodies another type of citizenship, which relates to equality and difference with a broader global orientation.[43]

Lein refers to the Israeli policy of setting a cap on the number of Palestinians in Jerusalem at 30 per cent.[44] Klein examines the contradiction between sovereignty over the city and its uncomfortable demography.[45] He describes how Jewish citizens have

> created their own separate areas, and have built not only protective walls with fences and security guards, walls for protecting particular identity, and symbolic walls such as raising the Israeli flag or giving a Hebrew name not only to their own residential area but to the entire neighbourhood.

Similar patterns have emerged through containment of the Palestinian inhabitants of Jerusalem. Klein states that 'One possibility is the "Belfastization" of the city' with this prospect constituting 'a radicalizing and destabilizing factor.'[46] It has also been demonstrated how state support for 400 Israeli settlers in Hebron disrupted the Oslo Accords, keeping 20,000 Palestinians under Israeli control.[47]

The reaction of the Israeli state to the grievances of localities within Israel and Palestine is to pay little attention, sometimes inflaming these feelings if the state believes they are secondary to its continued survival. Fundamental distrust over the character of the peace process and the harassment of the Palestinian population enables Palestinian militants to operate with broad popular support. In turn, this has meant that Israeli citizens are less likely to vote for political parties that treat Palestinian terror lightly. Meron Benvenisti wrote in *Hareetz* on 20 April 2006 that 'The public debate on the Israeli-Palestinian conflict focuses on political and security issues and is defined by maps – mainly maps of demography and settlements.'

The difference between the peace process in Northern Ireland and Israel could not be clearer; in Israel, the state is not doing the things that have led to a solution in Northern Ireland. The Israeli state is not developing new forums for participatory democracy, not funding Palestinian community groups, not seeking to reform its security forces, nor is it guaranteeing equality. This may be because the majority of Israelis wants nothing to do with Palestine, are weary of terrorism, and are prepared to move towards a two-state settlement. Paradoxically, this means a partial victory for the Palestinians. Gil Merom writes,

> [t]he Palestinians are all but certain to lose military encounters with Israel, but are nevertheless likely to realize most of their political goals. Specifically they will have an independent Palestinian state. Most Jewish settlements in the territories will be dismantled, and the settlers will be repatriated.[48]

The reason for this outcome is that 'the use of force, including terror, has bought the Palestinians some gains. Brutal force has apparently convinced Israelis to get closer to the Palestinian position, and prefer separation to occupation, even if unilateral'.[49]

The offer of the PLO to its enemy was an 'olive branch or a freedom fighter's gun' from the 1970s. Similarly, the IRA pursued its strategy of using the 'ballot box and the armalite' from the 1980s. The Palestinians have already gained as much as they can from violence – Merom (2003)

suggests it had already 'exceeded its utility'.[50] The same was true for the IRA in the 1980s. The peace process proved to be popular in Northern Ireland over time, with a state ready to give concessions such as releasing political prisoners thus helping to prevent factionalism among Republican ranks. The peace process was unpopular in Israel/Palestine, with an Israeli state not ready to give significant concessions thus heightening factionalism within Palestinian ranks.

Space has been used as a resource by Palestinian militants. Initially attacks were launched from sympathetic countries as the PLO embarked on its long journey from Jordan, Lebanon, Tunis back to the Occupied Territories. Long-distance nationalism has been a feature of Palestinian activity until recently when the Palestinians have won at least a section of their own state. In terms of space as resistance, the Palestinians have utilised peaceful demonstrations, the Intifada and the suicide bomb. Spatial solutions by the state include the decision by the Israelis to seal off the West Bank by constructing a Wall. This is partly a reaction to suicide bombing, in part a desire to redraw territory sealing off both Palestinian and settler alike, as well as dividing the West Bank from the Gaza Strip. Hamas and other factions use the Gaza Strip to launch rockets into Israel but with little effect. The PLO seeks to become more party-like in an area subject to checkpoints and daily harassment. In the absence of strong external pressure this 'solution', though nasty, may be the best that can be hoped for unless internal and external dynamics bring about more favourable political solutions.

Conclusion

Broadly, the underlying premise of this chapter is that the state, as part of a global system of states, is fundamentally at war with civil society in order to maintain power;[51] that civil society produces protesters who will always need 'safe' space for planning;[52] that the boundaries between civil society and the state are monitored and controlled by the state but are always open to recapture.[53] Protest movements survive because disorder or the threat of disorder is still the best weapon for those with grievances against authorities.

Under divided sovereignty, however, protest boundaries reinforce local ethnic boundaries and set in motion a cycle of localised protest and state repression. The framework provided above, examining four spatial manoeuvres by protest, four responses by the state, may help us discern how states and protest movements interact in highly contested local territory. For example, loyalists may use local boundaries to put a strain on a peace process they regard as unfavourable. Loyalists are concerned with Britain's lack of sovereign commitment to Northern Ireland, a gradual takeover by Southern Ireland and discrimination against their communities by the emerging regime established around London, Dublin, and Brussels. Ethnic violence has emerged in loyalist ghettoes, sometimes aimed at nationalists but often directed by opposing factions. The construction of new walls between the two communities since the beginning of the peace process reminds us that ethnic violence in some locales has not disappeared in Northern Ireland.

For Sinn Féin, the struggle over sovereignty is increasingly placed on the back burner; the main struggle is for equality. Therefore, Sinn Féin is the political party equivalent of the civil rights movement. However the need to defend ethnic-national areas from outside attack without using arms could confront Sinn Féin with the dilemma faced by the civil rights movement in August 1969: namely, how can a movement demanding equality avoid being forced into defending local areas? The key difference between then and now may be the extent of nationalists' trust in the Police Service of Northern Ireland to protect their local communities.

The Israeli government has decided unilaterally to construct a separate Palestinian state in the absence of negotiations. As a result, ethnic tensions have increased and there is pressure from the Arab states and the Middle East Quartet to reach joint agreement. In Israel, demographic pressures contribute to the majority population feeling threatened and result in the containment and isolation of Palestinians. This unilateral move by the state of Israel towards a two-state settlement, symbolised by the separation wall, differs from the state's attempt in Northern Ireland to bring the two ethnic-national groups together within a 'post-national' framework. The state in Northern Ireland has sought to disentangle ethnic boundaries from protest boundaries while the state of Israel has not. Within divided sovereignty local areas put forward national demands and potential solutions may or may not be found at different levels of government. The use of local space is integral to understanding how sovereign and popular power operates.

Notes

1. A. Kalyvas, 'Popular Sovereignty, Democracy, and the Constituent Power', *Constellations*, Vol. 12, No. 2, 2005, p. 226.
2. W. H. Sewell, Jr., 'Space in Contentious Politics' in R. R. Aminzade et al. (eds), *Silence and Voice in the Study of Contentious Politics*, Cambridge: Cambridge University Press, 2001, p. 68.

3. E. W. Soja, 'The Spatiality of Social Life' in D. Gregory and J. Urry (eds), *Spatial Relations and Spatial Structures*, London: Macmillan, 1985, p. 115.

4. Sewell 2001.

5. S. Elden, *Understanding Henri Lefebvre*, London: Continuum, 2004.

6. S. Tarrow, *Power in Movement: Social Movements, Collective Action and Politics*, Cambridge: Cambridge University Press, 1994.

7. J. Anderson and L. O'Dowd, 'Borders, Border Regions and Territoriality: Contradictory Meanings, Changing Significance', *Regional Studies*, Vol. 33, No. 7, 1999, pp. 593–604.

8. *Policing Disorder* (2004, 1999), http://www.homeoffice.gov.uk/docs/poldis. html.

9. Jane's Political Review Community, 'Protestors may be Mistaken for Terrorists', *Jane's Information Group*, 26 November 2004.

10. *Policing Disorder* (2004, 1999), http://www.homeoffice.gov.uk/docs/poldis. html.

11. D. Della Porta, Olivier Filleule, and Herbert Reiter, 'Policing Protest in France and Italy: From Intimidation to Cooperation?' in D. S. Meyer and S. Tarrow (eds), *The Social Movement Society*, Lanham, MD: Rowman and Littlefield, 1998.

12. D. Della Porta and M. Diani, *Social Movements*, Oxford: Blackwell, 2006.

13. J. D. Fearon and D. D. Laitin, 'Violence and the Social Construction of Ethnic Identity', *International Organization*, Vol. 54, No. 4, Autumn 2000, pp. 845–77.

14. Sewell 2001.

15. B. Graham and C. Nash, 'A Shared Future: Territoriality, Pluralism and Public Policy in Northern Ireland', *Political Geography*, Vol. 25, No. 3, 2006, pp. 253–78.

16. V. Kolossov, 'Border Studies: Changing Perspectives and Theoretical Approaches', *Geopolitics*, Vol. 10, 2005, pp. 606–32.

17. C. Tilly, *Social Movements, 1768–2004*, Boulder: Paradigm, 2004. Also C. Tilly, *Identities, Boundaries & Social Ties*, Boulder: Paradigm, 2005.

18. M. Farrell, *Northern Ireland: The Orange State*, London: Pluto Press, 1976.

19. P. J. Woodfield, 'Note of a Meeting with Representatives of the Provisional IRA' (21 June 1972), Document Reference PREM15/1009, http://cain.ulst. ac.uk/publicrecords/1972/prem15-1009-1.jpg .

20. A. W. Stephens, Head of Defence Secretariat, 'Operation Folklore' (16 November 1973), http://cain.ulst.ac.uk/publicrecords/1973/fco87_248_ special_1.jpg Document Reference FCO87/248.

21. See documents on this subject in http://cain.ulst.ac.uk/publicrecords/.

22. J. Tonge, *Northern Ireland*, Cambridge: Polity Press, 2006.

23. David McKittrick, Seamus Kelters, Brian Feeney, and Chris Thornton, *Lost Lives: The Stories of the Men, Women and Children Who Died as a Result of the Northern Ireland Troubles*, Edinburgh: Mainstream, 1999.

24. Ibid., p. 1482.

25. P. Doherty and M. A. Poole, 'Religion as an Indicator of Ethnicity in Northern Ireland – An Alternative Perspective', *Irish Geography*, Vol. 35, No. 2, 2002, pp. 75–85.

26. See J. Goodman, *Nationalism and Transnationalism*, Aldershot: Avebury, 1996; J. McGarry, *Northern Ireland and the Divided World: Post-Agreement Northern*

Ireland in Comparative Perspective, Oxford and New York: Oxford University Press, 2001 and W. Crotty and D. E. Schmitt (eds), *Ireland and the Politics of Change*, London and New York: Longman, 1998.

27. A. Guelke, 'The US, Irish Americans and the Northern Ireland Peace Process', *International Affairs*, Vol. 72, No. 3, July 1996, pp. 521–36.

28. D. Maguire, '"Here's a Wee Present for You": The Role of Civic Culture in the Governance of Northern Ireland', *Policy and Society*, Vol. 22, No. 2, 2003, pp. 144–63.

29. R. Rose, *Governing without Consensus: An Irish Perspective*, London: Faber and Faber, 1971.

30. A. Williamson (ed.), *Voluntary Action in Ireland: North and South: The Report of a Research Symposium*, Association for Voluntary Action Research in Ireland, Dublin and Coleraine 1998.

31. C. McCall and A. Williamson, 'Fledgling Social Partnership in the Irish Border Region: European Union "Community Initiatives" and the Voluntary Sector', *Policy and Politics*, Vol. 28, No. 3, 2000, pp. 397–410.

32. Hugh Orde, *Report of the Chief Constable 2002-2003-08-04*, Police Service of Northern Ireland, Belfast 2003.

33. D. Newman, 'From National to Post-National Territorial Identities in Israel–Palestine', *Geojournal*, Vol. 53, 2001, pp. 235–46.

34. I. Asya, 'The Israeli Newspapers' Coverage of Israeli Arabs during the Intifada', *Israel Affairs*, Vol. 9, No. 1, 2003, pp. 185–211.

35. On impact of migration see A. Shachar, 'Reshaping the Map of Israel: A New National Planning Doctrine', *Annals, AAPSS*, No. 555, 1988, pp. 209–18. On the geography of local planning see O. Yiftachel, 'Planning and Social Control: Exploring the Dark Side', *Journal of Planning Literature*, Vol. 12, No. 4, 1998, pp. 395–406.

36. Y. Bar-Gal, 'Boundaries as a Topic in Geographic Education', *Political Geography*, Vol. 12, No. 5, 1993, pp. 421–35.

37. M. Klein, 'Old and New Walls in Jerusalem', *Political Geography*, Vol. 24, 2005, pp. 53–76.

38. J. Williams, 'Territorial Borders, International Ethics and Geography: Do Good Fences Still Make Good Neighbours', *Geopolitics*, Vol. 8, No. 2, 2003, pp. 25–46.

39. Y. Lein, 'Behind the Barrier: Human Rights Violations as a Result of Israel's Separation Barrier', *B'Tselem*, April 2003.

40. H. Yacobi, 'In-Between Surveillance and Spatial Protest: The Production of Space in the "Mixed City" of Lod', *Surveillance and Society*, Vol. 2, No. 1, 2004, p. 61.

41. Asya, 2003, p. 195.

42. A. Bayet, '"The Street" and the Politics of Dissent in the Arab World', *Middle East Report*, Spring, No. 226, 2003, pp. 10–17.

43. N. Alfasi and T. Fenster, 'A Tale of Two Cities: Jerusalem and Tel Aviv in an Age of Globalization', *Cities*, Vol. 22, No. 5, 2005, pp. 351–63.

44. Y. Lein, 'Nu'man, East Jersusalem: Life under the Threat of Expulsion', *B'Tselem*, September 2003.

45. Klein 2005.

46. Ibid., p. 72.

47. D. Newman, 'Creating the Fences of Territorial Separation: The Discourses of Israeli-Palestinian Conflict Resolution', *Geopolitics and International Boundaries*, Vol. 2, No. 2, 1997, pp. 1–35.
48. G. Merom, *How Democracies Lose Small Wars*, Cambridge: Cambridge University Press, 2003, p. 258.
49. Ibid.
50. Ibid.
51. M. Foucault, *Society Must Be Defended*, London: Penguin, 2003.
52. Sewell 2001.
53. Ibid.

13
Consociational Peace Processes and Ethnicity: The implications of the Dayton and Good Friday Agreements for Ethnic Identities and Politics in Bosnia-Herzegovina and Northern Ireland

Rob Aitken

Peace building aims 'to create the conditions necessary for a sustainable peace in war-torn societies'.[1] Sustainable peace requires an end to hostilities, or at least a significant reduction in the level of violence, and the creation of stable political institutions.[2] One approach in attempting to promote stability in post-conflict situations is to 'identify traits by which the population has been divided during the conflict, and make sure each group defined by such traits is proportionally represented in the new state organs. Such variables could be everything from geography to gender to religion'.[3] However, in practice, international actors involved in peace processes have frequently singled out ethnicity as the predominant division in post-conflict societies.[4] In recent peace processes and interventions international actors have adopted this approach thereby conceiving of political legitimacy in terms of ethnically representative government.[5]

Consociational theory has provided the main theoretical framework for recent peace processes based on ethnic representation, although it was not originally developed to address ethnic divisions in post-conflict societies. Consociational theory argues that political stability in divided societies is best achieved through guaranteeing the participation and autonomy of significant groups within society. In order to achieve this it recommends power sharing, especially at the executive level; group autonomy on internal affairs, especially education and culture; proportional representation of some form in elections, and a mutual veto for groups.[6] Proportionality and power sharing provide guarantees of effective representation and participation in decision making to all significant groups. Group autonomy and the mutual veto provide reassurance for groups to participate in deeply divided societies characterized by a lack of trust. From this perspective, consociational democracy is argued to be the only viable form of government for deeply divided societies.[7]

Consociational solutions have been proposed for many recent conflicts including Bosnia-Herzegovina, Northern Ireland, Iraq, Southern Sudan, Cyprus and Macedonia. Many of these peace proposals might be better described as 'consociationalism plus' since consociational power-sharing arrangements have been supplemented by arrangements to accommodate ethno-nationalist demands for territorial autonomy (ethnic federalism), inter-state linkages and institutions, recognition of 'peoplehood' and in some cases the right to secede.[8] These peace agreements have successfully achieved an end to violence in conflicts such as Northern Ireland and Bosnia-Herzegovina. Consociationalists may have a point that the accommodation of some ethno-nationalist demands and the provision of guarantees are necessary to achieve an end to violence.[9]

Critics of consociationalism argue that consociational peace agreements institutionalize ethnicity and freeze ethnic divisions.[10] Consociational institutions, by conceiving of society as composed of discrete cultural groups whose interests are then protected through power sharing, vetoes and segmental autonomy, have the potential to reinforce these groups. In the case of ethnic consociational arrangements the risk is that the representation of society as composed of discrete ethnic groups, and the creation of institutions to protect the rights of these groups, maintains and strengthens those identities and limits the potential for ethnic identities to change in the future or other identities to become more politically salient. In seeking to provide guarantees to ethnic groups, they provide a powerful stimulus to ethnic organizations.[11]

In designing political institutions it is important to assess the impact that the introduction of different forms of democratic institutions is likely to have on the diverse cleavages in a post-conflict society.[12] Consociationalists have generally insisted that ethno-national identities are relatively stable and long lasting, although McGarry and O'Leary accept that ethno-national identities can change after a peace settlement.[13] However, they provide no analysis of how identities change after a peace process.[14] I argue that ethnic identities and the nature of ethnicity change significantly during conflicts. Not only does the salience of ethnicity increase during conflicts,[15] the nature of ethnicity can be transformed. The transformation of ethnicity during conflicts involves processes of boundary (re)definition, the politicization of ethnicity, territorialization of ethnic identities and the encapsulation of social relations within ethnic categories.

The dynamic character of ethnicity during conflicts should be recognized in peace processes. It raises at least the theoretical possibility that the salience and nature of ethnicity might change again once the pressures that produced processes of ethnicization are removed. This stands in contrast to traditional conflict management approaches that assume ethnicity is a relatively fixed political identity, as ethno-nationalists assert, and seek to peacefully manage relations between discrete ethnic groups. If ethnic identities are treated as stable and fixed, then there is a risk that peace processes will reinforce and continue the processes of ethnicization that occurred during the conflict.[16]

In this chapter I analyse the impact that institutions created by consociational peace settlements in Northern Ireland and Bosnia-Herzegovina have had on the transformations of ethnicity that occurred during the conflict to assess whether they reinforce the processes of ethnicization that occurred during the conflict or provide the space for identity change. I argue that the impact of consociational peace settlements is complex. The particular ways in which the peace settlements institutionalize ethnicity in the post-conflict institutions affect the outcomes.

Ethnicity before conflict

Ethnicity does not always take the form of discrete ethnic groups.[17] In Darfur until at least the 1960s and in the Southern Balkans in the late nineteenth century, ethnonyms described socioeconomic positions within a broader cultural system. In both cases the socioeconomic lifestyle defined the ethnic category a person was placed in. However, people could move into ethnic categories from different points of origin.[18] The social and political salience of ethnicity also varied. The ethnonyms now commonly used in Afghanistan were simply categories used by the state and anthropologists but without social meaning to the population; it was only with the war against the Soviets that ethnicization began.[19] In pre-conflict Afghanistan and Iraq identities and political loyalties were based primarily on networks of kinship and patronage, rather than on ethnic categories.[20]

In both Bosnia-Herzegovina and Northern Ireland ethnic categories were important identities institutionalized by state censuses and informal discrimination. However, they did not describe discrete cultural groups. Ethnographic accounts of the district of Ballybeg in the rural West of Northern Ireland in the 1950s and 1960s and the village of Dolina in central Bosnia in the 1980s portray a shared community life within which ethnic categories had social significance but were cross-cut by other identities.[21] Neighbours belonging to different ethnic categories socialized together and shared a common culture and set of values, although in Northern Ireland there was also significant social separation, religious intolerance and in general a Catholic or Protestant view on most issues. In both cases local religious communities formed an important part of social organization and identity but existed within a sense of a common community and culture. Social interactions were shaped by cross-cutting differences between the hill district and lowlands in Ballybeg or neighbourhoods within the village of Dolina as well as by the religious background of people.[22]

In pre-conflict situations ethnicity exists in diverse forms along a continuum between relatively open and fluid ethnic networks within larger cultural systems and the discrete cultural and political groups of ethno-nationalism.

The transformation of ethnicity during conflict

Conflict has the potential to transform ethnicity by raising the salience of ethnicity and reducing the fluidity of ethnic categories and boundaries.[23] Ethnic mobilization and violence sharpen the definition of ethnic boundaries and increase their social and political significance. The increased prominence of ethnicity reduces the sallence of other identities and differences which may have been the basis of social relationships between people in different ethnic categories or of cross-cutting cleavages between people within an ethnic category.[24]

Ethnic boundaries are complex and may be composed of multiple elements.[25] In pre-conflict situations this multiple construction of boundaries allows degrees of ambiguity and fluidity. In Bosnia-Herzegovina for much of the twentieth century a Muslim social or even political identity was not incompatible with a Yugoslav or Croat or Serb national identity.[26] However, during conflicts ethnic boundaries become more sharply defined reducing their fluidity.[27] Violence, propaganda and shifting practices of daily life increasingly conflate religious, cultural and political binary oppositions to form new sharp boundaries between ethnic categories.

Political tensions and ethnically targeted violence lead to increased social separation and avoidance of the ethnic 'other' even if previously friends.[28] Over time these new patterns of ethnicity may be institutionalized in the ethnic organization of diverse areas of social life. Social networks become increasingly encapsulated within ethnic categories and boundaries increasingly rigid. In the process ethnicity is transformed from one identity among many into the primary political identity.

In Bosnia-Herzegovina ethno-nationalist propaganda about the oppression of Christians under Muslim rule and Second World War atrocities emphasized the boundaries between 'Serbs', 'Croats' and 'Muslims', and placed the blame for perceived past wrongs on contemporary ethnic 'others'. Furthermore, the targeting of mosques and cultural buildings during the war destroyed not only physical evidence of Muslim presence in particular localities but also of centuries of shared culture and social life. The targeting of cultural buildings sought to rewrite history and deny that the different ethnic categories had ever lived together peacefully.[29] Not only were boundaries between ethnic categories sharpened during the Bosnian war, the social and religious category of 'Muslim' was transformed into a Bosniac national identity. In the process religious background, cultural identity and political loyalties were conflated. This does not mean that everyone accepts these new more rigid meanings of ethnic categories. There may be tensions between the emerging dominant identity category and individual's experiences and the meanings he or she places on categories.[30]

In Northern Ireland celebrations of community and tradition, as well as daily practices, emphasized boundaries between nationalists and unionists. Marches and murals reinforced the conflation of Catholic with nationalist and Protestant with unionist. The iconography used imposed particular histories, for instance of the Easter Uprising and the Battle of the Somme emphasizing Catholic-nationalist and Protestant-unionist identities respectively.[31] The effect of these material displays was to reinforce and maintain the ethnic boundary and deny legitimacy to histories and events that blurred this boundary, for instance, the history of Catholics who fought for the British Army in the First World War.

While ethnic mobilization and propaganda strengthens and sharpens the definition of ethnic boundaries it is not clear that by itself it necessarily leads to ethnic polarization and conflict. Widespread ethnic toleration and cooperation continued in Yugoslavia through the 1980s and into the 1990s despite increasingly virulent nationalist propaganda.[32] In cosmopolitan Sarajevo there was initially a strong resistance to the new nationalist discourses and defence of a multinational Bosnia-Herzegovina. However, violence gradually forced people to accept the logic that members of other groups posed a security threat and their own security depended on solidarity with the national group.[33]

The threat or reality of violence also transforms ethnicity through a territorialization of ethnic identities. Ethno-nationalist sentiments may lead to a shift in perceptions of space as particular neighbourhoods, localities and territories are defined as 'belonging' to a group, thereby constructing previous neighbours as 'strangers' and 'intruders' on their territory.[34] These claims may be enforced through genocide and ethnic cleansing of localities and territories as occurred in Bosnia-Herzegovina. Ethnic 'others' (and also moderate members of the dominant group) fled when ethno-nationalist militias and gangs seized power locally.[35] Ethnically targeted violence was used to systematically 'cleanse' claimed territories of ethnic 'others'. Visible symbols of the historic presence of other groups, such as religious buildings, have been targeted in conflicts.[36]

Changed perceptions of space may also lead to voluntary movements to areas of perceived greater security. The net effect is a greater segregation of ethnic categories and a strengthening of the association of localities and territories with particular ethnicities. This may result in broad ethnic territories, as was the result of ethnic cleansing in much of Bosnia-Herzegovina, but in other contexts results in a mosaic of local ethnic control and confrontation. Belfast, Sarajevo and Baghdad have all remained multi-ethnic during conflicts but local areas have been increasingly defined in ethnic terms as the degree of segregation increases.

In these contexts, territoriality and local conflicts over space became central to the reproduction of ethnicity and of sharp distinctions between ethnic categories. Claims to an area and exclusion of others reinforce ethnic identity and the distinction from other groups. Defence of a claimed area against perceived encroachment or a threat to the ethnic group's control of it reinforces the importance of the identity to members of the group resident in the area. Interface confrontations strengthened identities and perceptions of the threat of the other. Peace walls in Belfast, set up to prevent interface confrontations, created clear boundaries between ethnic territories in the most polarized areas and limited people's sense of space and movement. The prominent use of ethnic symbols, such as flags, banners and murals in Northern Ireland served not only to mark the territory as 'belonging' to a group but also to enforce a particular meaning of the ethnic identity.[37] This territorialization of identities means that the significance and experience of identities varies greatly by context. Ethnicity is different in highly segregated and politicized localities, such as around the peace walls in Belfast, and in more mixed areas of Northern Ireland.

Consociationalism and peace agreements

Consociational approaches to peacemaking offer ethno-nationalist leaders guarantees in the form of a share of power, cultural autonomy and veto rights. These rather static guarantees may be necessary to achieve a negotiated end to violence in an ethnicized conflict.[38] However, by accommodating ethno-nationalist groups as they exist at the end of the conflict, consociational agreements risk perpetuating the transformations of ethnicity that occurred during the conflict.

The Dayton Peace Agreement and the Good Friday Agreement both include the main characteristics of consociationalism: power-sharing executives, veto rights, proportionality and segmental autonomy.[39] Although the details of the institutions created and the ways in which they institutionalize ethnicity differ in the two cases, both peace settlements institutionalized ethnicity in the post-conflict institutions. The political system designed at Dayton was based on the representation of three groups recognized as the 'constituent peoples' of Bosnia-Herzegovina: Bosniacs, Serbs and Croats.[40] The three-person Presidency consists of a Bosniac and a Croat elected from the Federation and a Serb from the Republika Srpska.[41] The House of Peoples consists of 15 delegates 'two-thirds from the Federation (including five Croats and five Bosniacs) and one-third from the Republika Srpska (five Serbs).'[42] A majority of delegates from any constituent people have a veto over parliamentary decisions. The other chamber, the House of Representatives, is directly elected two-thirds from the territory of the Federation and one-third from the territory of the Republika Srpska.

The constitution of Bosnia-Herzegovina written at Dayton thus viewed the two entities within the state as representing Croats and Bosniacs (the Federation) and Serbs (the Republika Srpska). The entities also conceived of themselves in ethnic terms as the territories of particular ethnic groups. The constitution of the Federation enumerated only Bosniacs and Croats as constituent peoples, and that of the Republika Srpska spoke of the 'untransferable right of the Serb people to self-determination.'[43] However, in July 2000 the Constitutional Court ruled these provisions of the entities' constitutions illegal because they privileged some of the constituent peoples.[44] Negotiations to address this problem produced new constitutions that further institutionalized ethnicity in ethnic quotas at the entity level.[45]

Attempts by the international community to promote a move away from ethnic principles have been resisted by the main Bosnian political parties. The international community and European institutions have pressed for reforms to produce a more integrated and efficient state. In response to this the political parties in Bosnia-Herzegovina agreed on a constitutional reform in 2006. However, the agreement they reached maintained the ethnic principle of representation in government in Bosnia-Herzegovina.[46] The proposed amendments were defeated when some of the pro-reform politicians voted against them for not being integrationist enough.[47] In 2008 the Council of Europe again expressed its concern about the ethnic principles enshrined in the Bosnian constitution.

> The entity voting system in the House of Representatives and the excessively broad scope of the 'vital national interests' clause, together with the related veto mechanism in the House of Peoples, must be reformed for Bosnia and Herzegovina to become a genuine civic state for all those living in it. Members of Parliament should act as free and democratically elected representatives of all the citizens of Bosnia and Herzegovina and not as defenders of purely ethnic interests. The so-called 'Others' should be given an effective oppor- tunity to participate fully in political life, by running in the election for members of the presidency and participating in the designation of delegates to the House of Peoples.[48]

However, so far there has not been any reform to the provisions for ethnic representation and vetoes in the Bosnian constitution.

In contrast to the ethnic principles of power sharing enshrined in the Dayton Peace Accord, the Good Friday Agreement was based on power sharing between parties and not ethnic groups.[49] The 108-seat Assembly is elected by single transferable vote in 18 multi-member constituencies. Seats in the power-sharing executive and chairs of Assembly committees are allocated to parties by the d'Hondt formula based on the number of seats they hold in the Assembly. These features of the Good Friday Agreement are not based on ethnic principles, in that there is a single electoral roll and the allocation of portfolios in the executive and chairs of committees is based on party strength not ethnic identity.[50]

However, the Good Friday Agreement does enshrine ethnic princi- ples in its provisions for ethnic vetoes and its conception of Northern Ireland as composed of two communities. Members of the Legislative Assembly (MLAs) are required to declare themselves to belong to 'unionist', nationalist' or 'other' designations. Normal legislation is passed by a simple majority; however, key decisions require 'cross-community' support from both unionists and nationalists.[51] The Good Friday Agreement provided for the election of a First Minister and Deputy First Minister as a single slate by 'parallel consent', which requires a majority of both 'unionists' and 'nationalists.'[52] This rule ensured that the First

Minister and Deputy First Minister are from different 'communities' without formally requiring it. However, after talks to pave the way for the return to devolved government in 2007 the mechanism for the election of the First and Deputy First Ministers was reformed in the St Andrew's Agreement in a way that enshrined the ethnic principle but removed the requirement for 'parallel consent.'[53]

Despite the differences between the Dayton Peace Agreement and the Good Friday Agreement, both peace agreements institutionalized ethnicity through their representation of society as composed of discrete cultural communities who need to be represented and protected by vetoes. The evidence from Bosnia, and to a lesser extent Northern Ireland, is that politicians elected on the basis of ethnic representation are resistant to any future moves away from the ethnic principle. These peace processes based on consociational principles have institutionalized ethnicity and maintained patterns of ethnic politics in post-conflict situations.

Party politics and electoral engineering

In the uncertainty of immediate post-conflict context, elections risk legitimizing and confirming the power of ethno-nationalist parties, which present themselves as ethnic defenders and appeal to ethnic solidarity.[54] Electoral competition in highly ethnicized post-conflict situations takes two forms. On the one hand, there is inter-ethnic competition for control of governments and territories, and on the other there is intra-ethnic competition between parties within ethnic blocs for the greatest share of the votes of the ethnic bloc.

In Bosnia-Herzegovina war and ethnic cleansing had left ethno-nationalists in control of large swathes of territory. These areas had been largely ethnically cleansed to produce relatively homogenous ethnic territories. Initial elections were held in 1996 when ethno-nationalist militias were still in effective control of many parts of the country. The General Framework Agreement signed at Dayton contained provisions designed to undo the effects of ethnic cleansing and undermine the territorial control of ethno-nationalist parties. The right of refugees to return to their original domicile was included in the Framework Agreement.[55] Refugees and internally displaced persons (IDPs) were expected to vote in the municipality where they had been resident in 1991.[56] Elections might therefore have been expected to return to power the groups who had constituted majorities in municipalities before the conflict and help to undo ethnic cleansing.

The Framework Agreement, however, also allowed a citizen to 'apply ... to cast his or her ballot elsewhere'.[57] The main Croat and Serb ethno-nationalist parties (the HDZ and SDS respectively) used this provision as a tool to consolidate and legitimate the effects of ethnic cleansing. Displaced Croats and Serbs were pressured or forced to vote in municipalities where the HDZ and SDS respectively needed votes to consolidate their hold on power.[58] Control on the ground during the elections of 1996 remained for the most part in the hands of ethno-nationalist parties and their militias. The international peacekeeping force, IFOR, secured the boundary line between the two entities but did not provide security for refugees and internally displaced persons attempting to return home. Nationalist militias and mobs discouraged returnees with threats, violence and the destruction of houses.[59] The elections of 1996 were thus fought between the main ethno-nationalist parties to consolidate their control of territory. They functioned as an ethnic census vote that reinforced the changed demography after three years of war and ethnic cleansing. The elections entrenched and consolidated the power of the ethno-nationalist parties that had fought the war in Bosnia-Herzegovina. War leaders were legitimized as elected politicians, while the election of their supporters to power at the canton and municipal level consolidated their control on the ground. The effect of the confederal, consociational agreement reached at Dayton was at least initially to cement ethnic divisions and entrench ethnic politics in Bosnia-Herzegovina.[60] The ethnicization of Bosnia enshrined in the consociational and ethnic federal principles of Dayton has proved hard to undo despite an intensive international reconstruction programme.

Dominant ethno-nationalist parties were able to create fiefdoms in which they have significant control over ethnic populations. Once in control of municipalities and cantons as elected politicians, ethno-nationalist parties were able to use their access to state resources, and particularly jobs, to consolidate their power and control local populations. Access to state resources, and sometimes the vote, was conditioned on political support.[61] Without the support of the main parties people often lacked access to jobs and benefits since the war had allowed the ethno-nationalist parties to seize control of utilities, transport networks and industries in their territories.[62] Ethno-nationalists could also play on perceptions of threats to 'their' territory brought about by the return of refugees or international community's desire for a more integrated state to call for ethnic solidarity. The parties that had fought the war could also use this call for ethnic solidarity in their competition with other parties within their ethnic bloc.

In Northern Ireland election results are always analysed in terms of the shifts in numbers between the ethnic groups and the post-Agreement elections were a census vote in the sense that the vast majority of people voted within their ethnic bloc. However, unlike in Bosnia-Herzegovina there was no major threat to ethno-nationalist parties' control of territory or politics as the main parties were guaranteed seats in the power-sharing executive. Instead, the 1998 and 2003 elections were dominated by political competition within ethnic blocs. The struggle between pro- and anti-agreement unionists was the most important as this would determine the ability of the Assembly to elect a power-sharing executive. However, on the other side the SDLP and Sinn Fein competed to see who could gain most credit and reward for achieving the Good Friday Agreement. The non-sectarian parties saw their share of the vote drop.

In Bosnia-Herzegovina, although the 1996 elections involved contests between the wartime ethno-nationalist parties for control of territory, they were also fought to consolidate their control over their own group. Rivals from within their own ethnic group needed to be seen off to consolidate their own power. In addition the contradictory nature of the Dayton Peace Agreement meant that if non-nationalist parties won a more integrated state was possible and the ethno-nationalists could lose their gains in terms of ethnic territories. Since the late 1990s the main political competition in Bosnia Herzegovina has been between the ethno-nationalist parties that fought the war on the one hand and their ethnic rivals, often implicitly backed by the international community.

Attempts by the international community to promote multi-ethnic and non-nationalist parties in Bosnia-Herzegovina have had limited effect. Electoral rules and procedures were changed by the international community for each of the frequent elections in Bosnia-Herzegovina between 1996 and 2002 in attempts to promote the formation of moderate multi-ethnic or non-nationalist coalitions. This included the introduction of a preferential system for the election of the president of the Republika Srpska and changes to the indirect election of the Federation's House of People to allow all electors to vote for all delegates not just those from their ethnic group.[63] International actors brokered the formation of a ten-party reformist coalition in the aftermath of the November 2000 elections, which saw the wartime parties excluded from control of the federal and Federation governments.[64] Furthermore, some nationalist politicians were removed from office and banned from contesting again, including most notably the leader of the HDZ and Croat member of the Presidency, who was replaced in the Presidency by a Croat member of a multi-ethnic party. However, the 2002 elections saw a return to power of wartime parties. The SDS and HDZ in particular used a language of defence of ethnic interests. This ethnic outflanking of their more moderate competition was successful in 2002 though in the 2006 elections the wartime parties lost the elections. However, voting has remained largely within ethnic blocs.

Patterns of competition within ethnic blocs have maintained the salience of ethnicity as parties appeal to ethnic defence in their competition with rivals within their ethnic bloc. In both Bosnia-Herzegovina and Northern Ireland even the more moderate parties draw their support predominantly from one group and have to represent the interests of that group. They always face the risk of ethnic outbidding by the parties claiming to be more effective ethnic defenders.[65] Voters in Northern Ireland have shifted towards the parties seen as the more effective ethnic defenders: the Democratic Unionists and Sinn Féin. This has not precluded the possibility of compromise and co-operation as these parties have moderated their policies and become increasingly pragmatic over resource allocation while maintaining a strong position as ethnic defenders maximizing the ethnic group's share of resources.[66] However, while this may allow pragmatic co-operation between the more extreme ethnic parties, it reinforces the ethnic nature of the political system. Voting in Northern Ireland, as Mitchell, Evans and O'Leary argue, is increasingly based on 'who best stands up for us', who is most effective in representing the community's ethno-nationalist interests.[67] This pattern of 'ethnic tribune party' politics reinforces the view of Northern Ireland as two communities and politics as being the defence of ethnic interests. While Mitchell, Evans and O'Leary demonstrate that ethnic outflanking is not inevitable and moderation is possible, they also provide evidence that consociational agreements contribute to the ethnicization of politics.

Elections continue to be dominated by ethno-nationalist parties. In Northern Ireland the Democratic Unionist Party and Sinn Féin now dominate in their respective ethnic blocs. The four main unionist and nationalist parties took over 88 per cent of the vote in the Assembly elections in 2003. At the same time the non-ethnic parties have seen their share of the vote fall. The Alliance Party, which has traditionally maintained a 'one community' view, has seen many of its supporters align themselves with an ethnic bloc.[68] In Bosnia-Herzegovina the 2006 elections did see the wartime parties lose their hold on the presidency as for the first time all three seats were won by their rivals. However, the parties that replaced them, although more moderate and reformist in outlook, still draw their support predominantly from one ethnic group.

The political system remains one of competition within ethnic blocs although the more moderate parties have made considerable gains.

Elections in post-conflict Bosnia-Herzegovina and Northern Ireland have involved two forms of ethnic competition. First, elections involve a 'census vote' in that people are expected to, and overwhelmingly do, vote for parties representing 'their' ethnic group. Election results are interpreted in terms of the relative strength of the various ethnic groups. Second, given that people are not expected to vote across the ethnic lines, electoral competition is fiercest within ethnic blocs. Post-agreement elections involved intra-bloc competition between ethnic parties for the votes of members of their group. Institutional rewards and external interventions and threatened sanctions have not produced a reduction in ethnic politics. However, they have produced a moderation of parties or a move towards more moderate parties within an ethnic bloc.

Residential segregation and reintegration

In Bosnia-Herzegovina deliberate ethnic cleansing produced a radical transformation of settlement patterns. In Northern Ireland fear of violence, but more significantly voluntary movement due to changing perceptions of territory, led to a gradual movement out of mixed areas. In segregated areas the sense of territory combined with fear restricts the mobility of people.[69] This spatial segregation in Belfast remains unchallenged despite the peace settlement.[70] People are not yet moving into the other group's territory. While new integrated housing developments are planned there has not yet been a significant reintegration of residential patterns.

There has been considerable success in facilitating the return of refugees and displaced persons in Bosnia-Herzegovina. During the Bosnian conflict more than half of the pre-war population of 4.4 million was displaced. About half of these were displaced within Bosnia-Herzegovina, while the other half became refugees in neighbouring states or further afield.[71] By September 2004 the UNHCR had documented the return of more than one million refugees and displaced persons.[72] However, as a policy to reverse ethnic cleansing the results of the returns policy were limited in the initial years after Dayton. Most returnees in the period from 1996 to 1998 were refugees returning under voluntary repatriation schemes. The vast majority of these returned to areas where they felt secure, that is, part of an ethnic majority, and in the terms the international community applied to Bosnia, they were 'majority returnees'.

In the early years the international community did attempt to promote 'minority returns'; however, this met with limited success in the face of obstruction from ethno-nationalist politicians in control on the ground.

The main international agencies involved, the Peace Implementation Council, the Office of the High Representative and the UNHCR, responded to the obstructionism of ethno-nationalist parties by prioritizing 'minority' returns. This priority translated in 1998 into an agenda to 're-mix' Bosnia's separated ethnic groups by promoting domicile return over relocation as a permanent solution to the problem of displacement.[73] The number of minority returns increased significantly from 1997 onwards and peaked in the period 2000–2 before coming to a gradual end.[74] In the latest figures available (March 2009) over 467,000 'minority' returnees had gone back to their original domiciles.[75] However, only in relatively few cases did these returns change the demographic balance of the municipalities. Even where returns constituted a significant proportion of the pre-war population of that group in the municipality, resettled members of the new majority population in the area counterbalanced them.[76]

Minority returns have constituted a fifth of the population displaced during the conflict, while about half of all displaced persons have returned to their original homes as 'majority' or 'minority' returns. Economic and demographic factors as well as political ones have limited the number of returns. Young displaced Bosnians have been reluctant to return to rural areas, where there were frequently few economic opportunities, preferring to remain in the urban areas where they had taken refuge during the conflict.[77] Nevertheless the extent of the success of the 'minority returns' policy disproves sceptics such as Cox who doubted the ability of the international community to create a momentum behind minority returns.[78]

Although significant numbers of their displaced people have returned that does not necessarily reproduce old patterns of social integration. The continued high level of ethnicization in Bosnia-Herzegovina means that social reintegration is not an easy process. In some areas, the returns process has effectively produced new enclaves within, but separate from, the dominant population. For instance, in the Prijedor region in the Republika Srpska minority returnees, in this case Bosniacs, have a parallel existence to their Serb neighbours and continue to use social services in the Federation rather than ones they perceive to be 'Serbian'.[79]

The returns process in Bosnia-Herzegovina has been successful in reducing the dominance of a single group over large areas. It has at the very least succeeded in creating new minority enclaves in areas dominated by one group and increasing the proportion of minority populations. However, it has not produced a return to the pre-conflict demographic or political geography. Nevertheless it has produced a more complex pattern of coexistence than existed after the attempts by ethno-nationalists during the conflict to produce homogenous ethnic homelands. On the positive side more regular interaction and participation in local government together may produce a gradual process of integration. However, the institutionalization of ethnic politics limits the possibilities for a de-ethnicization of politics in Bosnia-Herzegovina. Furthermore, in the context of continued uncertainty about the political future and limited economic opportunities many people have sought security through voting for ethnic parties.

The territorialization of ethnic identities in conflicts provides a further obstacle to the reduction of the salience of ethnicity after a conflict. Not only are populations increasingly segregated reducing the possibilities of normal social interactions between them but neighbourhoods, towns and regions are frequently seen as ethnic territory. The returns policy in Bosnia limited the ethnic homogeneity of large territorial areas including the entities, cantons and municipalities, but did not recreate the integrated communities that had existed before the war. In segregated areas of Northern Ireland spatial segregation and senses of ethnic territories have yet to be challenged.[80]

Conclusions

In this chapter I have argued that ethnic identities should be understood as dynamic identities whose salience, meaning and nature can be transformed. During conflicts the salience of ethnicity often increases as mobilization on ethnic lines ethnicizes the conflict. Ethnicization in conflicts involves boundary making, ethnic polarization, increased encapsulation and the territorialization of ethnic identities. Ethnic boundaries are increasingly sharply defined as the language of ethnic mobilization in conflict uses history and myth to stress the differences between ethnic categories. Ethnically targeted violence leads many people to accept that their own security depends on solidarity with an ethno-nationalist group. An ethnicized conflict produces a polarization between ethnic categories represented by ethno-nationalists as distinct cultural groups unable to live together in peace, although people have been living together peacefully before the conflict. Social networks become increasingly encapsulated within ethnic boundaries. Increased segregation of populations and the territorialization of ethnicity contribute to the reproduction of ethnic identities. Ethno-nationalist understandings of ethnic categories as distinct 'peoples', rather than categories within a larger society, become increasingly dominant.

Consociational approaches to peace making can achieve peace in the short term by accommodating some of the demands of ethno-nationalists. However, the introduction of institutions to represent ethno-national groups risks perpetuating the ethnic boundaries and transformations of ethnicity produced during the conflict. From a dynamic perspective on identity, the best argument for consociational peace settlements is that the identity shifts they provoke will outweigh the degree to which the institutionalization of ethnicity will reproduce the ethnic identities and transformed ethnicity resulting from the conflict.[81] Analysis of the impact of the peace settlement in Bosnia-Herzegovina and Northern Ireland produces a complex picture of change but also the reinforcement of ethnic boundaries and politics. The dominant ethnic boundaries between unionists and nationalists, and between Serbs, Croats and Bosniacs, have been perpetuated and possibly reinforced. However, the maintenance of the ethnic boundary does not mean that ethnic identities are unchanged since the meaning of these identities can shift, albeit in complex and contradictory ways.[82]

The comparison of the impact of the Dayton Peace Agreement in Bosnia-Herzegovina and the Good Friday Agreement in Northern Ireland brings out the ways in which the details of the institutions created in consociational settlements affect the processes of identity change after the peace settlement. The Dayton Peace Agreement is based on ethnic power sharing, quotas and vetoes for the 'constituent peoples' of Bosnia-Herzegovina. These explicit quotas limit the flexibility of the system in response to political or demographic change. In contrast the Good Friday Agreement mandates power sharing between parties, but there are no requirements for quotas from different ethnic groups in parliament or the government. The greater flexibility in the Good Friday Agreement is important since once ethnic principles are embedded in consociational institutions they are difficult to reform. Despite pressure from the European Union and the Council of Europe, and the incentive of possible membership of the European Union and NATO, there has so far been no significant progress on constitutional reform in Bosnia-Herzegovina.[83]

The consociational approach to peace building can achieve an end to violence in ethnicized conflicts. However, peacemakers need to consider the processes of transformation of ethnicity that take place during a conflict and how any peace settlement will affect the dynamics of ethnicity after the peace. The end to violence may facilitate a gradual reintegration of society and reduction of the extent to which ethnicity dominates political identities and encapsulates social networks. However, the institutionalization of ethnic representation in a peace agreement may limit the potential of this peace dividend. The exact nature of the institutions created by consociational peace settlements affects the potential for further ethnicization or de-ethnicization in post-conflict situations.

Notes

1. Kofi Annan (1999) 'Report of the Secretary-General on the work of the Organization', http://www.un.org/Docs/SG/Report99/postconf.htm, United Nations General Assembly Official Records, Fifty-fourth session, Supplement 1 (A/54/1), paragraph 101, last accessed on 3 February 2007.
2. Chetan Kumar, 'Conclusion' in Elizabeth M. Cousens, Chetan Kumar and Karin Wermester (eds), *Peacebuilding as Politics Cultivating Peace in Fragile Societies*, Boulder, CO: Lynne Rienner Publishers, 2001, pp. 183–4.
3. Sven Gunnar Simonsen, 'Ethnicising Afghanistan?: Inclusion and Exclusion in Post-Bonn Institution Building', *Third World Quarterly*, Vol. 25, No. 4, 2004, pp. 711–12.
4. Simonsen 2004, p. 712. The most obvious, and least appropriate, cases of this ethnic representation were the appointment of interim governments in Afghanistan and Iraq based on the supposed ethnic demography of the countries, see Adeed Dawisha, 'The Prospects for Democracy in Iraq: Challenges and Opportunities', *Third World Quarterly*, Vol. 26, No. 4–5, 2005, pp. 727–8; Simonsen 2004, pp. 711–12.
5. Olivier Roy, 'Development and Political Legitimacy: The Cases of Iraq and Afghanistan', *Conflict, Security and Development*, Vol. 4, No. 2, 2004, pp. 167–9.
6. Arend Lijphart, 'The Wave of Power-Sharing Democracy' in Andrew Reynolds (ed.) *The Architecture of Democracy*, Oxford: Oxford University Press, 2002, pp. 38–9.
7. Ibid., p. 37.
8. John McGarry and Brendan O'Leary, 'Consociational Theory and Peace Agreement in Pluri-National Places: Northern Ireland and Other Cases' in Guy Ben-Porat (ed.), *The Failure of the Middle East Peace Process? A Comparative Analysis of Peace Implementation in Israel/Palestine, Northern Ireland and South Africa*, Basingstoke and New York: Palgrave Macmillan, 2008, pp. 84–6.
9. James Anderson, 'Partition, Consociation, Border-Crossing: Some Lessons from the National Conflict in Ireland/Northern Ireland', *Nations and Nationalism*, Vol. 14, No. 1, 2008, p. 98.
10. Rob Aitken, 'Cementing Divisions? An Assessment of the Impacts of International Interventions and Peace-Building Policies on Ethnic Identities and Divisions', *Policy Studies*, Vol. 28, No. 3, 2007, pp. 247–67; Donald L. Horowitz, 'The Northern Ireland Agreement: Clear, Consociational and Risky' in John McGarry (ed.) *Northern Ireland and a Divided World*, Oxford:

Oxford University Press, 2001, pp. 89–108; Benjamin Reilly, *Democracy in Divided Societies: Electoral Engineering for Conflict Management*, Cambridge: Cambridge University Press, 2001; Rupert Taylor, 'The Belfast Agreement and the Politics of Consociationalism: A Critique', *The Political Quarterly*, Vol. 77, No. 2, 2006, pp. 217–26; Robin Wilson, 'The Politics of Contemporary Ethno-Nationalist Conflicts', *Nations and Nationalism*, Vol. 7, No. 3, 2001, pp. 365–84.

11. Arend Lijphart, *Democracy in Plural Societies: A Comparative Exploration*, New Haven and London: Yale University Press, 1977, p. 41.

12. Timothy D. Sisk, 'Conclusions and Recommendations' in Timothy D. Sisk and Andrew Reynolds (eds), *Elections and Conflict Management in Africa*, Washington, DC: United States Institute of Peace Press, 1998, p. 160.

13. McGarry and O'Leary 2008, p. 88.

14. There are theories of processes of identity change in settlement processes by non-consociationalists, notably Jennifer Todd. Todd focuses on identity shift from individuals' responses to dissonance between the new post-settlement social order and established collective identities, as well as within the 'identity packages' that compose collective identities. Todd's analysis focuses on shifts in the meanings of ethnic boundaries and categories. However, in this chapter I argue that conflicts (and settlement processes) not only have impacts on boundary definition but also transform the nature of ethnicity. See Todd, this volume; Jennifer Todd, 'Social Transformation, Collective Categories, and Identity Change', *Theory and Society*, Vol. 34, No. 4, 2005, pp. 429–63; Jennifer Todd, 'Identity Shift in Settlement Processes: The Northern Ireland Case' in Guy Ben-Porat (ed.) *The Failure of the Middle East Peace Process?* 2008, pp. 195–216.

15. Sven Gunnar Simonsen, 'Addressing Ethnic Divisions in Post-Conflict Institution-Building: Lessons from Recent Cases', *Security Dialogue*, Vol. 36, No. 3, 2005, pp. 297–318.

16. Aitken 2007.

17. Rogers Brubaker, 'Ethnicity without Groups', *Archives Europeennes De Sociologie*, Vol. 43, No. 2, 2002, pp. 163–89; Andreas Wimmer, 'The Making and Unmaking of Ethnic Boundaries: A Multilevel Process Theory', *American Journal of Sociology*, Vol. 113, No. 4, 2008, pp. 981–2.

18. Gunnar Haaland, 'Economic Determinants in Ethnic Processes' in Fredrik Barth (ed.) *Ethnic Groups and Boundaries: The Social Organization of Culture Difference*, London: Allen and Unwin, 1969, p. 70; Laurie Kain Hart, 'Culture, Civilization and Demarcation at the Northwest Borders of Greece', *American Ethnologist*, Vol. 26, No. 1, 1999, p. 201.

19. Olivier Roy, *Afghanistan: From Holy War to Civil War*, Princeton, NJ: The Darwin Press, Inc., 1995, pp. 23–4, pp. 105–7.

20. Amatzia Baram, 'Neo-Tribalism in Iraq: Saddam Hussein's Tribal Policies 1991–96', *International Journal of Middle East Studies*, Vol. 29, No. 1, 2005, pp. 5–6; Adeed Dawisha, '"Identity" and Political Survival in Saddam's Iraq', *Middle East Journal*, Vol. 53, No. 4, 1999, pp. 562–7; Roy 2004, p. 178; Roy 1995, p. 22.

21. For Northern Ireland see Rosemary Harris, *Prejudice and Tolerance in Ulster: A Study of Neighbours and 'Strangers' in a Border Community*, Manchester University Press, Manchester 1972. For central Bosnia see Tone Bringa, *Being*

Muslim the Bosnian Way: Identity and Community in a Central Bosnian Village, Princeton, NJ: Princeton University Press, 1995.

22. Bringa 1995, pp. 65–84; Harris 1972, pp. 66–120.

23. On the increasing salience of ethnicity in conflicts see Simonsen 2005, pp. 297–318; Wimmer 2008, p. 982. On the decrease in the fluidity of ethnic boundaries during conflicts see Arjun Appadurai, 'Dead Certainty: Ethnic Violence in an Era of Globalization', *Public Culture*, Vol. 10, 1998, pp. 225–47; Anthony D. Smith, 'War and Ethnicity: The Role of Warfare in the Formation, Self-Images and Cohesion of Ethnic Communities', *Ethnic and Racial Studies*, No. 4, 1981, p. 375; Wimmer 2008, p. 982.

24. Anthony Oberschall and Hyojoung Kim, 'Identity and Action', *Mobilization: An International Journal*, Vol. 1, No. 1, 1996, pp. 73–81; Anthony Oberschall, *Conflict and Peace Building in Divided Societies*, London and New York: Routledge, 2007, p. 231.

25. Todd 2005, p. 438.

26. Ivo Banac, *The National Question in Yugoslavia: Origins, History, Politics*, Ithaca and London: Cornell University Press, 1984, pp. 374–5; Zachary T. Irwin, 'The Islamic Revival and the Muslims of Bosnia-Hercegovina', *East European Quarterly*, Vol. 17, No. 4, 1984, p. 449.

27. Appadurai 1998; Smith 1981.

28. Oberschall and Kim 1996, pp. 73–81.

29. John Chapman, 'Destruction of a Common Heritage: The Archaeology of War in Croatia, Bosnia and Herzegovina', *Antiquity*, Vol. 68, 1994, pp. 120–6; András Riedlmayer, 'From the Ashes: The Past and Future of Bosnia's Cultural Heritage' in Maya Shatzmiller (ed.), *Islam and Bosnia: Conflict Resolution and Foreign Policy in Multi-Ethnic States*, Montreal and Kingston: McGill-Queen's University Press, 2002, p. 114.

30. For an analysis of the tensions and shifting identities of Muslim Sarajevans during the conflict see Ivana Maček, 'Predicaments of War: Sarajevo Experiences and Ethics of War' in Bettina E. Schmidt and Ingo W. Schröder (eds) *Anthropology of Violence and Conflict*, London and New York: Routledge, 2001, pp. 207–9.

31. Neil Jarman, 'Commemorating 1916, Celebrating Difference: Parading and Painting in Belfast' in Adrian Forty and Suzanne Kuchler (eds), *The Art of Forgetting*, Oxford: Berg, 1999.

32. Randy Hodson, Duško Sekulič and Garth Massey, 'National Tolerance in the Former Yugoslavia', *American Journal of Sociology*, Vol. 99, No. 6, 1994, pp. 1534–58.

33. Maček 2001, p. 208.

34. Bringa 1995, pp. 56–7.

35. John Mueller, 'The Banality of "Ethnic War"', *International Security*, Vol. 25, No. 1, 2000, pp. 53–4.

36. For lists of the numbers of mosques and other Muslim religious buildings destroyed, see Riedlmayer 2002, pp. 99–100.

37. See Neil Jarman (1997) *Material Conflicts: Parades and Visual Displays in Northern Ireland*, Oxford: Berg, 1997; Jarman 1999.

38. Anderson 2008, p. 98.

39. On Bosnia-Herzegovina see Sumantra Bose, *Bosnia after Dayton Nationalist Partition and International Intervention*, London: C. Hurst, 2002, pp. 216–7.

On Northern Ireland see Brendan O'Leary, 'The Belfast Agreement and British-Irish Agreement: Consociation, Confederal Institutions, a Federacy, and a Peace Process' in Andrew Reynolds (ed.), *The Architecture of Democracy*, Oxford: Oxford University Press, 2002, pp. 292–356.

40. 'Others' were also mentioned in the Constitution agreed at Dayton but not given any specific representation; see annex 4 of Dayton Peace Agreement (1995) 'The General Framework Agreement for Peace in Bosnia and Herzegovina', http://www.ohr.int/dpa/default.asp?content_id=379, Office of the High Representative, last accessed on 22 April 2009.

41. This has the effect not only of preventing a Bosniac, a Croat or a Serb from the 'wrong' entity from being elected to the Presidency, but also of preventing 'others' (e.g. Jews or Roma) from holding a seat in the Presidency.

42. Annex 4, Article 4, paragraph 1 of Dayton Peace Agreement (1995).

43. International Crisis Group (2002), *Implementing Equality: The 'Constituent Peoples' Decision in Bosnia & Herzegovina*, Europe Report No. 128, Sarajevo/ Brussels, International Crisis Group, p. 3.

44. Ibid., pp. 3–5.

45. International Crisis Group 2002.

46. Parliamentary Assembly of the Council of Europe (2006) *Resolution 1513: Constitutional reform in Bosnia and Herzegovina*, adopted on 29 June 2006.

47. European Forum for Democracy and Solidarity (2006) 'Bosnia's parliament rejects constitutional reform', available at http://www.europeanforum.net/ news/152/bosnia_s_parliament_rejects_constitutional_reform, last accessed 3 May 2009.

48. Parliamentary Assembly of the Council of Europe (2008) *Resolution 162: Honouring of Obligations and Commitments by Bosnia and Herzegovina*, adopted on 30 September 2008.

49. McGarry and O'Leary refer to this as liberal consociationalism as opposed to corporatist consociationalism, McGarry and O'Leary 2008, p. 88.

50. J. McGarry and B. O'Leary, 'Consociational Theory, Northern Ireland's Conflict, and its Agreement 2. What Critics of Consociation can Learn from Northern Ireland', *Government and Opposition*, Vol. 41, No. 2, 2006, p. 271.

51. 'Cross-community support' can be achieved by one of two procedures: 'parallel consent' or 'weighted majority'. Parallel consent requires an overall majority, a majority of 'unionists' and a majority of 'nationalists' to vote for a measure. 'Weighted majority' requires 60 per cent of all members plus 40 per cent of 'unionists' and 40 per cent of 'nationalists' to support a measure.

52. O'Leary 2002, p. 299.

53. The First Minister is now nominated by the largest party in the Assembly and the Deputy First Minister by the largest party in the other main designation. See section 8 (in particular the revised section 16C (6)) of Office of Public Sector Information (2006) 'Northern Ireland (St. Andrews Agreement) Act 2006'. Available at http://www.opsi.gov.uk/acts/acts2006/ukpga_20060053_ en_1, Office of Public Sector Information, last accessed on 19 April 2009.

54. In Bosnia-Herzegovina the September 1996 elections, the first held after the conflict, saw the three parties that had fought the war take 86 per cent of the seats in the federal House of Representatives in a party list electoral system. Mirjana Kasapovic, '1996 Parliamentary Elections in Bosnia and Herzegovina', *Electoral Studies*, Vol. 16, No. 1, 1997, p. 119. In the 1998

Northern Ireland Assembly elections almost 80 per cent of the first preference votes went to the four main unionist and nationalist parties.

55. Dayton Peace Agreement (1995), annex 7 (as cited at note 40).
56. 'A citizen who no longer lives in the municipality in which he or she resided
    in 1991 shall, as a general rule, be expected to vote, in person or by absentee
    ballot, in that municipality.' Dayton Peace Agreement (1995), annex 3, arti-
    cle 4, paragraph 1.
57. Ibid., annex 3, article 4, paragraph 1.
58. Carrie Manning and Miljenko Antic, 'Lessons from Bosnia and Herzegovina:
    The Limits of Electoral Engineering', *Journal of Democracy*, Vol. 14, No. 3,
    2003, p. 52; John Malik, 'The Dayton Agreement and Elections in Bosnia:
    Entrenching Ethnic Cleansing through Democracy', *Stanford Journal of
    International Law*, Vol. 36, No. 2, 2000, pp. 323–6.
59. Malik 2000, pp. 323–9.
60. Ibid., pp. 352–5.
61. Ibid., pp. 336–8.
62. Manning and Antic 2003, p. 56.
63. Ibid., p. 53.
64. International Crisis Group, *Bosnia's Alliance for (Smallish) Change*, Europe
    Report No. 132, International Crisis Group, Sarajevo/Brussels, 2002.
65. Roger Mac Ginty and Cathy Gormley-Heenan, 'Ethnic Outbidding and Party
    Modernization: Lessons from the Democratic Unionist Party', *Ethnopolitics*,
    Vol. 7, No. 1, 2008, pp. 43–61.
66. Paul Mitchell, Geoffrey Evans and Brendan O'Leary, 'Extremist Outbidding
    in Ethnic Party Systems is not Inevitable: Tribune Parties in Northern
    Ireland', *Political Studies*, Vol. 57, No. 2, 2009, pp. 397–421.
67. Ibid., pp. 410–12.
68. Jon Tonge, 'Polarisation or New Moderation? Party Politics since the GFA'
    in Michael Cox, Adrian Guelke and Fiona Stephen (eds) *A Farewell to Arms?
    Beyond the Good Friday Agreement* (2nd edition), Manchester: Manchester
    University Press, 2006, p. 86.
69. For the case of Belfast, see Peter Shirlow, 'Segregation, ethno-sectarianism
    and the "new" Belfast' in Michael Cox, Adrian Guelke and Fiona Stephen
    (eds), *A Farewell to Arms? Beyond the Good Friday Agreement*, 2006, pp. 230–3.
70. Shirlow 2006, p. 230.
71. Gearóid Ó Tuathail and Carl Dahlman, 'The Effort to Reverse Ethnic
    Cleansing in Bosnia-Herzegovina: The Limits of Returns', *Eurasian Geography
    and Economics*, Vol. 45, No. 6, 2004, pp. 439–40.
72. United Nations High Commissioner for Refugees (2004) 'One Millionth
    Returnee goes Home in Bosnia and Herzegovina', UNHCR Briefing Notes,
    available at http://www.unhcr.org/news/NEWS/414ffeb44.html, last accessed
    on 25 April 2009.
73. Ó Tuathail and Dahlman 2004, p. 443.
74. See United Nations High Commissioner for Refugees Return Statistics avail-
    able at http://www.unhcr.ba/return/index.htm.
75. United Nations High Commissioner for Refugees (2009) 'Statistics Package',
    available at http://www.unhcr.ba/return/pdf%202009/SP_03_2009.pdf, last
    accessed on 24 April 2009.
76. Ó Tuathail and Dahlman 2004, p. 444.

77. Ibid., p. 449.
78. Marcus Cox (1998) 'Strategic Approaches to International Intervention in Bosnia and Herzegovina', Center for Applied Studies in International Negotiations, available at http://www.casin.ch/web/pdf/cox98rapportfinal. pdf, last accessed on 19 April 2009.
79. Daniela Heimerl, 'The Return of Refugees and Internally Displaced Persons: From Coercion to Sustainability?' *International Peacekeeping*, Vol. 12, No. 3, 2005, p. 385.
80. Shirlow 2006.
81. Todd, this volume.
82. Todd 2008.
83. Parliamentary Assembly of the Council of Europe (2008) *Resolution 1626*.

Index